Footprint Handbook

Trinidad & Tobago

LIZZIE WILLIAMS

This is
Trinidad &
Tobago

The most southerly of the Caribbean arc of islands, Trinidad and Tobago are only just off the coast of Venezuela, yet they share little of the culture of South America. The people now living on the islands are descendants of immigrants from far-flung homelands – French, Dutch and English colonialists, as well as their West African slaves and indentured labourers from India and China, brought over to work on the islands' plantations. This cosmopolitan mix of people is best introduced at Trinidad's world-famous ebullient pre-Lent Carnival. Fuelled by rum and street food, thousands parade in brilliantly gaudy costumes through the streets of Port of Spain, carried along by the crowds and 'jumping up' to the sounds of calypso and soca music.

At other times, and elsewhere on Trinidad, there are few typical tourist attractions, although the island does have a magnificent north coast, lapped by the gentle Caribbean Sea and studded with beautiful and peaceful coves and sandy beaches. But Trinidad's economic mainstay comes from oil, gas and manufacturing, rather than tourism, and much of the south of the island is an industrialized zone, which, while successful, has little appeal to the visitor. It's a different story on the sister island of Tobago, though, where even Trinidadians ('Trinis') like to go for the well-developed beaches and hotel zones in the southwest. And Tobago still has some wonderful empty coastlines with nothing more than rural fishing villages, glorious bays, offshore islets and idyllic stretches of crescent-shaped sands where accommodation options are small and low key.

Away from the beaches, both these islands have impressive mountainous areas of thick and emerald-green forests, as wells as coastal wetlands of mangroves and swamps, which are brimming with flora and fauna. Birdwatching is a major attraction, and the species found here are directly related to those found in South America, as well as in the other Caribbean islands. There are several protected areas and wildlife sanctuaries where, in addition to the birds, you can find monkeys, iguanas, caimans and sea turtles.

Lizzie Williams

Best of
Trinidad & Tobago

top things to do and see

❶ Trinidad Carnival

Be part of the biggest party of the year when Port of Spain explodes in a riot of colour, music, revelry and creativity, and watch the parade of fantastic costumes from a grandstand on the Queen's Park Savannah. Page 34.

❷ The Abbey of Mount St Benedict

Drive up to this hilltop monastery in the Northern Range for afternoon tea at the

Pax Guesthouse and sweeping views over central Trinidad. Page 50.

❸ Asa Wright Nature Centre

Admire the delicate hummingbirds fluttering around the feeders on the veranda at an old plantation house of this nature centre in Trinidad's forested Northern Range. Page 52.

❹ Turtle watching at Grande Riviere

Take an after-dark excursion to see giant leatherback turtles crawl up the beach to nest and lay their eggs, or the tiny hatchlings emerge from the sand, on this gorgeous beach. Page 56.

❺ Caroni Swamp and the scarlet ibis

Go out on the afternoon boat trip into this mangrove wetland on Trinidad's Gulf of Paria to see magnificent flocks of vivid red ibis coming home to roost at dusk. Page 59.

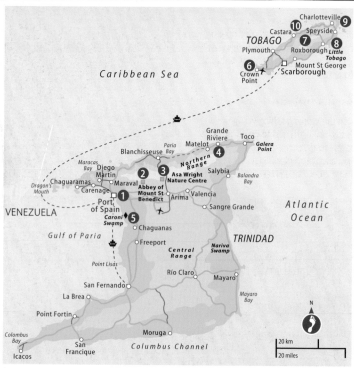

❻ Crown Point

Join the holidaying Trinis at this southwest corner of Tobago for the beaches, watersports, restaurants and nightlife as well as snorkelling and boat trips out to Buccoo Reef and Nylon Pool. Page 89.

❼ Main Ridge Forest Reserve

Employ the services of an expert Tobago birdwatching guide to explore the trails and spot the magnificent birdlife in what is one of world's oldest protected conservation areas. Page 102.

❽ Little Tobago

Explore the coral reefs around this tiny island from a glass-bottomed boat or through a diving or snorkelling mask, then hop ashore to see colonies of seabirds. Page 104.

❾ Charlotteville

Visit this working fishing village on Tobago's north coast to go diving, walk to the near-deserted beach at Pirate's Bay, and watch glorious sunsets over horseshoe-shaped Man O War Bay. Page 105.

❿ Castara Bay

Spend a night or two in peaceful and rustic accommodation in one of Tobago's prettiest villages and friendliest communities, and enjoy the stunning views of the bay dotted with colourful fishing boats. Page 107.

Leatherback turtle hatchlings, Grande Riviere, Trinidad

Route planner

While together they form one nation, Trinidad and Tobago are perhaps an unlikely pairing of islands. Trinidad is bustling, with many cosmopolitan influences, it has a strong tie to industry that makes it one of the most prosperous islands in the Caribbean, and a lively character reflected in its nightlife, music and yearly Carnival. Tobago, on the other hand, is a sleepy and uncrowded island, whose beaches and forests remain undisturbed and where a fishing trip is about as busy as it gets. Although some direct flights go to Tobago, the busier international airport is on Trinidad; quick and frequent flights linking the two islands are known as the 'Air Bridge'. Wherever you arrive, Trinidad and Tobago are both small and can be easily explored on short trips.

Four to seven days
urban attractions, birds and north coast bays

Assuming you have arrived at Piarco International Airport, it is recommended you spend at least four days visiting Trinidad's major attractions before you hop over to Tobago. The airport is in a convenient location in the heart of the residential suburbs on the east–west highway across the island and at the foot of the Northern Range. These mountains harbour woodland and untrammelled forest which is home to great birdlife, while at the north end of the island the mountains drop down to the Caribbean Sea in a series of beautiful bays. To the west of the airport, the small capital of **Port of Spain** is worthy of a day to see some of the historic sights, or enjoy the good restaurants and nightlife. A leisurely day trip north of the city will take you around the **Chaguaramas Peninsula** and up to **Maracas Bay** and the pretty **North Coast Road**. East of the airport and north up the wilder Atlantic coast you'll come across quiet beaches and rustic villages that are a far cry from the industrialized and less appealing south of Trinidad. Few drives or bus journeys between the major attractions take longer than two or three hours, and if you're short of time it's perfectly feasible to do a mini-circumnavigation along the major roads between Port of Spain and **Manzanilla** in the east and **San Fernando** in the south in one day. Take extra time for a boat ride to see the scarlet ibis at **Caroni Swamp**, a night or two at

Grande Riviere if it's leatherback turtle-watching season, and of course you'll need at least a long weekend to enjoy the boisterous and colourful **Carnival**.

One to two weeks

lazy days, beaches and forests

Tobago has some of the prettiest beaches in the Caribbean, with glorious white sand backed by rainforest, where it's impossible not to relax next to the turquoise ocean and soak up the sun. Most visitors, including holidaying Trinidadians, will arrive at **Crown Point** in the southwest, which has the greatest concentration of accommodation, watersports and restaurants. It's a fun and lively area, typical of many Caribbean resorts. But if you're seeking solitude then the real attraction is the north of Tobago, and where the tourist industry has hardly made a dent into the island way of life. Again you can drive around the whole island in one day, and a leisurely one at that, on a circular road that scenically dips up and down along both the Caribbean and Atlantic coasts. But extra days staying in one of the smaller fishing villages like **Castara**, **Charlotteville** or **Speyside** will give you the opportunity to experience the relaxed pace at a more local level. With its lovely forests, quiet bays and coral reefs, Tobago offers plenty to keep nature lovers busy, starting with a snorkelling and glass-bottomed boat trip to **Buccoo Reef** and **Nylon Pool** from Crown Point, and then perhaps birdwatching in the deep valleys running north and south of the **Main Ridge**, scuba-diving off **Little Tobago**, or hiking to waterfalls where deep pools offer refreshing swimming. Equally important are a few days for simply lazing on the beach, floating in the warm ocean, and enjoying a rum punch or two while admiring a gorgeous sunset.

When to go

… and when not to

Climate

As with everywhere in the Caribbean the climate is tropical and temperatures reach a maximum of 30-31°C year round. Trinidad and Tobago are hilly, forested islands that attract plenty of rain to keep them lush and green. The driest time of year is usually January to April, coinciding with the winter peak in tourism, when daytime temperatures are normally in the high 20°s, tempered by a cooling northeast trade wind, and at night it's a comfortable average of about 21°. At other times of the year greater humidity can make it feel hotter if you are away from the coast. The wettest months are June to December, with a short dry period about mid-September to mid-October known as Petit Carême; similar to what temperate climes know as an Indian Summer and which offers a warm, invigorating change from dull weather. But even during the wetter months, rain tends to fall in the afternoon and not for very long. Trinidad and Tobago are far enough south to escape the worst of the hurricane season, which afflicts most of the Caribbean between June and November. However, occasional severe tropical storms can cause flooding and mudslides.

Weather Trinidad and Tobago

January	February	March	April	May	June
29°C	30°C	30°C	31°C	31°C	30°C
21°C	21°C	22°C	23°C	23°C	23°C
70mm	40mm	30mm	40mm	110mm	250mm

July	August	September	October	November	December
30°C	31°C	31°C	30°C	30°C	29°C
23°C	23°C	23°C	23°C	23°C	22°C
240mm	230mm	180mm	170mm	190mm	140mm

Carnival

Carnival in Trinidad (on the Monday and Tuesday before Ash Wednesday) is great fun; it's the biggest party in the year, and has the best carnival parades and music in the Caribbean, managing to be both well-rehearsed and spontaneous at the same time. If you plan to attend, book travel early. It's worth arriving a few days before Carnival Monday to watch the various side events, such as practice sessions of steel pan bands, and feel the excitement build up before the big event. For accommodation in Port of Spain, make reservations months in advance – many Trinidadians and Tobagonians living overseas return each year for the 'mother of all limes'. For more information, visit the website of the **National Carnival Commission of Trinidad and Tobago** (www.ncctt.org). For more information on the Carnival, see box, page 34. For other festivals and public holidays, see page 136.

What to do

Birdwatching

With tropical savannahs, rainforests, woodlands and mangrove swamps, birdwatching is one of the most popular activities on both Trinidad and Tobago. Trinidad has some 430 species, many of them South American, while Tobago has around 220. Trinidad in particular boasts one of the largest concentrations of hummingbirds in the Caribbean, and is where you can see the spectacular sunset display of the scarlet ibis, while Tobago is home to a broad variety, from tiny forest motmots to the huge frigate bird. There are plenty of birding hotspots: on Trinidad visits to the **Caroni Bird Sanctuary**, **Asa Wright Nature Centre** and the **Pointe-a-Pierre Wildfowl Trust** are all very rewarding, and on Tobago specialist bird walks can be organized on the delightful trails in the Main Ridge Forest Reserve. **Discovering the Birds of Trinidad and Tobago**, www.birdsoftt. com, has good online bird lists, while the best field guide is *A Guide to the Birds of Trinidad and Tobago*, by Richard ffrench.

Cycling

Cycling is not particularly popular on either island, although amateur road racers participate in the Tobago Cycling Classic; a one-day race around the island in October.

For visitors, though, bike hire is available in Crown Point for anything from a short ride to the beach at Pigeon Point Heritage Park to longer trips along the coast. For the mountain biker, the options progress from organized guided tours on forested trails on Tobago suitable for beginners to challenging cross-country routes for advanced riders.

Fishing

The islands have some of the world's most exciting game fish, including blue marlin, white marlin, swordfish, wahoo, tuna, barracuda, mahi mahi and shark. There are a number of operators that organize deep-sea fishing charters as well as angling off the coast; **Fishing TnT**, www. fishingtnt.com, has a full list of operators. On Trinidad's east and north coast, and from any of the villages around Tobago, there is also the option of negotiating to go out with a friendly local fisherman. Several fishing tournaments are organized on both islands: see the website of the **Trinidad and Tobago Game Fishing Association**, www.ttgfa.com.

Hiking

With their hilly terrain and lovely coastlines, there are numerous options for hiking on the islands whether it is a short stroll along a magnificent beach lined with coconut

ON THE ROAD

Music

Calypso

Calypso music first developed in the 18th century with the arrival of French planters and their slaves who used the music as a form of communication to sing about their masters. Its rhythms can be traced back to West African kaiso, a highly rhythmic music characterized by harmonic vocals, with sometimes witty and often scurrilous lyrics, which was mostly sung in patois (Creole French) and led by a *griot* (a West African historian, storyteller, poet and/or musician). Calypso was popularized after the abolition of slavery in 1834.

From the early 1900s, calypso spread throughout the Caribbean and around the world, and in 1914 the first calypso recording was made by the Victor Gramophone Company of New York (by the 1950s Trinidad had its own recording studios). The late 1920s saw the rise of the first Port of Spain calypso tents; at that time, bamboo structures were used as the venue for calypsonians to practice and perform during Carnival. Today, official, permanent performing halls showcase the new music of the Carnival season in the weeks leading up to the competition's final. During this time the songs blast from radio stations and sound systems all over the islands. Then, at the Sunday night Dimanche Gras show, the last six or so calypso bands battle it out for the title of Calypso Monarch. Immediately after is the official start of J'Ouvert, at 0400 on the Monday morning, marking the beginning of Carnival proper.

palms where you can paddle as you go, or a full day in the forests to waterfalls where you swim in clear cool pools. You can head off on your own into Trinidad's Northern Range or Tobago's Main Ridge, but there are also guides who will help you appreciate the flora and fauna, especially the birds. Another option is to just walk on any of the pretty coastal roads away from the urban areas and see where you get to (and get public transport back). **Island Hikers**, www.islandhikers.com, a good resource for trail information, also organizes group hikes for residents and visitors.

Sailing

Trinidad and Tobago are islands after all, so there are opportunities to enjoy the waters from the deck of a boat. Boat excursions can be organized from Chaguaramas, Trinidad, out to the string of islands off the northwest peninsula in the Bocas del Dragón (Dragon's Mouths) between Trinidad and Venezuela. Chaguaramas is also the yachting centre of the islands and many yacht owners retreat here during hurricane season. On Tobago a popular day trip is to go out on a catamaran for a sail up the Caribbean coast with snorkelling and a barbecue lunch on a remote beach. There are plenty of other options such as snorkelling, glass-bottomed boat trips or sunset cruises to Buccoo Reef and Nylon Pool, or you can simply charter a boat with a skipper and crew and head off just about anywhere.

Over the years, calypso music has changed, spawning sub-groups, which attract wider audiences to the genre. **Soca** (also known as the soul of calypso) developed in the 1970s and 80s, with influences of funk and soul (and electric guitars). **Chutney** is an Indian version of calypso sung in Hindi and especially popular since the advent of radio stations devoted only to Indian music; **chutney soca** is a combination of both; **ragga soca** is a fusion of soca and Jamaican dancehall, also originating in the 1970s with lyrics sung in the reggae dub style; **rapso soca** is an even newer breed, fusing soca and rap music.

Steel pan

Steel pan music has a shorter history, and some argue that this was the only acoustic instrument to be invented in the 20th century. It originated in the urban tenements of Port of Spain in the 1930s when the tamboo-bamboo bands created percussion instruments from tins, dustbins, pans and lengths of bamboo. By the end of the Second World War (during which Carnival was banned) some ingenious souls had discovered that huge oil drums could be converted into expressive instruments, their top surfaces tuned to all ranges and depths (the ping pong, or soprano pan, embraces 28-32 notes, including both the diatonic and chromatic scales). While to an outsider the banging of steel pans may look primitive, it's actually one of the most innovative ideas in music. Each pan represents a different instrument – cello, guitar, tenor bass and so on – and there are frontline, mid-range, and background pan sections, like a full orchestra; steel pan musicians are called pannists. Carnival of 1940 witnessed the first public appearance of the steel pan, and today the steel bands compete in the Carnival's Panorama competition. The preliminary rounds take place in the respective panyards and the finals at the Queen's Park Savannah over the main Carnival weekend.

Scuba-diving

Trinidad does not have the clear blue waters typically associated with the Caribbean, because of the silt washed around the island by the outflow of Venezuela's Orinoco River. However, there are a couple of operators (see page 82) that offer diving off the Chaguaramas Peninsula and the Bocas islands where the plankton and nutrients attract huge manta rays and large pelagics. Tobago, though, has average water temperatures of 24-29°C, visibility of 15-37 m, and is surrounded by rich and colourful reefs with more than 300 species of coral and over 700 species of fish, suitable for beginners and advanced divers; there are numerous operators around the island offering single dives to week-long courses. Snorkelling is excellent too, and if you don't want to get wet, glass-bottomed boat trips are a good option.

Watersports

Around Crown Point in Tobago there are numerous play options, from wind- and kitesurfing and hobie cat sailing to jet-skiing, boogie-boarding and snorkelling. Watersports centres are at the most popular beaches and at some of the larger hotels, and activities can be arranged off the beaten track: surfing to remote beaches or catamaran sailing up the coast. Sea kayaking and stand-up paddling (SUP) are also available, and a number of centres and hotels around both Trinidad and Tobago rent out the equipment.

Improve your travel photography

Taking pictures is a highlight for many travellers, yet too often the results turn out to be disappointing. Steve Davey, author of Footprint's *Travel Photography*, sets out his top rules for coming home with pictures you can be proud of.

Before you go

Don't waste precious travelling time and do your research before you leave. Find out what festivals or events might be happening or which day the weekly market takes place, and search online image sites such as Flickr to see whether places are best shot at the beginning or end of the day, and what vantage points you should consider.

Get up early

The quality of the light will be better in the few hours after sunrise and again before sunset – especially in the tropics when the sun will be harsh and unforgiving in the middle of the day. Sometimes seeing the sunrise is a part of the whole travel experience: sleep in and you will miss more than just photographs.

Stop and think

Don't just click away without any thought. Pause for a few seconds before raising the camera and ask yourself what you are trying to show with your photograph. Think about what things you need to include in the frame to convey this meaning. Be prepared to move around your subject to get the best angle. Knowing the point of your picture is the first step to making sure that the person looking at the picture will know it too.

Compose your picture

Avoid simply dumping your subject in the centre of the frame every time you take a picture. If you compose with it to one side, then your picture can look more balanced. This will also allow you to show a significant background and make the picture more meaningful. A good rule of thumb is to place your subject or any significant detail a third of the way into the frame; facing into the frame not out of it.

This rule also works for landscapes. Compose with the horizon two-thirds of the way up the frame if the foreground is the most interesting part of the picture; one-third of the way up if the sky is more striking.

Don't get hung up with this so-called Rule of Thirds, though. Exaggerate it by pushing your subject out to the edge of the frame if it makes a more interesting picture; or if the sky is dull in a landscape, try cropping with the horizon near the very top of the frame.

Fill the frame

If you are going to focus on a detail or even a person's face in a close-up portrait, then be bold and make sure that you fill the frame. This is often a case of physically getting in close. You can use a telephoto setting on a zoom lens but this can lead to pictures looking quite flat; moving in close is a lot more fun!

Interact with people

If you want to shoot evocative portraits then it is vital to approach people and seek permission in some way, even if it is just by smiling at someone. Spend a little time with them and they are likely to relax and look less stiff and formal. Action portraits where people are doing something, or environmental portraits, where they are set against a significant background, are a good way to achieve relaxed portraits. Interacting is a good way to find out more about people and their lives, creating memories as well as photographs.

Focus carefully

Your camera can focus quicker than you, but it doesn't know which part of the picture you want to be in focus. If your camera is using the centre focus sensor then move the camera so it is over the subject and half press the button, then, holding it down, recompose the picture. This will lock the focus. Take the now correctly focused picture when you are ready.

Another technique for accurate focusing is to move the active sensor over your subject. Some cameras with touch-sensitive screens allow you to do this by simply clicking on the subject.

Leave light in the sky

Most good night photography is actually taken at dusk when there is some light and colour left in the sky; any lit portions of the picture will balance with the sky and any ambient lighting. There is only a very small window when this will happen, so get into position early, be prepared and keep shooting and reviewing the results. You can take pictures after this time, but avoid shots of tall towers in an inky black sky; crop in close on lit areas to fill the frame.

Bring it home safely

Digital images are inherently ephemeral: they can be deleted or corrupted in a heartbeat. The good news though is they can be copied just as easily. Wherever you travel, you should have a backup strategy. Cloud backups are popular, but make sure that you will have access to fast enough Wi-Fi. If you use RAW format, then you will need some sort of physical back-up. If you don't travel with a laptop or tablet, then you can buy a backup drive that will copy directly from memory cards.

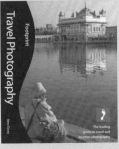

Recently updated and available in both digital and print formats, Footprint's Travel Photography by Steve Davey covers everything you need to know about travelling with a camera, including simple post-processing. More information is available at www.footprinttravelguides.com

Where to stay

from fun-loving beach resorts to peaceful rustic cottages

Places to stay on the islands include large and small hotels, guesthouses, B&Bs and self-catering apartments or cottages. The islands are notable for having a large number of independent, privately owned hotels, with very few international chains represented. The **Hilton**, **Hyatt** and the **Radisson** in Port of Spain are the exceptions rather than the rule and exist mainly for the business market. Most properties have been audited by the **Trinidad and Tobago Bureau of Standards** (TTBS) and have met the minimum requirements established under the **Trinidad and Tobago Tourism Industry Certification** (TTTIC) programme. Nonetheless, quality of accommodation varies considerably across the budget range and many are criticized for poor service, lack of maintenance and being in need of renovation. In Tobago in particular (where the tourism industry began way back in the 1960s) you may find some of the resort-style places stuck in a time warp in terms of furnishings and decor. Even some of the business hotels on Trinidad appear circa 1980s in style (this was when the oil boom really took hold of the island). However, in saying this, there is a clutch of good modern and stylish properties, where cleanliness and standard of comfort is rarely

> **Tip...**
> Tourist authority websites (see page 141) provide details of accommodation. Almost all places on Trinidad and Tobago have websites to book direct and request further information; alternatively, you can book through the likes of www.expedia.com and www.booking.com.

Price codes

Where to stay	
$$$$	over US$300
$$$	US$150-300
$$	US$75-150
$	under US$75

Price codes refer to a standard double/twin room in high season.

Restaurants	
$$$	over US$30
$$	US$15-30
$	under US$15

Price codes refer to the cost of a two-course meal, excluding drinks or service charge.

an issue, and where most rooms are well equipped with almost all having air conditioning, cable TV and Wi-Fi (even at the budget end). Some of the older or simpler properties can be quite charming too – staying at a rustic beachside inn in a beautifully remote location or at a full-blown

Tip...
Hotel tax (10%) and service (10%) are charged across the board, usually as a single charge of 20%; you must remember to factor this in as it's rarely shown on published rack rates but is added to you bill at the end of a stay.

holiday resort with lots of activities can be very enjoyable; in most cases, it is the location that is the important factor when choosing accommodation.

Hotel rooms vary from US$70 for a double/twin in the cheaper guesthouses to US$300 + in a chain hotel like the **Hyatt**. Very few places include breakfast in room rates, and the cost of breakfast (when available) can be the equivalent of US$5 for a simply local breakfast of saltfish and bake to US$20 for a full buffet. The best option for budget travellers – especially a group or family – is to book an apartment. Most have at least two double beds and/or pull-out sofa beds, and costs can be brought down further by cooking for yourself instead of relying on restaurants for all your meals. Peak season for accommodation is November to April, with further peaks at Christmas/New Year and Easter. Other popular times are special events such as **Carnival on Trinidad** (see box, page 34) or the **Tobago Jazz Experience** in April, as well as fishing festivals or beach parties (fetes). For most of the year, hotels in Port of Spain cater almost exclusively for business visitors and rooms can be hard to find if your visit coincides with a conference. If you intend to stay in Trinidad for Carnival, you must book a hotel well in advance – even by months; most hotels raise their prices steeply and some insist you stay for a minimum period and will ask for a deposit in advance. If arriving at Carnival time without a reservation, the tourist office at the airport may help to find you a room in a hotel or with a local family, though both options will be expensive and are far from guaranteed. On Tobago peak times are long public holiday weekends, which are popular with holidaying Trinidadians, although for most weekends it's best to book accommodation and the 'Air Bridge' flights across from Trinidad in advance.

Food
& drink

from bake and shark to tropical fruit salad

Food

The food on Trinidad and Tobago has influences from all over the world. Their distinctive fusion cuisine is the result of the islands' occupation by the Spanish, French and British, who in turn used the labour of the Amerindians, Africans, Chinese and East Indians, supplemented later by immigrants from the Middle East and Portugal. The variety of one-pot stews, hearty dishes relying on meat and carbohydrates, comes from the traditions of African slaves. Curries were brought from India, with emphasis on vegetables and pulses. Many of the very sweet desserts and snacks can be traced to Indian roots and southern Trinidad is famous for its Indian cooking. The ubiquitous Chinese restaurant is on nearly every street in Trinidad (far less so on Tobago), with chefs adapting their repertoire according to local ingredients.

Chicken, goat and, to a lesser extent, lamb are the most popular local meats. Beef, on the other hand, is often imported, usually from the USA. Cow-heel soup and chicken-foot and pig-foot souse are other popular meat dishes. Naturally the availability of fish is plentiful and the waters around the islands teem with delicious seafood. In particular, lobster and shrimp are excellent. The climate and the fertile soil contribute to a reasonable harvest of farmed fruit and vegetables, though these become less readily available in the dry season, January to April, when many of the more upmarket restaurants (and supermarkets) rely on imported produce. However, many tropical fruits and vegetables grow naturally, including large and juicy pineapples, pawpaws, very good sapodillas, and starchy eddoes and yam tanias. Varieties of bananas include the mini sweet siquier, the large plantain (eaten fried) and the savoury green fig (a banana, not a fig). Citrus season is January to March, and later in the year look out for mangoes (a huge variety: julie, graham, peter, starch, pineapple, long, doudou, etc) and large, creamy avocados (locally called *zaboca*). Salt prunes (Chinese) and red mango are on sale almost everywhere. Use the local pepper sauce in moderation unless you are accustomed to chilli dishes. Non-meat eaters are well catered for.

ON THE ROAD

Roti

A wrapped roti is the most popular lunch on-the-go in Trinidad and Tobago, a hand-held meal equivalent of the British sandwich. It is also fuel for more partying and the late-night pit stop, much like the ubiquitous kebab or a burrito. Rotis are eaten widely across the West Indies, especially in countries with large Indo-Caribbean populations such as Trinidad and Tobago, and were originally introduced by indentured laborers who came from India in the mid-1800s. They can be filled with split peas, dhalpuri, and/or a variety of vegetable and conch, goat, beef and shrimp curries. The favourite is curried chicken accompanied by curried potato and chickpeas (channa), curried mango, pumpkin or other relishes and sauces. Some offer boneless chicken, but Trinidadians and Tobagonians generally prefer the flavour of the meat on the bone, sucking and licking clean anything that isn't edible. Sada is a plain roti, dosti is two-layered, and 'buss-up-shut' is a torn paratha reminiscent of a torn shirt with the curry on the side to dip the bread into.

Everyone has their favourite place to get roti and arguments can break out over each chef's merits regarding the thickness of the roti or the silkiness of the paratha. 'Roti shops' can be found across the nation – by corners, beaches, main roads and back roads – and are (almost) as ubiquitous on the islands as 'rum shops'.

Eating out

In Port of Spain and the larger towns on Trinidad, and at Crown Point and (to a lesser extent) Scarborough on Tobago, there are plenty of options for eating out, both for local and international cuisine. Away from these areas, there are a few formal restaurants dotted around the islands, often in scenic locations so you can enjoy a pleasant lunch overlooking a bay or beach, or sip a sunset cocktail on a veranda before dinner. Other than that, the choice is limited to hotel restaurants, local 'snackettes' (small takeaway kiosks), rum shops that may also serve a hot plate of food, US-style fast-food joints like KFC, and roti shops. Street food is also an option in the urban areas – choosing the vendors with the longest queues usually means the food is good. Items include doubles, barbecue and jerk meats, Creole corn soup, fried chicken and fish, and hotdogs and burgers.

Opening hours listed for restaurants are liable to change at short notice, and many places close on Sundays and public holidays and sometimes another day of the week. In Port of Spain, restaurants may close or reduce their hours during Carnival when most customers are too preoccupied to eat properly and staff are otherwise engaged. Smaller less busy places in the villages around the islands may not even have formal

Tip...
For the best restaurant listings on the islands, visit TriniChow; www.trinichow.com.

ON THE ROAD

Limin'

A 'lime' is not just something to garnish a rum and coke – it also denotes a 'hanging out' session, whether impromptu or pre-arranged. In order to be considered 'liming', there must be no greater purpose to the hanging out than sharing food, drink, conversation and laughter with others – be it a family group enjoying a liming picnic on a beach at the weekend, or a group of friends sharing the after-work lime on a step outside a rum shop. Liming is an important part of Trinidad and Tobago's culture, and everybody goes out of their way to make time for it. No visit to the islands would be complete without a 'lil lime'.

opening times at all – where only one person does all the cooking, they are more likely to be open 'any day, any time'.

Restaurant prices vary and a higher cost for a meal does not always indicate better food. Rotis and street food snacks start at about TT$15 (less than US$3); portions of local stew, fried chicken or bake and shark on the beach will be about TT$30 (nearer US$5). You can also find some pretty good food in the cheaper Indian or Chinese canteens at around TT$40 (US$6 per plate). Beyond that, menu prices steadily increase to about TT$400 (US$60) per head for a two- to three-course dinner with wine in a smart Port of Spain restaurant or an upmarket hotel.

Drink

Fizzy soft drinks are plentiful, as are fresh juices, both also used in cocktails and rum punches. A local non-alcoholic drink is *mauby*, slightly bitter and made from the bark of a tree. Sorrel is a bright red Christmas drink made from sepals of a plant from the hibiscus family. There is also ginger beer, and you can get sorrel and ginger beer shandy. Fresh lime juice is recommended; it is sometimes served with a dash of **Angostura** bitters. There are plenty of rums to try (most Trinidadians and Tobagonians have a strong tolerance for rum; the uninitiated should take it easy), and these vary from potent local brews with a high alcohol percentage to the smoother, more palatable fine rums produced by the likes of **Angostura** (www.angostura.com; see also **House of Angostura**, page 49), many of which are better without punch or coke and

> **Tip...**
> Coconut water – the clear liquid inside young green coconuts – is very refreshing to drink. Look for barrows and stalls piled high with coconuts and a machete-wielding vendor who will slice the nut open to drink fresh; in Trinidad good places are around the Queen's Park Savannah and Independence Square in Port of Spain; in Tobago, try the market in Scarborough or some of the Beach Facility car parks.

Menu reader

bake and shark the ultimate Trini beach snack; a spicy fried bread sandwich of fried shark with a variety of sauces such as tamarind, garlic, *chadon beni* (kingfish-and-bake, mahi mahi-and-bake and shrimp-and-bake are alternatives).

benny balls a somewhat jaw-breaking local sweet in Tobago, made from baked sesame seeds.

buljol salt fish with onions, tomatoes, avocado and pepper.

callaloo a thick soup based on dasheen leaves.

chadon beni a distinctive local herb, which tastes a bit like coriander.

crab-and-dumplings stewed crab with curry and coconut milk served over flat flour dumplings, especially popular in Tobago.

doubles curried chickpeas (*channa*) in two pieces of fried *barra* (mini pancakes), eaten for breakfast and bought from street stalls across the country.

hops a crusty bread roll.

oil-down breadfruit with salted meat boiled down in coconut milk and oil.

pastelles/pastilles maize flour parcels stuffed with minced meat, olives, capers and raisins, steamed in a banana leaf and eaten at Christmas.

pelau savoury peas with rice and meat cooked with coconut and pepper.

pholouri fritters made with split peas.

roti Indian-inspired chapatti pancake in various forms and filled with curries; very good and cheap and seen almost everywhere (see box, page 21).

saheena deep-fried patties of spinach, dasheen, split peas and mango sauce.

saltfish the local name for smoked herring and salt cod, often eaten with a fried bake (pan-fried bread), especially for breakfast.

sugar cakes made with grated coconut.

zaboca large, creamy avocados.

savoured on the rocks. Local beers are **Carib** and **Stag,** both owned by the same company, which also brews **Carlsberg, Mackeson, Royal Stout** and **Guinness; Samba,** a Pilsner-type lager, is produced by a local independent brewery. From the same company is **Stud Power Stout,** a European-style sweet and darkly coloured stout, which (as the name suggests) contains several herbs such as ginseng that are considered aphrodisiacs. Wine (imported from Argentina, California and Europe) is generally not cheap but widely available in restaurants, supermarkets and hotel bars, and the boxed variety can often be seen on the shelf of a rum shop too.

Trinidad

Trinidad is one of the most diverse islands in the Caribbean. Its metropolitan areas are vibrant and it has a great range of natural features to explore. The lush northern coast, with its golden beaches, picture-book crescent bays and stunning headlands is backed by densely forested mountains where there is good hiking and excellent turtle watching. Elsewhere there are swamps, mangroves and wetlands, home to innumerable birds – from tiny hummingbirds to the magnificent scarlet ibis – and other creatures such as manatee or caiman. Another range of hills runs down the centre of the island and along the south. Forest reserves protect wildlife, preserving habitats and biological diversity. In the south are unusual geological features such as the Pitch Lake, a huge area of tar, and active mud volcanoes.

Trinidad, with its oil and gas industries, is the economic powerhouse of the twin island nation, and its people work hard and play hard. It is the more extrovert of the two islands, full of energy, from sports to nightlife. Sprawling Port of Spain is the heart of business and finance but the city is known for its cultural and artistic creativity, most dynamically witnessed in Carnival, where music, dance, colour, shape and form whirl together in the parades and parties. Calypso, soca and steel pan were all created here; the urban streets throb with rhythm and beat, while the latest calypsos are matters for debate and political commentary.

Unlike most islands in the Caribbean, Trinidad is not dependent on tourism for income and job creation. There are several top-notch hotels in Port of Spain, but these mainly cater to business travellers, and there are no all-inclusive tourist resorts or holiday-type enclaves. As a result, the opportunity here is to appreciate the genuine warmth of the people and experience Trinidadian life at its own pace and style.

Essential Trinidad

Finding your feet

Piarco International Airport (Golden Grove Road, Piarco, T669 4880, www.tntairports.com/piarco), is 27 km east of downtown Port of Spain (see page 131).

Immediately outside the arrivals exit is the desk for the **Piarco Airport Taxi Cooperative Society**, T669 1689; fares to all destinations around the island are on a notice board. For example, a taxi to Port of Spain costs US$30, and to the Chaguaramas Peninsula, US$50. Note: fares between 2200 and 0600 attract a surcharge of 50%. All drivers accept Trinidad and Tobago dollars and US dollars cash. Alternatively, you can ask your hotel when reserving a room to send a car to collect you, but these will be taxis too so costs are the same.

There is a **Trinidad and Tobago Public Service Corporation** (PTSC; T623 2341, www.ptsc.co.tt) bus which leaves from the concourse in front of the airport to Port of Spain – the last stop is the City Gate terminal on South Quay. The service runs every 30 minutes Monday-Friday 0630-2000 but not at weekends or public holidays; TT$4 one way. At the airport, tickets are bought from the newsstand in the atrium near the ATMs – it's best to buy two tickets so you have one for the return trip too. The car hire companies have desks immediately after the arrivals exit.

Best Port of Spain restaurants

Aioli, page 72
Angelo's, page 72
Apsara, page 72
Buzo Osteria Italiana, page 73
Jaffa at the Oval, page 73

Best drives

Around Queen's Park Savannah, page 35
Chaguaramas Peninsula, page 41
Port of Spain to Maracas Bay, page 46
Up to the Abbey of Mount St Benedict, page 50
To Grande Riviere on the northeast coast, page 56

If arriving by ferry from Scarborough on Tobago, the **Trinidad and Tobago Inter-Island Ferry Service** (TTIT; T625 4906/3055, www.ttitferry.com) ferry terminal is in Port of Spain on Wrightson Road opposite the western end of South Quay. Taxis are available and its a 650-m walk to the City Gate teminal for **PTSC** buses.

Getting around

You can see most of the sights of Port of Spain by walking around the city centre. For further afield, however, there are regular taxis, **PTSC** buses and privately run maxi taxis (the main terminus for both is City Gate on South Quay), route taxis along some of the quieter roads, and car hire. There are dual carriageways from Port of Spain south to San Fernando, west to Diego Martin and east to Arima, but elsewhere the secondary roads may be slow, narrow and winding. The rush hour in Port of Spain starts early and ends late, and there may also be traffic jams at surprising times; for example, returning from beaches at Chaguaramas or Maracas Bay on Sunday afternoons. Allow a full day if going from Port of Spain to Grande Riviere in the northeast or to the far southwest, if you want to have time to see anything or relax before returning.

Port of
Spain

Port of Spain lies on a gently sloping plain between the Gulf of Paria and the foothills of the Northern Range. The capital city of Trinidad and Tobago, it is a busy port city with the constant coming and going of shipping, as well as being an important financial centre and business hub. It was founded in 1757 by the Spanish but, apart from its name, there is not much about the city to recall that era. Street and place names, as well as the historical buildings, hark back to the days of the British colony, while skyscrapers, fast-food joints and shopping centres reveal the influence of the USA on the modern city. Today it is part of a larger conurbation stretching from Chaguaramas in the west to Arima in the east, and this rapidly developing region on the plains of central Trinidad is estimated to have a population of around 600,000. While Port of Spain doesn't have much traditional sightseeing or many places to visit, some fretwork wooden architecture and old 18th-century mansions still remain among the modern concrete and office towers, and it has plenty of open spaces such as the Queen's Park Savannah and Royal Botanical Gardens. It is a multicultural city that is full of life, famous for its music, pre-Lenten Carnival and delicious food.

Woodford Square

At the heart of the (rather run-down) old city centre is Woodford Square, named after former Governor Sir Ralph Woodford, who developed the town along a square grid plan. On the south side is the fine **Anglican Cathedral of the Holy Trinity** (consecrated 1823), with an elaborate hammer-beam roof festooned with carvings. It was built during Woodford's

1 Trinidad

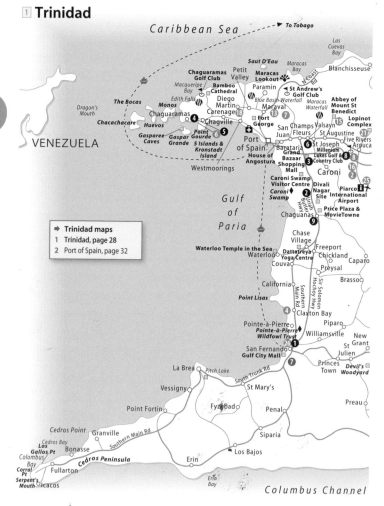

governorship (1813-1828) and contains a very fine monument to him. On the west side of the square, the **Red House** was originally built in 1844 as the seat of Parliament. When it was built, and Trinidad was preparing to celebrate the Diamond Jubilee of Queen Victoria, the building was painted red. This first Red House was destroyed by fire in 1903 during riots over an increase in water rates but was extensively rebuilt in 1907, and the tradition of painting it red has continued to this day. For many decades the Red House was the home of the House of Representatives, the Senate and various government departments, but Parliament is today housed in the Port of Spain International Waterfront Centre next

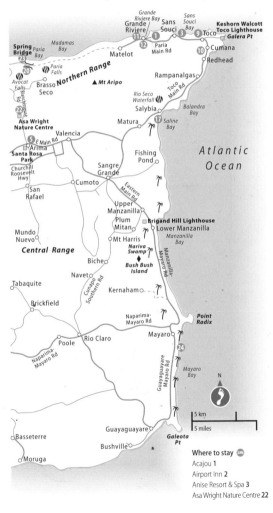

Cara Suites 4
Chateau Guillaume 5
Crews Inn Hotel
  & Yachting Centre 6
CrossWinds Villa B&B 7
D'Lime 18
Holiday Inn Express 8
Hosanna Toco Resort 9
J&J Big Yard Guest House 10
Laguna Mar Beach Resort 23
Le Grand Almandier 11
Mc Haven Resort 12
Monique's Guesthouse 13
Mount Plaisir Estate Hotel 11
Pax Guest House 15
Piarco Village Suites 16
Playa del Este 17
RASH Resort 24
Regent Star 25
Royal 26
Salybia Nature Resort 17
Second Spring B&B Inn 20
Trade Winds 26
Xanadu Tropical Resort 21

Restaurants 🍴
Art d'Manger 1
Bootleggers 8
Buffet King 9
Canboulay Restaurant
  & Lounge 1
Krave 1
More Vino, More Sushi 1
Passage to India 9
Pêche Pâtisserie 2
Rasam 3
Sails Restaurant & Pub 5
Soongs Great Wall 1
Valpark Chinese 6
Woodford Café 9
Zanzibar by the Sea 4

Bars & clubs 🍸
LIV Nightclub 7
The Rig Restaurant
  & Lounge 7

Where to stay 🛏
Acajou 1
Airport Inn 2
Anise Resort & Spa 3
Asa Wright Nature Centre 22

BACKGROUND
Trinidad's history

Trinidad's recorded history began on 2 August 1498, when Christopher Columbus and his fleet of three small ships (the *Santa María*, *Pinta* and *Nina*) sailed into the bay between Los Gallos Point and Corral Point. Whether he named the island after the day of the Holy Trinity, or after the three hills that he spied from the sea (now the Trinity Hills) is a matter of dispute. When the Spanish settled on the island a century later there were about seven Amerindian tribes living there; many of them died in the aftermath and, by 1824, their numbers had been reduced to fewer than 900.

Trinidad remained under Spanish rule until 1797, when it was captured by the British; the island was formally ceded to Britain by Spain in 1802 under the Treaty of Amiens. Soon after, the Bristish erected Fort Picton and Fort George on high hilltops to secure the island against enemy attack, although neither fort has ever seen any military action.

African slaves were imported to work in the sugar fields, introduced by French planters. After the abolition of slavery in 1834, the colonists had to look for alternative sources of labour. Several thousand immigrants from neighbouring islands arrived between 1834 and 1848; some North Americans came from Baltimore and Pennsylvania in 1841; Madeiran 'Portuguese' migrants also came seeking employment and were joined by small numbers of European – Scots, Irish, French, Germans and Swiss. The first batch of labourers from India arrived aboard the *Fatel Razack* on 30 May 1845 and, by 1917, 141,615 Indians had arrived for an indentured period of five years (although many returned to India afterwards, the majority settled). Chinese labourers were also brought to the island between 1848 and 1852.

The British had had control of neighbouring Tobago since 1803, and in 1889 incorporated the two islands into one crown colony (see box, page 34, for the colonial history of Tobago). The first political organizations in Trinidad and Tobago developed in the 1880s, and then the economic depression of the 1930s spurred the formation of labour movements. Full adult suffrage was introduced in 1946 and political parties began to develop. In 1956, the People's National Movement (PNM) was founded by the hugely influential Dr Eric Williams, who dominated local politics

to the Hyatt Regency Trinidad. The Red House is now sadly derelict, although the fine red Beaux-Arts style façade is in good condition and the whole structure is presently housed under a giant corrugated-iron roof awaiting restoration.

On the west side of the Red House, at the corner of St Vincent and Sackville streets, is Port of Spain's **Central Police Station**, built in 1876 on the site of former West Indian Regiment barracks. It has quite a striking gothic design with two square towers and arched verandas, and also once accommodated police housing and a magistrate's court. Also in the southwest corner of Woodford Square, on Hart and Abercrombie, is the striking, modern **National Library** building, next to the restored **Old Fire Brigade Station** (1897), which has been incorporated into the new complex. On the opposite side of the square to the cathedral are the modern **Hall of Justice** and the **City Hall**, with a fine relief sculpture on the front.

until his death in 1981. The party won control of the new Legislative Council, under the new constitutional arrangements which provided for self-government, and Dr Williams became the first Chief Minister. In 1958, Trinidad and Tobago became a member of the new Federation of the West Indies, but after the withdrawal of Jamaica, in 1961, the colony, unwilling to support the poorer members of the Federation, sought the same Independence rights for Trinidad and Tobago. The country became an independent member of the Commonwealth on 31 August 1962, and became a republic within the Commonwealth on 1 August 1976. Dr Williams remained Prime Minister until his death in 1981, his party drawing on the support of the ethnically African elements of the population, while the opposition parties were supported mainly by the ethnic Indians.

The PNM remained in power following the death of Dr Williams, but its 30-year rule ended in 1986, when the National Alliance for Reconstruction (NAR), a multi-ethnic coalition aimed at uniting people of Afro-Trinidadian and Indo-Trinidadian descent, won a landslide victory and Tobago's Arthur Napoleon Raymond Robinson became Prime Minister.

But the NAR began to break down when the Indian component withdrew in 1988, and in the 1991 elections, the PNM again took the majority of votes and returned to power. Again the PNM was ousted in 1995 by an alliance of the NAR and the United National Congress (UNC), returned again in 2002 elections and, in 2010, elections were won by a coalition called the People's Partnership, comprising the UNC, Congress of The People (COP) and Tobago Organisation of the People (TOP), with Kamla Persad-Bissessar being sworn in as the country's first female Prime Minister. But yet again – in another hotly contested election in 2015 – the PNM returned to power under Keith Rowley – the eighth Prime Minister of Trinidad and Tobago since 1962.

Meanwhile, the President of Trinidad and Tobago is the head of state. The office was established when the country became a republic in 1976, before which the head of state was Queen Elizabeth II. The President is formally chosen by an electoral college consisting of members of both houses of Parliament, but is the nominal source of executive power and, in practice, authority is exercised by the Prime Minister and his or her cabinet. The current President of Trinidad and Tobago is Anthony Carmona, a former high court judge.

Independence Square and around

Independence Square is two blocks south of Woodford Square and runs from east to west across 10 blocks. Formerly called Marine Square, it was renamed in honour of Trinidad and Tobago's independence from Britain in 1962. At the eastern end is the **Roman Catholic Cathedral of the Immaculate Conception**, built on the shoreline in 1832 but since pushed back by land reclamation. Built of limestone in the shape of a cross and with two grand towers framing the entrance and some fine stained-glass windows, it was completed in 1836 and reopened after extensive restoration in 2015. Behind the cathedral is Columbus Square, with a brightly painted statue of the island's European discoverer. The central and western area of Independence Square, from the cathedral to Wrightson Road, has been made into a pedestrian area known as the **Brian Lara Promenade** in honour of the Trinidadian cricketer and former West Indies captain. A bronze statue of him, unveiled in 2011, is at the Wrightson Road end and shows the batsman in his signature 'pull shot'

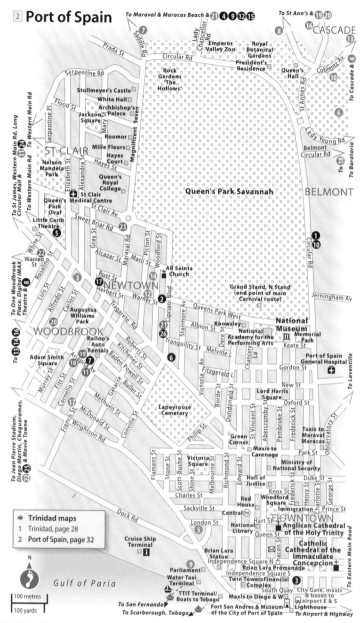

2 Port of Spain

To Maraval & Maracas Beach & 21 4 9 12 15   To St Ann's & 19 20

To St Ann's & CASCADE

Prada St

Saddle Rd

Lady Chancellor Rd

Emperor Valley Zoo

Circular Rd

Rock Gardens 'The Hollows'

Royal Botanical Gardens

President's Residence

Queen's Hall

Coblentz Av

To Cascade & 4

Serpentine Rd

Stollmeyer's Castle

White Hall

Archbishop's Palace

Jackson Square

St Anns Rd

6

Serpentine Pl

Flood St

Roomor

Mille Fleurs

Hayes Court

Lady Young Rd

Belmont Circular Rd

To Barataria

ST CLAIR

Nelson Mandela Park

Hayes St

Queen's Royal College

Mary

Magnificent Seven

Elizabeth St

Alexandra St

Queen's Park Oval

St Clair Medical Centre

St Clair Av

Queen's Park Savannah

BELMONT

Little Carib Theatre 5

Sweet Briar Rd 23

1
10

White St

Gray St

Picton St

Woodford St

Marli St

Circular Rd

22

Rosalino St

Warren St

To One Woodbrook Place, Digital IMAX & 8

Luis St

Rust St

Alcazar St

All Saints Church

Jernigham Av

3

Alfredo St

Carlos St

17

Herbert St

NEWTOWN

Warner St

12

2

14

Cipriani Blvd

Grand Stand, N Stand (end point of main Carnival route)

Augustus Williams Park

Tragarete Rd

Stanmore Av

Queens Park West

20

WOODBROOK

Roberts St

Kitchener St

Albion St

Knowsley

National Academy for the Performing Arts

National Museum

Memorial Park

To 13 14 15 16

Adam Smith Square

18

Kalloo's Auto Rentals

19

21

26

Tranquility St

Melville L

Dere St

Keate St

Murray St

Fitt St

Cornelio St

Ariapita Av

11

Baden Powell St

6

Victoria Av

Fitzgerald L

Chancery La

Port of Spain General Hospital

To Laventille

Galacie St

Buller St

Borde St

17

Methuen St

Conville St

New St

Lord Harris Square

Oxford St

Gordon St

Taxis to Maraval Maracas

Frederick St

Park St

French St

Wrightson Rd

McDonald St

Lapeyrouse Cemetery

Philip St

St Vincent St

Abercromby St

Pembroke St

Charlotte St

Observatory St

Flament St

Stone St

Scott-Bushe St

Shine St

Victoria Square

Melbourne St

Richmond St

Edward St

Green Corner

Maxis to Carenage

Ministry of National Security

Duke St

Henry St

George St

Charles St

Sackville St

Red House

Woodford Square

Hall of Justice

Knox St

Immigration

Prince St

To Eastern Main Road

Dock Rd

London St

Central (P)

Hart St

Queen St

National Library

DOWNTOWN

Anglican Cathedral of the Holy Trinity

Cruise Ship Terminal i

Parliament

Water Taxi Terminal

9

Brian Lara Statue

Independence Square N

Brian Lara Promenade

Independence Square S

Chacon St

Catholic Cathedral of the Immaculate Conception

Gulf of Paria

N

100 metres

100 yards

TTIT Terminal/ Boats to Tobago

Twin Towers Financial Complex

South Quay

Maxis to Diego & W

3

City Gate, maxis & buses to airport E & S

To Jean Pierre Stadium, Diego Martin, Chaguaramas, & Movie Towne

To San Fernando

To Scarborough, Tobago

Fort San Andres & Museum of the City of Port of Spain

Lighthouse

To Airport & Highway

→ Trinidad maps
1 Trinidad, page 28
2 Port of Spain, page 32

Where to stay 🛏

Carlton Savannah **10**
Chancellor **19**
Coblentz Inn Boutique
  Hostel **4**
Courtyard Port of Spain -
  Marriott **22**
Culture Crossroads Inn **11**
Forty Winks Inn **12**
Gingerbread House **3**
Heritage Inn **13**
Hilton Trinidad **6**
Hyatt Regency Trinidad **9**
Inn at 87 **14**
Kapok **7**
Kiskadee Korner **21**
L'Orchidée Boutique Hotel **16**
Melbourne Inn Trinidad **17**
Normandie **8**
Radisson Hotel Trinidad **5**
Samise Villa **20**
Thanna's Place **18**

Restaurants 🍴

Aioli **4**
Angelo's **7**
Apsara **1**
Buzo Osteria Italiana **2**
Chaud Café & Wine Bar **8**
Creole Kitchen **9**
D'Bocas **3**
Dianne's Tea Shop **12**
Hakka **13**
Hotte Shoppe **24**
IrieBites Jerk Centre & Grill **14**
Jaffa at the Oval **5**
Jenny's on the Boulevard **6**
Joseph's **15**
More Vino, More Sushi **16**
Patraj Roti **17**
Tamnak Thai **10**
Texas de Brazil **25**
Town Restaurant & Bar **26**

Bars & clubs 🍸

51 Degrees **21**
Aria Lounge **18**
Drink Lounge & Bistro **22**
Shakers Cocktail Bar **11**
Stumblin On The Avenue **19**
Trotters **23**
Tzar Nightlife **20**

stance standing on one leg on a globe. The promenade is lively in the evening with people liming and drinking beer and there are plenty of fast-food outlets and vendors selling coconuts or snacks, such as doubles.

South of Independence Square, between Edward and St Vincent streets, is the **Twin Towers** financial complex, two 92-m-tall towers, and **Eric Williams Plaza**, housing the Central Bank and Ministry of Finance. A little to the south of the square on South Quay is the old neoclassical railway station, now known as **City Gate**, which is the transport terminal for PTSC buses, maxi taxis travelling between Port of Spain and outlying towns. Opposite City Gate and close to the waterfront on South Quay is **Fort San Andres**, built in 1785 to protect the harbour of Port of Spain (known to the Spanish as Puerto de los Hispanioles). It is the last surviving fortification from the period of the Spanish occupation of Trinidad, which came to an end in 1797 with the capture of the island by the British. In 1845, the Port of Spain town council approved the filling of the waterfront to the northern side of Fort San Andres, and later in the 19th century the shoreline was again filled to its present line, completely land-locking the fort. The fort fell into disuse and later a newer structure was built on the foundations to become the home of the harbour master and various other government offices. In 1995 the remains were restored and the newer building was converted to the **Museum of the City of Port of Spain** ⓘ *T623 5941, www.nmag. gov.tt, Tue-Fri 0900-1700, free.* It serves as a branch to the **National Museum and Art Gallery** (see page 39), but there are only a few exhibits here covering archaeology and Amerindian history, although several of the fort's original cannons survive and the foundations bear the date 1785.

To the west of Independence Square along the waterfront proper on Wrightston Road, are the **Trinidad and Tobago Inter-Island Ferry Service** (TTIT) ferry terminal

ON THE ROAD

Carnival

The main event of the year in Trinidad is the pre-Lenten Carnival, or 'De Mas' as locals call it (a shortened version of masquerade), which is attended by thousands of revellers from across Trinidad and Tobago and other parts of the Caribbean. It is an explosion of colour, music, creativity and spontaneity, and is a vibrant time to be on the island. Carnival is held in Port of Spain on the Monday and Tuesday before Ash Wednesday, which is itself 40 days before Easter (excluding Sundays). So Ash Wednesday can be as early as the first week in February or as late as the second week in March.

Today's glittering Carnival dates back to the 18th century, when the French Catholic planters held elaborate balls at Christmas before the long lean period of fasting in the Lenten season leading up to Easter. In the meantime, their slaves held festivities around the burning and harvesting of the sugar cane (this was known as *cannes brûlées*, anglicized as Canboulay or Camboulay). The slaves began mimicking (and mocking) the lavish ballroom festivities of their French masters with their ornate costumes and dances by making and wearing elaborate masks and costumes of their own, while at the same time creating their own music using household items like sticks and pans. Eventually, the complex rhythms and melodies of these improvised orchestras evolved into the calypso music that forms the backbone of Trinidad's Carnival to this day (see box, page 14). After emancipation in 1838, the freed slaves took their Carnival to the streets and, as each new immigrant entered Trinidad, a new flavour was added to the festivities. Canboulay became a symbol of freedom and defiance and, in response, the British colonial government tried to suppress drumming, stick fighting, masquerading and general merriment. But it eventually settled on a regular date (the Monday and Tuesday before the first day of Lent) and was adopted as a symbol of Trinidadian culture. In 1950 the National Carnival Commission was formed, and then its success was copied; London's Notting Hill Carnival was started by immigrants from Trinidad and Tobago in 1966, and today there are also carnivals on other Caribbean islands, New York, Miami and Toronto.

Today, Trinidad's Carnival is a bawdy, rum-flavoured feast of the senses. It not only features masquerades, but also costumes of beads, sequins and feathers, limbo dancers, marching bands and minstrels – as well as dancing, eating, drinking and sweating – and all to a backdrop of calypso, soca, reggae, chutney and steel pan. It kicks off at about 0400 on Carnival Monday with J'Ouvert (pronounced 'Jou-vay, derived from French patois and meaning 'day open'), which marks the official start of the two-day carnival and the first revellers hit the streets. This ritual represents the original Carnival-goers rebellion against slavery. Some dress as devils known as jab jabs, but most will just get doused in oil, cocoa and mud. Other events over the two days include a Kings and Queens costume competition, a re-enactment of Canboulay, the Kiddie's Carnival, and the Parade of the Bands ending in Queen's Park Savannah. All this accompanied, of course, with plenty of partying all over Port of Spain well into the night.

for ferries to Scarborough on Tobago, and the **Water Taxi Terminal** for services to San Fernando. Between these and the Cruise Ship Terminal (accessed from Dock Road), is a complex known as **No 1 Wrightson Road**. This includes the 26-storey **Port of Spain International Waterfront Centre**, which was completed in 2009 and, at 120 m, is Trinidad's tallest building (home to Parliament and a large conference facility), and the 22-storey **Hyatt Regency Trinidad** hotel.

Queen's Park Savannah

To the north of the city centre is Queen's Park Savannah, a large, vaguely circular open space with many sports fields and a favourite haunt of joggers and kite-flying families at the weekend. Known simply as the Savannah, it covers over 100 ha and the distance around its perimeter is 3.5 km; some regard it as the world's largest roundabout – if you are driving around it and miss a turn-off, you will indeed have to go all the way around again. Once sugar land owned by the Peschier family, it was bought by the town council in 1817 to use as a public space. From 1913 and Frank Boland's aerial display (see box), the Savannah was used as Port of Spain's airstrip until 1931, when a development contract was given to local engineer who chose Piarco as the new site (now Piarco International Airport). Apart from a ring of trees round its perimeter, the Savannah was never really landscaped, except for the small area in its northwest corner called the Hollows, a former reservoir now drained and made into the **Rock Gardens**, with lily ponds and flowering shrubs. The Savannah was the site of Trinidad's main racecourse for decades, until racing was moved to Arima in the early 1990s (see page 51). On the Savannah's southern side, the **Grand Stand**, formerly used for viewing horse races, is now used for various spectator events, most notably the Carnival.

Opposite the Savannah on the northern side, are the 25-ha **Royal Botanic Gardens** ① *Circular Rd, T622 1221, daily 0600-1800, free*, founded in 1818 by Sir Ralph Woodford as the garden for the residence of the governor of the colony. There are more than 700 trees here and an amazing variety of tropical and subtropical plants and shrubs from around the world; about 15% of the gardens are planted with species indigenous to Trinidad and Tobago. There is very little signage but it is a popular place for a shady walk and is mostly flat. Next to the gardens is the official presidential residence, a colonial-style building in an 'L' shape that was built for Governor James Robert Longden (1870-1874). Adjoining the Botanic Gardens on the eastern side is the small **Emperor Valley Zoo** ① *Circular Rd, T622 3530, www.zstt.org, 0900-1800 except Christmas Day and Carnival Mon and Tue, no tickets after 1730, US$4.50, children (under 12) US$2.25*. It opened in 1952 and initially specialized in animals living wild on the island, including iguanas, boas and the spectacled caiman, but there are now caged lions, tigers, giraffes and other non-native species, as well as a butterfly garden. Despite recent upgrading of the facilities, it remains small and cramped for the animals. Just off the

Tip...

For great views of the city, harbour, sea and mountains, drive into the hills above Port of Spain up Lady Young Road (named after the wife of Hubert Winthrop Young, Governor of Trinidad and Tobago 1938-1942). From Queen's Park Savannah, follow it up past the Hilton and after about 3 km you reach a lookout some 170 m above sea level where you can pull over. The road continues to join the Eastern Main Road at Barataria, and while it's not on a public transport route, some taxis take this route between Port of Spain and the airport.

ON THE ROAD

Early Aviation at the Savannah

Ten years after the Wright Brothers had made their first motorized flight, an American called Frank Boland landed the first plane on Trinidad; he landed on the Savannah in his little biplane in January 1913. An aerial demonstration was scheduled for the 23rd, and hundreds of Trinidadians came out in their Sunday best, the ladies in long skirts, carrying parasols, and the men in elegant hats. Boland took off, and the spectators saw the wonder of a flying machine in action for the first time. But after only a few minutes, tragedy struck when Boland attempted to land near the hollows at the western end, where the Magnificent Seven (see below) stood in brand-new splendour. He lost control of his plane and crashed to the ground, dying instantly. A month after Boland's death, Trinidadians were able to witness a more successful flying demonstration by George Schmidt, also from the US. Boland and Schmidt were two of many dare-devil US aviation pioneers, who, in winter time, took to the warmer climate of the Caribbean for their flying demonstrations. They hopped from island to island in their minuscule wooden planes, like circus artistes, while making money from their novelty aerial acrobatics. Doubtlessly, there must have been some youngsters in the crowd at the Savannah who were bitten by the flying bug: when the First World War broke out, many enlisted in the British Royal Air Force. In total, 84 Trinidadian and Tobagonian men joined the RAF between 1914 and 1918, about 25 of whom became fighter pilots.

Savannah (on St Ann's Road) is **Queen's Hall** ⓘ *1-3 St Ann's Rd, T624 1284, www.queenshalltt. com*, a theatre and conference venue that is also home to the National Academy for the Performing Arts. It hosts concerts, plays, shows and other live entertainment – check the website for what's on.

The Magnificent Seven

There are several other Edwardian-colonial mansions along the west side of Queen's Park Savannah on Maraval Road, built between 1904 and 1910 and known as the Magnificent Seven. The plots for the mansions were sold off after the government moved its farm from St Clair to Valsayn in 1899. The auction in 1902 was specifically for the construction of grand and luxurious mansions. From south to north, they are the Queen's Royal College; Hayes Court, the residence of the Anglican Bishop; Mille Fleurs, or Prada's House; Roomor or Ambard's House; the Archbishop's Palace; White Hall; and Killarney, also known as Stollmeyer's Castle. Apart from Hayes Court, which was built in 1910, all were built in 1904. However, after decades of abandonment, most are now seriously dilapidated and are in need of extensive restoration; only a couple of the buildings are still functioning.

Queen's Royal College This, the most imposing of the Seven, was built to a Germanic design at the corner of St Clair and Maraval avenues. It is known for its clock tower, with its chiming clock, as well as for being the leading boys' school on the island (www.qrc. edu). Although it was built to contain six classrooms for 30 boys each, the lecture hall is big enough for 500. After careful restoration, the school now sports its original colours, and features from the first part of the 20th century have been preserved.

Hayes Court Built as the official residence for the Anglican bishop, Hayes Court was named after Thomas Hayes, who was the second Bishop of the Anglican Diocese of Trinidad and Tobago, although he died in 1904 before he could take possession of it. The first occupant of the house was the third Bishop of Trinidad and Tobago, the Right Reverend John Francis Welsh, and it remained the home of the bishop for several decades after. It has a pleasant mixture of French and English architectural styles and features high ceilings, a mahogany staircase, wrought-iron fretwork and wood panelling. But today, while the exterior is in relatively good condition, the five bedrooms are uninhabitable and modern offices for the diocese have been built alongside the main house. In 2014, the Hayes Court Restoration Project was launched by the present Anglican Bishop of Trinidad and Tobago, the Right Reverend Claude Berkley, to refurbish Hayes Court when funds can be raised.

Mille Fleurs This graceful and elegant house in French provincial style with lovely decorative work was built as the residence of the Prada family, who occupied it from 1904 until 1923, when it was sold to Joseph Salvatori. He and his wife lived there until they both died and their daughter sold the house in 1973. It was subsequently bought by the government with the aim of making it the offices of the National Security Council, but it is currently unoccupied, boarded up and in an advanced state of deterioration.

Roomor Built for Lucien Ambard and designed by a French architect, Roomor looks like a mini chateau and most of the materials were imported from France, Italy and Scotland. Unfortunately, Ambard could not keep up his mortgage payments and the house was sold and then rented out until Timothy Roodal bought it in 1940. His granddaughter, Dr Yvonne Morgan, now lives in the house and the name is a contraction of their surnames, Roodal and Morgan. It is the only one of the Seven to remain a private residence and it is still largely as it was when it was built.

Archbishop's Palace This was built by the fifth Roman Catholic Archbishop of Port of Spain and has remained in the church ever since. Its Irish architect took Indian styles as his influence, but unfortunate modernization in the 1960s led to a complete remodelling of the ground floor, with concrete walls and aluminium doors replacing the original timbers. Only the first floor, the sacristy and the chapel are in their original state.

White Hall The largest of the Seven, White Hall was commissioned by Joseph Leon Agostini, a cocoa planter, who wanted a residence in the Mediterranean style to remind him of his native Corsica. However, the bottom dropped out of the cocoa market, Agostini died in 1906, and the family could not afford to finish the construction. So, in 1907, the property was sold to an American businessman, Robert Henderson, who lived there with his family and changed its name from the original Rosenweg to White Hall, after giving it a coat of white paint. The house was taken over by US forces during the Second World War until 1944 and then subsequently occupied until 1949 by the British Council, who used it as a cultural centre and sub-let space to libraries and artistic groups. After remaining empty for a few years, it was bought by the government in 1954 and in 1963, after independence, became the Office of the Prime Minister, Dr Eric Williams. White Hall continued to be occupied by the Office of the Prime Minister until 2009, but today, like the Red House (see page 29), is covered in its entirety by a huge corrugated-iron roof to protect it further from decay.

Gingerbread houses

Trinidad's signature architectural style is that of the gingerbread house, which features delicate wooden filigree, jalousie windows, peaked roofs, dormers, and a welcoming gallery at the front (a gallery is the local name for a porch or terrace). George Brown, a Scottish architect who came to Trinidad in 1880, was the pioneer of this movement; he built his own house in this elaborate Victorian style and its charm was copied and spread across the island. The architectural style adapted equally well to the stately mansions of the planters and merchants as it did to the humble cottages of labourers and tradesmen. To see some of best gingerbread houses in Port of Spain, go to the suburb of Woodbrook, especially the popular restaurant and nightlife area along Ariapita Avenue. Originally a sugar estate founded in 1786, Woodbrook was laid out in cheap housing lots around 1899 and became a respectable suburb for a new emerging middle class. Those who belonged to this group strove to emulate the finer graces of the ruling elite, and this was reflected in the quaint houses, which though small in size, often exhibited the neat elegance of the gingerbread style to full effect. Woodbrook is now the premiere liming spot for Trinis, but it remains a living museum of architecture as well.

Killarney Built for Charles Fourier Stollmeyer by a Scottish architect, Robert Gillies, Killarney may have been designed along the lines of a wing of Balmoral Castle in Scotland. However, the baronial style was too ostentatious for Mrs Stollmeyer and the house was passed on to their son, Conrad. Although occupied by US forces during the Second World War, the house remained in the Stollmeyer family until 1972, when it was sold. In 1979 it became the property of the government and has since then been unoccupied. As a result, while outwardly the stone and brick façade looks robust and in good condition, the timber floor and roof structure are in dire need of structural repairs.

Around the Savannah

A walk along the north and west sides of the Savannah is best in the early morning (before it gets too hot), arriving outside Queen's Royal College as the students are arriving and the coconut sellers are waking up outside. The 19th-century **Anglican All Saints Church** ⓘ *13 Queen's Park West, on the corner with Marli St, T627 7004, www.allsaintschurchtt. com*, is worth a visit to see its fine stained-glass windows. **Knowsley**, another beautifully constructed 1904 building that could easily belong to the group of Magnificent Seven mansions, occupies an entire block facing Queen's Park Savannah and bounded by Chancery Lane, Dundonald Street and Albion Lane. It was built as the residence of William Gordon Gordon: a massive status symbol, using imported yellow bricks, local coral limestone, marble from Italy for the veranda and green heart timber from Guyana for the magnificent staircase. Since 1956 and until recently, Knowsley (which has been well restored and looked after) has been occupied by the Ministry of Foreign Affairs; now it is earmarked to become the new home of the National Museum and Art Gallery (see below).

On the southeast corner of the Savannah is the unmissable **National Academy for the Performing Arts (NAPA)** building, a vast metal and glass domed structure, part of the University of Trinidad and Tobago (UTT), which was completed in 2009 in time to host the opening ceremony for the Commonwealth Heads of Government Meeting. Chinese-built, it was closed down in 2014 because of structural faults and there's no indication of when it will reopen. Near here, at the corner of Frederick and Keate streets, is the small **National Museum and Art Gallery** ⓘ *117 Frederick St, T623 5941, www.nmag.gov.tt, Tue-Sat 1000-1800, free*, in the former Royal Victoria Institute built in 1892. It has sections on petroleum and other industries, Trinidad and Tobago's natural history, geology, archaeology and history, carnival costumes, sport, photographs of kings and queens, and art exhibitions. These include a permanent exhibition of the work of the 19th-century landscape artist, Michel-Jean Cazabon (1813-1888), who is regarded as Trinidad's first internationally known artist and is renowned for his paintings of Trinidad scenery and for his portraits of planters, merchants and their families. The museum's exhibitions are somewhat tired but are comprehensive and a visit is well worthwhile.

Fort George
Fort George Rd, daily 1000-1800, free.

From Fort George, a short drive north from the city centre and 335 m above Port of Spain, there are excellent views over the Gulf of Paria as far as the Caroni Swamp and even the hills of Venezuela. The signal station dates from 1802 and the fort was built around 1804. It was formerly called **La Vigie** (the Lookout) before it was renamed in honour of King George III. The original cannon with his Coat of Arms can still be seen. There were additional fortifications at the foot of the hill at the water's edge and ships on standby. Although it was never used to defend the island, in times of danger people from Port of Spain brought their valuables up here for safe keeping. The fort ceased military operations in 1846. The Victorian signal station you see today was built around 1883 but decommissioned in the 1960s when modern signal towers were built on top of a hill to the north. To reach it from the city centre, take the St James route taxi from Woodford Square and ask to get off at Fort George Road. From here it is about one hour's walk uphill passing through some fairly tough residential territory, or take a private taxi from the corner of Western Main Road and Bournes Road in St James, from where Fort George is a 10-minute drive. If you have your own car, it is a precarious 3.5-km drive up the hill, but there is plenty of parking space and good restrooms at the top. While it's a popular place at weekends, at other times go in a group, not alone, as there have been robberies at the fort.

Tip...
Fort George is a lovely place to take your lunch (there are picnic benches), and later in the day around December and January you may be lucky to see the sunset before closing time.

Around
the island

If Port of Spain is your first destination on the island, then there are easy and leisurely day trips to the north; Chaguaramas Bay, the closest point to the South American mainland, is a lively yachting centre, while the beaches around Maracas Bay are a fine introduction to the iridescent blueness of the warm Caribbean Sea. Beyond these, you don't need to use Port of Spain as a base for exploration of the rest of Trinidad. Piarco International Airport is located on the flat savannah region of northwest Trinidad and has easy access to the east–west Churchill Roosevelt Highway (one of the island's major roads). You can branch off directly from the airport in a hire car. East and south is the Atlantic coast, a blustery place on a windy day but with long empty beaches backed by giant coconut palms that make for an isolated drive. Northeast is Trinidad's beautiful wild coast that tips at Galera Point – the closest point of the island to Tobago – where the rich forests of the Central Range mountains meet sleepy villages of quaint wooden houses and the soft sands of quiet beaches. The south of the island is less alluring, it's long been the location of Trinidad's oil and gas industry, but among the ugliness of the industrial plants and dull satellite suburbs, there are a few sights worth making time for; particularly the boat trip to see the fantastic scarlet ibis in the Caroni Swamp.

The Chaguaramas is Trinidad's northwest peninsula and the closest part of the island to South America. A former US naval base, it is today a national park surrounded by an archipelago of five islands and eight islets, and is where the hills, forests and valleys share many of the features of the mainland. Here you can find red howler and capuchin monkeys, anteaters, iguanas and a host of birds, butterflies and insects. From the hilltops you can get glorious views over the Gulf of Paria, back to Port of Spain and on a clear day across to Venezuela. Western Main Road, the peninsula's main artery up the coast, also provides access to marinas that are a safe bolthole from hurricanes further north for a multitude of yachts of all sizes. In parts this road is not particularly pretty – marine-based industries, vast dry docks and defence force and coastguard headquarters blot the landscape – but it is a thriving area for local tourism: there are bars and restaurants, and its beaches are popular at weekends and holidays with residents of Port of Spain, which, if the traffic is kind, is only a 20-minute drive away.

Port of Spain to Diego Martin Valley
After leaving Port of Spain via Wrightson Road, which then becomes the Audrey Jeffers Highway, the drive northwest to Chaguaramas first passes the looming apartment towers and commercial development in the featureless modern suburb of Westmoorings. Here is the junction of the Western Main Road westwards to Chaguaramas and the Diego Martin Highway that snakes northwards through the hills and the densely populated **Diego Martin Valley**. At the junction, the huge, modern **Falls at West Mall** is one of the nicest large shopping malls on Trinidad, with a good choice of upmarket shops and cafés (see page 80). Named after a Spanish explorer Don Diego Martín, the valley was settled by French planters and their slaves in the 1780s, and was once filled with a number of sugar and cocoa estates. But Diego Martin is today one of Port of Spain's biggest dormitory suburbs, and the only real attraction is at the north end. The **Blue Basin Waterfall** is a picturesque waterfall and series of pools on the Diego Martin River surrounded by luxuriant tropical vegetation and is a lovely place for a refreshing dip. To get there, drive to the end of Diego Martin Highway and then take either St Lucien Road or the Diego Martin Main Road and turn right on to North Post Road, and right again on Blue Basin Road. Near the waterfall the road goes up a steep incline and you can park at the base; from there it's a five-minute walk upstream to the waterfall. Unfortunately the area has had crime problems; it is advisable to go in a group and leave nothing of value in your car.

Western Main Road to Chaguaramas
Beyond Westmoorings, the Western Main Road narrows along the coast and offers many good views of the Gulf of Paria, especially of the Five Islands and the nearby Carrera Island Prison (which dates from 1854). About 2 km past The Falls at West Mall, the road goes past the **Trinidad and Tobago Yacht Club** (TTYC) – opposite Goodwood Park, where the rich live – and to **Carenage**. This name is derived from the French *carénage* or 'careen', meaning to beach sailing vessels

Tip...
If you are not driving, the No 6 PTSC bus and maxi taxis operate seven days a week between City Gate in Port of Spain and Chaguaramas, along Western Main Road.

for maintenance; the practice still takes place in the village, where there is also a fish market and a little church, **St Peter's Chapel**, on the waterside.

The Western Main Road then leads to **Chaguaramas**, on the bay of the same name. This whole area once belonged to the US Navy (see box) but is now under the management of the **Chaguaramas Development Authority (CDA)** ① *T225 4232, www.chaguaramas.com*. Most of the old military buildings are still there, with new uses such as the coastguard training school or satellite campuses for universities. Over the years the CDA has spent a lot of time and money on improving this stretch of coastline; primarily by re-sanding beaches and constructing public beach boardwalks in three phases between **Williams Bay** and **Chagville Beach**. The boardwalks are made from recycled plastic, the lighting is solar-powered, and there is wheelchair access, seating areas under gazebos, car parks, changing facilities and toilets. It is a pleasant area, particularly popular at weekends, but the water along this northwest coast is not exactly pristine (there's better swimming at Macqueripe Bay, see below) and parts of the development seem to have come to a standstill as there are a number of unfinished construction sites around. But Williams Bay provides kayaking opportunities in relatively sheltered ocean waters and it is sometimes possible to see iguanas on the rocks from the ocean; the **Kayak Centre** ① *T633 7871, see Facebook, daily 0600-1800*, is signposted off Western Main Road and rents out kayaks for around US$6 per hour.

Between Williams Bay and Chagville Beach, on your left is **Pier 1** ① *www.pier1tt. com, Mon-Fri 0800-1600*, a small marina with restaurant and function facilities, and then **Pier 2** where the CDA and private operators offer boat trips to the offshore islands (see below). Then, at the far end of Chagville Beach next to the coastguard training ground and the heliport, is the **Chaguaramas Military History and Aerospace Museum** ① *T634 4391, www.militarymuseumtt.com, daily 0900-1700, US$4.50, children (under 12) US$1.50*. Displays are built around the theme, 'Five Hundred Years of Military History' from the Amerindians who lived on the island before the arrival of Columbus, followed by Spanish rule, the British capture of the island in 1797, up to Trinidad's role in both world wars. There are a surprisingly large number of items, from ancient weapons and model ships, to military uniforms and photographs, and the staff are knowledgeable and will happily show you around. Perhaps the most extraordinary exhibit is the turquoise L1011 jet parked in the grounds (once part of BWIA West Indies Airways fleet – Trinidad and Tobago's now defunct national airline).

Continuing along Western Main Road past part of the old US military base (still a fenced area and headquarters of the Trinidad and Tobago Defence Force), another 2 km or so brings you to **Crews Inn Hotel & Yachting Centre** ① *www.crewsinn.com, see also page 67*, on Point Gourde on the left-hand side. This multi-functional venue is the centre of the yachting industry in the Chaguaramas (see box, opposite), and is where the customs and immigrations offices are. But it also has a good hotel and is a worthwhile port of call for landlubbers for the great views over the yachts in its attractive marina and mini candy-striped lighthouse, from the boardwalk Crew's **Caffe Del Mare** or more formal upstairs **Lighthouse Restaurant** (see page 75). There's also a **Massy Stores Express supermarket** (Monday-Friday 0800-2000, Sunday 0800-1600), an ATM and duty free shops.

The Western Main Road continues for another 3-4 km to an abrupt end at the coastguard base at the tip of the peninsula. On the way you'll pass (among others) the Coral Cove Marina, Power Boats, Peake's, CL Marine Ltd, and Industrial Marine Services (IMS), all offering services to the yachting clientele; some have their own bars/restaurants which are open to casual visitors. This area is packed with boats stacked on land or in the water.

BACKGROUND
Chaguaramas Military History

Strategically located on the northwest peninsula of Trinidad, the earliest history of Chaguaramas dates back to the Amerindian occupation between AD 100 and 400; Chaguaramas itself is an Amerindian word describing the once palm-fringed shoreline. In 1498, Columbus sailed through the Bocas del Dragón (Dragon's Mouths) – the name of the straits separating the Gulf of Paria from the Caribbean Sea. Then, in 1797, after being harassed and outgunned by the British following 300 years of Spanish rule, Rear Admiral Apodaca, scuttled his fleet in Chaguaramas Bay. In 1806, there was a slave revolt on the French-owned Chaguaramas sugar plantations and, eight years later, in 1813, the re-invasion of Venezuela by patriots was launched from Chacachacare, an island off the Chaguaramas Peninsula. In 1941 its strategic location really came into prominence, and it was one of the eight famed Second World War "Destroyer Bases". Under the Destroyers for Bases Agreement between the US and Britain, 50 mothballed Caldwell, Wickes, and Clemson-class US Navy destroyers were transferred to the Royal Navy in exchange for land rights on British possessions. One of these was on Trinidad and, by 1943, Chaguaramas had become a fully operational US naval base; in 1966 one of the world's eight global-range radio Omega Navigational Systems was constructed there. Meanwhile though, after Trinidad and Tobago gained independence in 1962, there were demands for a return of Chaguaramas to the people. Large areas of the peninsula were returned to the government in 1967; in 1972 Chaguaramas was opened to the public and the government set up the Chaguaramas Development Authority (CDA) with a mandate to develop the peninsula; the Omega station was finally vacated by the US in 1978.

Tucker Valley

Near the Chaguaramas Military History and Aerospace Museum and just after the police post that marks the start of the old military base, turn right for the Tucker Valley. The road heads north through open fields and towering saman trees; the old **Mount St Pleasant** village is on the right. This was the home of workers on the Tucker Estate during the colonial period but was emptied to make way for US forces; a half-ruined church and a cemetery can still be seen. Tucker Valley Road then leads across the peninsula and ends at the boom gate to the car park for **Macqueripe Beach** ① *daily 0600-1800, US$3 per car, changing rooms/toilets US$0.30 per person*. The beach itself is at the base of a hill and is accessed by a steep concrete walkway – on the way down the view of the bay is spectacular and on a clear day you can see the Güiria Peninsula of Venezuela. Macqueripe is not great for sun bathing – the tropical forest-covered hillsides around the bay create shade from the sun and there's not much sand to spread out a towel – but the generally calm, deep waters are great for swimming and snorkelling. The bay was a submarine station during the US occupation and, before then, was the picturesque backdrop for the (now-demolished) Macqueripe Beach Club (established in 1924 and used from 1941 as an entertainment centre for the families of the American officers). Today there are public toilets and changing rooms, a children's play area, picnic tables and benches, and a lifeguard station; this beach also gets crowded at weekends. **Macqueripe Bay** is the location for a zip-line and canopy walk run by **Zip-Itt (Ziplining in Trinidad and Tobago)**

ON THE WATER

Yachting in Chaguarama Bay

Trinidad has evolved into an important yachting storage and repair centre as it lies below the critical 'hurricane belt' – the northern part of the Caribbean Sea and the Gulf of Mexico. Yachts can be moored up here in the several marinas along the sheltered Chaguarama Bay, which have both dry storage and stern-to docks. Provisioning is excellent and there are boat repair and maintenance services from air-conditioning and electronics, to sail-making and woodworking (local teak costs a fraction of US prices). Workmen are highly skilled, spare parts can be imported duty free for in-transit yachts, and yacht-owners and their crew are granted a stay of up to six months. Additionally, yacht insurance is reduced if vessels are kept below the hurricane line in season – below the 12° north latitude zone according to insurance carriers – and insured boats must either duck below this line between July and November (hurricane season) or leave the Caribbean altogether. The position of Chaguarama Bay is 10°40.5'W, 61°38.3'W. Further information can be found from the **Yacht Services Association of Trinidad and Tobago (YSATT)**, www.ysatt.org, which has its own marina and represents much of the yacht services industry on the Chaguaramas Peninsula. **Crews Inn Hotel & Yachting Centre** (see page 67) at the eastern end of Chaguaramas Bay is the centre of yachting activity in the area and is also where customs and formalities are completed for in- and outgoing yachts.

Adventure Tours ① *T303 7755, see Facebook, Tue-Fri 1000-1600, Sat, Sun and public holidays 1000-1630, 1 hr, US$21, children under 12 US$10.50, no bookings required.* There are seven zip-lines and five net bridges/canopy walks, giving you a wonderful view of the bay and the forest, and you can also rent mountain bikes from the office.

Turnings to the left from Tucker Valley Road lead to the nine-hole/18-tee **Chaguaramas Golf Club** (see page 83), built by US servicemen during their occupation of the peninsula for their own private use. Part of the course was built on the Macqueripe Estate tonka bean plantation and some of the trees, now well over 100 years old, still grow there and are particularly pretty when in bloom, with a swathe of purple blossom in July and August. Golfers may also come across red howler monkeys, iguanas, blue emperor butterflies and many birds while on the course. It became public in 1974 after the last US forces left the island and their caddies later formed the golf club; the club house is a good place for a drink. Also from the club is the short and easy trail to **Edith Falls**, a nice walk of 20 to 30 minutes through the old tonka bean and cacao plantation, and again red howler monkeys or orange-winged parrots may be spotted, but there is barely a trickle of water in the three-level falls except in the rainy season (June-December).

Another interesting feature off Tucker Valley Road is the **Bamboo Cathedral**, also known as Bamboo Cazabon. The 300-m stretch of bamboo on Radio Tower Road arches over either side of the road forming a tunnel. In existence for more than 150 years, it was much painted by the 19th-century Trinidadian artist Michel-Jean Cazabon, after whom it has become known.

The Bocas del Dragón (Dragon's Mouths) between Trinidad and Venezuela is broken by a series of lovely islands, which during colonial days supported a flourishing whaling industry, coconut plantations and small communities of fishermen. Today the closest ones to the Chaguaramas Peninsula are increasingly popular with wealthier Trinidadians as sites for their holiday homes. A trip to these from Chaguaramas is known locally as 'down de islands' or 'DDI', as opposed to 'up the islands', meaning a trip northwards to other countries in the Caribbean chain.

For a boat excursion from the jetty at Pier 2 on Western Main Road, you need to book through the **CDA** (see page 42), or a tour operator such as **Caribbean Discovery Tours** or **Trinidad & Tobago Sightseeing Tours**, see Tour operators, page 84. Alternatively, you can organize it at the **Island Property Owners' Association Marina** ⓘ *near CL Marine Ltd, Western Main Rd, T634 4331.*

The most popular and worthwhile trip is to the **Gasparee Caves** on **Gaspar Grande Island**, which is about a 20-minute boat ride. The landing stage is at the west end of Gaspar Grande (where there are many weekend homes), and the caves are about 15 minutes from the landing stage up a good path through woods, but quite steep in places and hot. The complex of caves is large but you are only shown one, with steps leading down and naturally lit from a blow hole. There is a beautiful lake (tidal) at the bottom with stalactites which the guide will light. Swimming is allowed in the cave on less crowded days. There are also trips to explore the coves and beaches at **Scotland Bay** on 'mainland' Trinidad (the area around the coastguard base at the tip of the peninsula), which is considered to be 'down de islands' because it is only accessible by boat. Other trips go to **Monos Island** at the west tip of Trinidad, which has many deep caves and white sandy beaches popular for weekend houses; it was so named as it was once home to red howler monkeys – *monos* being the Spanish word for monkeys. **Chacachacare**, a larger uninhabited island and the closet to Venezuela, is much frequented by boats and yachts at the weekend but virtually deserted during the week. It has an old lighthouse, ruins of a former leper colony and eight good beaches, including nesting sites for the hawksbill turtle. Boat trips land at the jetty at La Tinta beach and then you have a 3-km guided walk to the lighthouse, built in 1896 and still in operation, perched on the highest point (273 m) from where there are fantastic views of the other Bocas islands, as well as Trinidad and Venezuela.

Tip...

For island boat excursions, expect to pay from US$30 per person for two hours to US$150 per person for a full-day trip, but prices vary depending on arrangements and how many in a group.

The North Coast Road is stunningly beautiful, running along magnificent bays and across hilly promontories and giving access to some of the best beaches on the island. The Northern Range of mountains tumble like crushed green velvet into the Caribbean Sea, providing a safe habitat for wildlife and hiking trails for the intrepid. Maracas Beach is one of the most popular on the island, peaceful and idyllic during the week, turning into a party place at weekends and something of a culinary adventure. The road peters out at Blanchisseuse; it is not possible to drive the length of the north coast.

Port of Spain to Maracas Bay

From the northwest corner of Queen's Park Savannah, take Saddle Road, which after 2.5 km takes you through **Maraval**, one of Port of Spain's high-income residential areas popular with diplomats and expats. Stay on Saddle Road towards Maracas Bay or, for a detour up into the hills, head left off the main Maraval crossroads up Saut D'eau Road to **Paramin** (occasional 4WD taxis make the run up from Maraval). This sprawling, steep and mountainous village is not much more than a junction with a few shops, primary school and a Roman Catholic Church, and most of its inhabitants live and work on farms etched into the high hillsides of the Maraval Valley. There isn't much to do here but the views are good and, interestingly, several families still speak French Creole. There is an annual Parang music festival just before Christmas.

Back on Saddle Road, and just beyond Maraval at Moka, is the very picturesque 18-hole **St Andrews Golf Club** (see page 83). Beyond here, the North Coast Road branches left onto Saddle Road – look for the two stone gateposts on the left on the brow of a hill; Saddle Road itself runs back down the hills to meet the Eastern Main Road at San Juan. From the junction, the North Coast Road leads to Maracas Bay, Las Cuevas and Blanchisseuse, and as you come over the range you get a magnificent view of the heavily indented bays of the north coast and the rocks and islets offshore. The largest of these is Saut d'Eau Island, off Medine Point, which is a nesting site for brown pelicans, swifts and wood rails. About 8 km from the junction, be sure to pull over at the **Maracas Lookout** to take photos; several stalls offer fruit, snacks, drinks and handicrafts to weekend visitors from Port of Spain. A track goes steeply down to a secluded beach on **La Vache Point** and you can explore **Balata Bay**.

Maracas Bay

Some 16 km from the capital, Maracas Bay has a sheltered half-moon-shaped, 2-km-long sandy beach fringed with coconut palms. Despite small waves there can be a dangerous undertow here; do not swim far out, watch the markers, and swim at the east end away from the river mouth. It can be very crowded on Sundays and holidays with loud music and parties, but fairly quiet otherwise. It is also the place people come on Ash Wednesday to relax after the rigours of Carnival. Lifeguards are on duty until 1800; there are changing rooms (TT$2), showers, beach chairs, car parking and cabanas for beach vendors. This is also the place to come for bake and shark; a traditional Trinidadian dish of fried shark fillets stuffed in a pocket of deep-fried bread. Opinions vary over which stall sells the best. **Richard's** is the most famous, but **Mom's** is reputed to serve the best fish and **Natalie's** the crispiest bake. All offer sauces and a buffet station of vegetables and salads as toppings to customize your meal. You don't have to eat shark; there are other fish such as butterfish and kingfish, shrimp or even vegetarian options. There are route taxis from Port of Spain, but all transport is irregular and infrequent. It is easy at weekends to reach but less so during the week. The best bet is by hire car or taxi and it's a pleasant drive of not much more than 45 minutes.

North coast beaches

Next to Maracas Bay is **Tyrico Bay** (lifeguards and toilets), another half-moon beach with undertow, which is quieter than Maracas and has greyish-brown sand. Approximately 8 km east of Tyrico is **Las Cuevas Bay** (changing rooms and showers; TT$2, lifeguards, snack kiosk, and occasional surfing at the far end), a picturesque bay with a wide sandy beach, calm waters popular with families and with fishing boats moored at the east end (beware of the sandflies in the wet season). The west end is very beautiful but can be isolated, so it is best to go in groups. It is busy on Sunday but quiet during the week. The bay gets its name from the Spanish word for caves, of which there are many along the edge.

There are smaller beaches beyond **La Fillette** and at **Blanchisseuse**, about 11 km beyond Las Cuevas; this is a particularly wild and rugged stretch of coast, where fishermen learn to manoeuvre their tiny craft between rocks and reefs, and to carry their boats and engines up steep cliffs to the main road. The name of Blanchisseuse is derived from the French for 'washerwoman' and is divided between the Upper Village and Lower Village, with the Arima road as the dividing line. There is a post office, health centre, Roman Catholic Church, government offices and police station in Lower Village, while Upper Village has the recreation field, school and several artisans working in wood and leather. It has become a popular weekend getaway with holiday homes and self-catering apartments and is the starting point for hikes.

Marianne Bay, at the far end of Blanchisseuse where the road begins to fizzle out, has the largest and most popular beach, and there's a freshwater lagoon at the eastern end where the river runs into the sea. This is a popular place for river bathing, and a great alternative for swimming when the sea here gets too rough, which often occurs between November and April. But watch out for sandflies and for mosquitoes at dusk. The place is kept clean by the owners of **Cocos Hut restaurant/Laguna Mar Beach Resort** (see page 68), which sits in a small nature reserve on the banks of the river.

Marianne River is dramatically beautiful with overhanging vines, buttress roots of trees, boulders, pools and lots of birds, including spotted sandpipers, kingfishers and striated herons. A 40-minute hike upriver will take you to the **Three Pools**, beautiful bathing spots with natural slides and jacuzzis. You can also rent a kayak at the river mouth; however, kayaking here is only really worthwhile towards the end of the rainy season when the water level is high enough to allow you to paddle the entire trip to Three Pools (during the dry season low water levels require you to walk the kayaks part of the way).

All this part of the coast is very beautiful with the forest tumbling down to the sea. The paved road continues to some luxury villas across the Spring Bridge and over the Marianne River, but then peters out and is little more than a rutted dirt track, formerly used as a donkey trail to service the old cocoa plantations along the way. From **Spring Bridge** a one-hour trail leads

Tip...
The isolation of the north coast east of Blanchisseuse means that it is also used by those with less benign intent, such as drug smugglers. Hiking is safest at weekends or in a group, and always carry plenty of water and a picnic.

the spectacular **Avocat Falls**. The footpath, shaded by the canopy of the forest, ascends steeply to the top of the ridge and then descends to the river and the 15-m Avocat Falls, where the base is encircled by huge boulders and has a lovely pool for bathing. You can return from the falls via the Three Pools (above).

Tip...
Leatherback turtles nest along all the beaches of the north coast in season (March-August), but the best place to see them is on nightly excursions from Grande Riviere (see page 56).

You can hike east along the coast from Spring Bridge to **Paria Bay** – a distance of around 8 km that begins on the gravel road and then continues along a forest trail interspersed with beautiful views of the Caribbean Sea. It takes about two hours and the trail is wide and clear and has moderate inclines. It goes via Turtle Rock and Cathedral Rock (or Paria Arch) and on to the beach in Paria Bay, which is possibly the best beach on the island – the silky smooth sand stretches for 1.5 km and the crashing waves are quite inviting and similar to those of Maracas Bay. There is a primitive shelter on the beach but no other facilities, so take provisions with you. At its eastern end is the mouth of the Paria River where the riverbed has accumulated sand by the backlash of seawater during high tide you'll see a variety of small marine fish. A 15-minute walk alongside the river will lead to **Paria Falls** with its fresh, clean water coming from remote areas of the Northern Range and its large pool to swim in.

An alternative to the hike between Blanchisseuse and Paria Bay is to drive or take a taxi from Arima towards Blanchisseuse; 4.5 km past the Asa Wright Nature Centre (see page 52) turn right on to the twisting mountain Paria–Morne Bleu Road for 6.5 km to the village of **Brasso Seco**. From here a 13-km forest trail runs to Paria Bay.

If you choose to continue hiking after Paria Bay to Matelot (see page 56), which is at the end of the tarred section of Paria Main Road on the northeast coast west of Grande Riviere, the trail rambles over a succession of small ridges, crossing several streams, until you get to **Gran Tacarib**, a 1.2-km crescent-shaped beach. From Gran Tacarib the trail continues to **Madamas Bay** (and the river and the beach of the same name), after which it is a series of ups and downs (some moderate, others strenuous) to the **Petite Riviere**, then the **Matelot River** and the village of Matelot. The total distance between Spring Bridge at Blanchisseuse and Matelot is 32 km, and usually takes two days, so most hikers camp overnight on the beach; experienced hikers have been known to cover the stretch between Paria Bay and Matelot in about 10 hours.

The east–west corridor from Port of Spain is a line of industrial and residential suburbs linked by the Eastern Main Road and, more quickly, by the Churchill Roosevelt Highway and its priority bus/taxi route. This is Trinidad's most densely populated area, and the older centres along the route, San Juan, Curepe, Tunapuna, Arouca and Arima, have merged into one continuous urban chain. They are lively, with shops, small bars, Chinese restaurants and fruit and vegetable markets that jam up the traffic even on Sunday morning. But although the flat bits are mostly unattractive, it's quick and easy to leave the heat and suburban sprawl and you are never more than a kilometre or two from the many cool valleys of the Northern Range. Here, among the peaceful hills are wonderful views of Central Trinidad and across to the Gulf of Paria.

House of Angostura
Corner Eastern Main Rd and Trinity Av, Laventille, T623 1841, www.angostura.com, 2-hr tours Mon-Fri 0930-1530, US$10, bookings required at least 3 days in advance, groups preferred.

Just east of Port of Spain on Eastern Main Road is the House of Angostura rum distillery. It sits on an 8-ha site, with its colour-coded stills towering up like an oil refinery. The tour begins with a short film on the history of the company and its famous bitters, a visit to the Angostura museum and one-of-a-kind Barcant Butterfly Collection, and a behind-the-scenes tour of the 'Bitters Manufacturing Room'. Visitors can then ride on an open-air tram down to the state-of-the-art rum distillery and bottling plant, followed by rum tasting and shopping. Angostura Ltd is one of the Caribbean's foremost rum producers whose portfolio includes award-winning and internationally acclaimed rum brands such as 1824, 1919, Single Barrel Reserve, Reserva, 5 Year Old and 7 Year Old. It is also the world's market leader for its aromatic Angostura bitters, the recipe for which has not been changed since its inception in 1824 and for which there is a royal warrant to the Queen. They also make a non-alcoholic drink known as LLB (Lemon, Lime and Bitters).

To St Joseph
Continuing on the Eastern Main Road, just to the east of the House of Angostura in San Juan, is the turn-off to the north on Lady Young Road, which is an alternative route back to Queen's Park Savannah in Port of Spain. Then, a couple of kilometres further on, is the turn-off on to Saddle Road, which provides a route northwards to Maracas Bay without going back through the city. Beyond here on the Eastern Main Road at **Champs Fleurs,** is the **Carib Brewery**, which sold its first bottle of beer back in 1950 and today produces Carib and Stag beers and a range of shandy products which are sold throughout the Eastern Caribbean islands. Then, after passing the Mount Hope teaching hospital, you reach **St Joseph**, which is considered the oldest town in Trinidad and Tobago and which served as the capital of Spanish Trinidad between 1592 and 1783 as San José de Oruña. The imposing **Jinnah Memorial Mosque** stands here. Completed in 1954, the green and white mosque is named after the founder of Pakistan, Quaid-I-Azam Mohammed Ali Jinnah. In the centre, the 7.3-m-high main dome is 18 m in diameter, surrounded by glass louvres and crowned by the crescent and star. Four half domes around the main dome each have a door allowing onlookers to see both the inside of the dome and the prayer

Angostura bitters

Angostura bitters are a crucial component in many cocktails, classic and modern, such as the Old Fashioned, Bloody Mary and Singapore Sling, and dashes of the concentrated ruddy orange tonic are used to add colour and aroma as well as flavour without changing the sweetness level. It is said to contain over 40 ingredients — although few can know for sure, since the recipe, which was developed as medicine by a German doctor, JGB Siegert, in the town of Angostura in Venezuela in 1824, is still a closely guarded secret. It is, however, known to contain water, vegetable and plant flavouring extracts, and a bitter root called gentian. Although it contains 44.7% alcohol by volume, each dash contains such an insignificant amount of alcohol, it is classed as non-alcoholic by the food and drink retail industry.

hall on the ground floor, which can hold some 600 worshippers. Beyond them, six small domes with spires stand at the corners of the hexagonal structure and on the very outside are two tall minaret towers, also capped with domes.

Maracas Valley

North of St Joseph is the Maracas Valley (there is no road to Maracas Bay, just a footpath). People refer to the area as Maracas-St Joseph to distinguish it from Maracas Beach on the other side of the mountains. The valley was one of the first areas to be settled and the Maracas Royal Road running up the valley is one of the oldest on the island. The river running through it is called the **St Joseph River** or the **Maracas River** and is a major tributary of the Caroni River. A pleasant area, its main tourist attraction, the 91-m-high **Maracas Waterfall**, is about 8 km north of St Joseph and reached by a good trail 30 minutes from Waterfall Road (you can park at the Wasa Pump Station situated next to the red flamboyant tree). The trail weaves through the forest with its myriad plants, birds and butterflies until you get to a pretty glade. In the dry season the waterfall is like smoke cascading down the rocks, but in the wet season it is more impressive and you can bathe in the pool at its foot (take care when walking on the slippery rocks).

Abbey of Mount St Benedict

At the top of St John's Rd, 3.5 km north of St Augustine on Eastern Main Rd, T662 2259, www.mountstbenedictabbey.org, check the website for mass/prayer times; shop open Mon-Sat 0800-1600, Sun 0630-1600.

Further east, high on a forested hill some 240 m above sea level on the edge of the Northern Range, is the Abbey of Mount St Benedict, which is easily visible from Eastern Main Road. It is also known as the Abbey of Our Lady of Exile and is the oldest Benedictine complex in the Caribbean. Although the original monastery was founded by a Belgian, the first Benedictine monks came from Bahia, Brazil, in 1912, fleeing religious persecution. It started with a *tapia* hut but construction of the main building on Mount Tabor began in 1918. Today the abbey's estate covers 243 ha and at the main complex is the lovely church (open to all for morning and evening prayer and at least one mass daily, plus three masses on Sunday), dwellings for the monks, lots of educational facilities, a drug rehabilitation centre, a farm and the **Pax Guest House** (see page 69), which is popular with birdwatchers and walkers – more than 140 bird species have been recorded up here. The monks run a little shop next to the church selling religious items, books, pictures, rosaries, candles, etc, and a café for cold drinks, sweets, snacks and home-made cakes, pies and pastries (although not hot drinks). They also make their own yoghurt and delicious yoghurt drinks with tropical flavours: guava, soursop, pineapple, almond and more. There are marvellous views over the Caroni Plain to the sea and a picnic area from which to enjoy them. The **Pax Guest House** (see page 76) offers pre-booked lunch and an excellent afternoon tea; try to get a seat on the peaceful terrace and watch the hummingbirds at the feeders.

To get here, the abbey operates a white van shuttle service (TT$4), marked St Benedict, which leaves from outside Scotia Bank on the corner of Eastern Main Road and St John's Road in St Augustine every 30 minutes between 0600 and 1700. A priority maxi taxi from Port of Spain to St Augustine takes 20 minutes, then a route taxi up St John's Road and then St Michael's Road will take you close to the monastery; but unless you pay to go off route it is still a stiff walk uphill. Otherwise take the shuttle or a private taxi all the way.

Lopinot Complex
Lopinot, T684 9358, daily 0600-1800, free.

A little further along the Eastern Main Road at **Arouca** is the turn-off along Golden Grove Road (crossing Churchill Roosevelt Highway on the way) to the residential and industrial town of Piarco, which fans out around Piarco International Airport and where there is a decent selection of airport accommodation. Then back on Eastern Main Road, Lopinot Road turns off north and winds 10 km up into the forested foothills of the Northern Range to the Lopinot Complex. This estate was built in 1806 by French Count Lopinot de la Fresillière, who had fled to Trinidad in 1791 to escape the Haitian revolution and was granted 478 acres (193 ha) of land for services rendered to the British crown. The count established a cocoa estate on the land and called it La Reconnaissance, and he contributed significantly to the development of cocoa production on Trinidad, which by the end of the 19th century was the fourth largest producer in the world. The estate is now a popular picnic spot and destination for school trips, well-maintained by the Forestry Division; the Lopinot River is a short walk away if you want to cool down. The old plantation house and slave quarters have been turned into a small museum about the history of the estate, which hosts a parang music festival before Christmas. There is a bar across the road, open, like most others in Trinidad, 'anyday, anytime' and close by in the village of Lopinot, the **Café Mariposa** (T669 8647, www.mariposalopinot.com) is open daily for lunch and dinner.

Arima
Arima is 25 km east of Port of Spain and easily reached by bus or route taxi as the priority bus/taxi route from the capital ends here. The landmark at the centre is the **Dial**, an old public clock (originally powered by steam) donated to the town by the mayor in 1898 after he bought it in Nice, France. It was repaired after an argument with a heavy truck several years ago, but no longer chimes. Arima is also the focus of Trinidad's Amerindian heritage and still has a recognized Carib community. The town was founded in 1757 when Capuchin monks arrived to convert the local people to Christianity, and built the **Santa Rosa Roman Catholic Church**, and many were relocated here when their lands were seized in 1783 for cocoa plantations. A group of local people regard themselves as descendants of the original Amerindians of the area. They are now largely Roman Catholic although they do have a ceremonial figurehead **Carib Queen** and call themselves the **Santa Rosa First Peoples Community** (www.santarosafirstpeoples.org). To celebrate Arima's special identity as an area of Spanish, Catholic and Amerindian heritage, the feast

of **Santa Rosa de Limais** is held on the last Sunday in August with a special mass at the church and a parade through the streets led by the Carib Queen. Arima is also the location of Trinidad's only horse-racing track, Santa Rosa Park (see page 83).

Asa Wright Nature Centre

Spring Hill Estate, off Blanchisseuse Rd, T667 4655, www.asawright.org, daily 0900-1700, US$10, children (under 12) US$6, which includes a 1½-hr guided walk at 1030 or 1330, advance reservations required. Buffet lunch in the dining room 1200-1300, Mon-Sat US$21, Sun US$30, children half price, sandwiches on the veranda 1100-1600, accommodation available (see page 68). Drive or get a taxi from Arima, ask the driver to wait for you, or tour operators and taxi drivers can arrange an excursion from Port of Spain for around US$80 per car.

About 14 km north of the Eastern Main Road at Arima, and off the road to Blanchisseuse, is the Asa Wright Nature Centre, an old plantation house for the former cocoa/coffee/citrus Spring Hill Estate overlooking a wooded valley and a must for bird-lovers – 166 species of bird have been recorded here, and hummingbirds, bananaquits, honeycreepers and tanagers are the most common. It is so named as it was bought in 1947 by a retired English lawyer, Newcome Wright, and his Icelandic wife Asa. When Newcome died, he entrusted the land to a conservation area and a trust was established in 1967. The centre now owns nearly 600 ha (1500 acres) of protected forest in the Arima and Aripo valleys of the Northern Range. There is a beautiful man-made pool where you can swim, a network of trails and guided walks, and you can sit on the veranda and watch the hummingbirds (there are six different species present on the island) while you have a sandwich and drink – sublime. The rangers are very knowledgeable and can tell you about the birds as well as the plants and insects. The centre can organize visits to see the rare fruit-eating nocturnal oilbirds in **Dunstan Cave**, but obviously only if you stay overnight.

Tip...
Wear insect repellent and take binoculars and a camera, as the hummingbirds are fairly tame and you can get close to them at the feeders.

Northeast coast
time-lost villages and remote beaches backed by emerald rainforests

Where the Atlantic and Caribbean currents collide in the passage between Trinidad and Tobago, the northeast coast is one of the most remote and unspoiled parts of the island. This is partly because the road does not extend along the whole of the north coast from Blanchisseuse, and this northeast corner of the island is time-consuming to get to, but well worth the effort for its peace and serenity. Long stretches of sand attract nesting leatherback turtles and numerous birds and butterflies live in the forest where the eastern end of the Northern Range dips its toes in the sea.

From Arima northeast to Toco

Beyond Arima, the Eastern Main Road continues 12 km to the small town of **Valencia**. It is here that Toco Main Road forks northeast and leads to Matura, Salybia and around Galera Point to the north-coast villages of Toco, Grande Riviere and Matelot. (Eastern Main Road heads southeast to Sangre Grande.) The journey to Toco has some interesting places to visit en route, and the road itself becomes prettier (and more winding) as it goes through small villages, woodland and eventually joins the coast at **Salybia** (affectionately known as Sally Bay), 24 km from Valencia.

Matura Beach The rural village of Matura is the first of the leatherback turtle-watching locations that you come across along this coast (see box, page 54). During nesting months (1 March-31 August), excursions to the protected Matura Beach where the leatherbacks nest are organized by **Nature Seekers** ① *Toco Main Rd, Matura, T668 7337, www.natureseekers.org, tours depart at 2000 and last approximately 2½ hrs, US$20, children (under 12) free, turtle-watching permit TT$5, children (under 12) TT$2*, although permits need to be obtained in advance (the nearest Forestry Division office is in Sangre Grande, T668 3825); it is less complicated to continue to Grande Riviere (see below) where permits are available on site. However, **Nature Seekers** do offer a number of other interesting walks into the Matura forests to see birds, iguanas and red howler monkeys.

Saline Bay At **Salybia**, there are two mediocre but comfortable beach resorts next to each other (see page 70), and just around the next bend after the village, off the road to the right, is a good beach overlooking Saline Bay (also called Salybia Bay). This is a long, scenic bay, often windswept, with surging breakers and a small fringing reef. There are lifeguards, changing rooms/toilets (TT$2), and a hut renting out kayaks for use on the small lagoon formed by the mouth of the Salybia River. The sea can be rough here – it's a popular surfing spot between October and April when the waves are up – so ensure you don't swim far from the lifeguard hut.

Rio Seco Waterfall A trail to the falls, which are on the Rio Seco River, a tributary of the larger Salybia River, begins just after the bridge over the Salybia river mouth; look out for the sign for the **Salybia Matura Trace**. There are two options here: you can either park and hike to the falls from this point, which takes around an hour and a half, or you can do the 20-minute, rather rough drive up to the top of Salybia Matura Trace, park there, and walk the remaining 30 minutes. This final part of the trail is quite enchanting; it is situated on the top riverbank and is shaded by the canopy of the rainforest, numerous tree roots spread diagonally across the footpath, and there are two gentle streams to cross. The waterfall is not very high (about 5 m) but what makes Rio Seco so appealing is its large basin and pristine waters, which reflect vibrant colours of emerald green from the surrounding trees. There is also a picnic area. Alternatively, you can visit the falls on three- to four-hour guided hike with **Nature Seekers** in Matura (see above).

Tip...

If you are a good swimmer; it is quite feasible to jump (carefully) from the top of the waterfall into the pool, which has a depth of about 6 m.

ON THE ROAD

Leatherback turtles

The leatherback (*Dermochelys coriacea*) is the world's largest turtles, and is easily differentiated from other sea turtles (like the green and Hawksbill) by its lack of a bony shell. Instead, the carapace of the leatherback is covered by skin and oily flesh, which is an inky-blue colour and somewhat flexible – almost rubbery – to the touch (hence the name); ridges help give it a more hydrodynamic structure. They are also the world's fourth-heaviest reptile (behind three different types of crocodile) and adults can weigh 250-900 kg, with a total length measurement (from flipper to flipper) of 1.8-2.2 m. A large pair of front flippers powers the turtles through the water and, like other sea turtles, the leatherback has flattened forelimbs adapted for swimming. They dive to depths of 1200 m – far deeper than any other turtle – and can stay down for up to 85 minutes.

Leatherbacks have the widest global distribution of all reptile species, and possibly of any vertebrate. They can be found in the tropic and temperate waters of the Atlantic, Pacific, and Indian oceans, as well as the Mediterranean Sea, and, given that they can retain body heat to survive in cold water, adults have been seen as far north as Canada and Norway and as far south as New Zealand and the bottom of South America. Leatherbacks undertake the longest migrations between breeding and feeding areas of any sea turtle, averaging 6000 km each way – a turtle seen in the Caribbean may have come from as far away as Madagascar.

After mating at sea, females come ashore during the breeding season to nest. The night-time ritual involves hauling herself up on to the beach through the surf, excavating a hole in the sand with her back flippers, depositing eggs, re-filling the nest, leaving a large, disturbed area of sand that makes detection by predators difficult, and finally returning to the sea. They visit up to nine times per season, laying 75 to 120 eggs in one 'clutch', each time about 10 days apart. Incubation time is 60 days, so about two months later, the eggs hatch, and the baby turtles ('hatchlings') dig themselves out of their nests and hustle – awkwardly and adorably – to the open sea. The temperature inside the nest determines the sex of the hatchlings. A mix of male and female hatchlings occurs when the nest temperature is approximately 29°C, while higher temperatures produce females and cooler temperatures produce males. Female

Galera Point After Salybia, Toco Main Road winds its way past the entrance to **Balandra by the Bay**, an exclusive gated community of villas currently under construction overlooking the bay of the same name, through a couple more villages including **Cumana**, where there's a petrol station, a couple of bars, a small supermarket and a guesthouse (see page 71), before it makes a sharp left to Toco and becomes Paria Main Road. Opposite, the right turn goes 3 km to Galera Point, and on the way you can stop at **Toco Beach** where you can pull your car up almost right to the surf line; there are toilets and showers (TT$2) and, at busier times, a few beach vendors selling drinks and beach apparel. Be wary of swimming, however, as the sand shelf to the sea is steep. From here, go over a rickety wooden bridge to the small, pretty lighthouse at Galera Point. This was built in 1897 and is marked with Queen Victoria's initials as it opened the same year as her Diamond Jubilee. It was rechristened the **Keshorn Walcott Toco**

hatchlings that make it to the sea will roam the oceans until they reach sexual maturity. Astonishingly, they then return to the very same beach where they themselves hatched to produce their own offspring. Males spend the rest of their lives at sea.

However, only about one egg in a thousand produces a hatchling that actually survives and makes it back to the sea – the eggs either do not incubate, or the eggs or the hatchlings get taken by crabs, birds or dogs. There are other dangers too and leatherbacks are classed as critically endangered – in 1980 there was an estimated global population of nesting females of around 120,000, but in 2016 figures were put at around 40,000. The population of males is unknown as they never come out of the sea and are rarely seen. Hazards to them are sharks (they are soft to munch through, after all), many get caught up in fishing nets or are struck by boats, and leatherbacks can also die if they ingest floating plastic debris mistaken for their favourite food – jellyfish. Other threats include poachers (turtle meat is known as the 'beef of the sea' in some communities), disconcerting man-made light (they only follow the light of the moon), beach erosion and pollution, such as oils spills.

Trinidad and Tobago are two of the world's most important turtle nesting grounds, and the season is from the beginning of March to the end of August. Trinidad takes on a very special role – the second largest leatherback turtle nesting site in the world (after Gabon in West Africa) is the beach at Grande Riviere. But the turtles also come up on numerous north and east coast beaches around the islands, many of which are protected and public access is prohibited at night. On Trinidad, these beaches include Matura and Fishing Pond on the east coast; and Paria, Tacaribe and Grande Riviere on the north coast. And on Tobago they include Great Courland Bay (known as Turtle Beach), Stonehaven Bay, Bloody Bay and Parlatuvier. Turtle watching is a fascinating experience – whether you see the females nesting or the hatchlings run to the sea – and excursions, always at night, can be organized at a number of these beaches for which permits are required. For Grande Riviere see page 56, and for details of the other options, visit the website of the Turtle Village Trust (www.turtlevillagetrust.org), the umbrella organization for all the Trinidad and Tobago turtle conservation groups: Nature Seekers, Grande Riviere Nature Tour Guides Association (GRNTGA), the Matura to Matelot Network, the Fishing Pond Turtle Conservation Group, and Save Our Sea Turtles (SOS) Tobago.

Lighthouse after the Toco-born javelin thrower won Trinidad and Tobago's first gold medal in 36 years at the 2012 London Olympics. The lighthouse isn't open, but around its base is a pleasant picnic ground with concrete seats and tables, and you can walk right on to the rocks at the point to admire the views. This is often lauded as the point where the two oceans meet – the Atlantic to the east and the Caribbean to the west. Legend also has it that those rocks were the final resting place for dozens of Amerindians who, in an ultimate show of desperation, threw themselves into the water, choosing death rather that forced conversion to Christianity at the hands of a Capuchin priest. The waves can be impressive, crashing against the rocks and forming blowholes, and you may spot brown pelicans dive-bombing into the sea. This is the closest point to Trinidad's sister island Tobago, which can be seen 35 km to the northeast.

Grande Riviere

The drive between the village of Toco and Grande Riviere is only 16 km, but the road twists and turns and it can take nearly an hour. But the recently surfaced road is good and it's a beautiful drive through dense forest of overhanging trees and at Sans Souci the road runs right along the coastline no more than a metre above the waves.

Tip...

Grande Riviere is 118 km from Port of Spain, and 85 km from Piarco International Airport, so can be reached on a comfortable three- to five-hour drive on the same day as a turtle-watching excursion in the evening.

Grande Riviere is a small village lying in the forested headlands of the Northern Range, from which the river flows down on to the long and lovely quartz-rich sandy beach, where it forms a shallow lagoon where you can swim and kayak. Guesthouses here can organize birdwatching or hiking tours into the forest and along the path to Matelot and Blanchisseuse; but most people come to see the leatherback turtles. Where the river flows into the sea, strong waves are formed giving the turtles the extra push they need to haul themselves on to the sand at nesting time. Grande Riviere is believed to be the world's largest nesting site for the leatherback turtle after Gabon in West Africa, and more than 6000 females visit the beach here each season. In fact, even though the beaches in northern Trinidad are also the nesting/hatching grounds for Hawksbill and green turtles, the volume of leatherbacks at Grande Riviere is so great, there is simply no room for these other smaller turtles to come ashore.

From 1 March to 31 August it is prohibited for anyone to go on to the beach between 1800 and 0600, unless you are with a guide. On the organized nightly excursion you can to watch the turtles laying their eggs in the sand, then, later in the season, see the thousands of hatchlings dig their way out of the nests and make their way to the sea. In Grande Riviere these visits are organized by the non-profit, community-based organization, the **Grande Riviere Nature Tour Guides Association (GRNTGA)** ① *Hosang St, just behind the beach, T670 4257/469 128, office opens at 1900 when you register, you can then go back to your accommodation for dinner and tours depart 2000-2400 and last approximately 1½ hrs, US$15, children (under 12) US$8, plus TT$5 permit fee per person.* It is an extraordinary experience watching these curious creatures – their behaviour appears to be chaotic and clumsy and sophisticated and determined all at the same time. There are few places in the world where turtle watching is so accessible, and a couple of the guesthouses in Grande Riviere (**Le Grand Almandier** and **Mount Plaisir Estate Hotel**, see page 70) are almost directly on the sand, so early risers may spot turtles at first light too.

Grande Riviere is easy to reach by private car and possible, but not so easy, by public transport – give yourself lots of time. From Port of Spain take a bus (faster than a maxi) to Arima, and then go on to Sangre Grande (much more of a transport hub than Valencia), where buses, maxis and route taxis all stop in the same place on Bus Station Road, just north of Eastern Main Road in the centre. It is relatively easy to get a maxi to Toco and possibly on to Sans Souci, but this still leaves another 16 km on through the woods to Grande Riviere. Some maxis and route taxis leave in the morning from Grande Riviere to Sangre Grande, returning at about 1600. And, for the right price, a route taxi in Sangre Grande will become a private taxi, which is how the guesthouses at Grande Riviere will arrange to pick you up. Whichever way you go, the effort is worthwhile.

Beyond Grande Riviere the tarred road ends at the tiny and peaceful fishing village of **Matelot** (10 km from Grande Riviere and 26 km from Toco), after which the only way westwards along the north coast is on foot (see page 48 for details of hiking between here and Paria Bay and Blanchisseuse Spring Bridge). Matelot has a pleasant beach and the 3-m-high **Matelot Falls** are about an hour's hike upstream on the stony bed of the Matelot River. Again they have a deep clear basin to swim in.

East coast
coconuts, oil, swamps and two sweeping bays along the wind- and wave-lashed Atlantic coast

Sangre Grande (with its rather confusing one-way system) is the largest town in northeastern Trinidad, and is about half an hour's drive or just over 20 km from Arima via the Eastern Main Road. The name means 'big blood' and it has been suggested that the town was named after a battle that took place between the Amerindians and the Spanish settlers. From here it's another 15 km southwest to the Atlantic coast at Manzanilla, where the Eastern Main Road becomes the Manzanilla–Mayaro Road and heads south. The east coast here is divided into two huge sweeping bays – Manzanilla and Mayaro – and there is an almost uninterrupted line of gracefully bent coconut palms (*Cocos nucifera*) along the shore, testimony to the days when most of the area was covered with coconut plantations. Both bays have beautiful sandy beaches, but the Atlantic currents are consistently strong with dangerous undercurrents during high tide, and this can make swimming dangerous. Sadly, too, these currents also wash ashore debris – from pungent seaweed to plastic rubbish accumulated from further out in the ocean. The large waves also tirelessly erode the shoreline, and it's quite common to see collapsed coconut trees drifting in the surf. Nonetheless, it's a pleasant drive to enjoy the fresh sea breeze and watch the breakers rolling in, and the Manzanilla–Mayaro Road is flat, straight and in good condition.

The beach at **Lower Manzanilla** is sheltered, with a car park, snack bar, picnic tables and changing rooms with showers and toilets (TT$2), as well as the very run-down D'Coconut Cove Holiday Beach Resort (not recommended). Next the road runs southwards alongside the beach and lines of windswept coconut palms, a stretch known locally as 'The Cocal'.

Beyond the southern end of Manzanilla, past St Joseph Village, is the start of **Mayaro Bay**. At Mayaro village fishermen

Tip...

Shortly before you reach the coast, and just after Upper Manzanilla, you can take Plum Mitan Road to the right for about 4 km to the stocky **Brigand Hill Lighthouse** (1958) that shares Brigand Hill with TV/radio masts. From here there are spectacular views of the entire east coast, the Nariva Swamp and the central plains towards the Northern Range.

can be seen pulling in their nets on the beach. There are several beach houses to rent and a clutch of equally poor and dated concrete holiday resorts – popular at long weekends for liming (Mayaro is one of the traditional places for Trinis to spend the Easter holidays). There are lifeguards and public toilets at the beach. The peaceful character of Mayaro is somewhat marred at night, however, by the glow from the offshore oil platforms, which stand out luridly against the black horizon.

Beyond Mayaro, the road meanders on for several more kilometres to the southeastern tip of Trinidad at **Guayaguayare** (often simply called Guaya) at **Galeota Point**. This has been oil country for more than a century (the first commercially viable wells were drilled in

1902) and today it's a major operational centre occupied by tank farms for oil companies. Driving this far is like stumbling on to a large military base. Maps show a public road from here northwest to Rio Claro, but there is in fact no access without prior arrangement from Petrotrin, the state oil company, so you will need to turn back. The option then is to either retrace your route back to Sangre Grande via the coast, or to turn onto the Naparima–Mayaro Road at Mayaro. Once at Rio Claro you can either head north to Sangre Grande on the Cunapo Southern Road, or westwards across the island through the wooded parts of the Central Range to San Fernando or Chaguanas.

Nariva Swamp

Access is usually from the village of Kernaham, which is reached from the Manzanilla–Mayaro Rd; the turn-off is about 20 km south of Lower Manzanilla.

Not too far from the rumble and tumble of the Atlantic waves, is the 60-sq-km Nariva Swamp, immediately inland from Manzanilla Bay and the largest freshwater swamp in Trinidad. Along the northern border, a small portion has been reclaimed for rice cultivation, but for the most part it is wild wasteland. Within the wetland is an elevated peninsula known as **Bush Bush Island**, an area of lowland tropical rainforest measuring 15-sq-km. The biodiversity within the system is extremely high owing to a varied mosaic of distinct vegetation – marshy swamps, mangroves, grassy savannahs and a variety of hardwood, fig and palm trees. Like Caroni Swamp (see page 59), it is a **RAMSAR Wetland of International Importance**, and more than 200 species of bird have been recorded here. These include the snowy egret, black-crested antshrike, savannah hawk, orange-winged parrot, yellow-capped Amazon parrot, red-breasted blackbird, red-bellied macaw and numerous flycatchers and kingfishers. It's also the habitat of an array of beautiful butterflies, at least three dozen types of bat, mammal species including red howler monkeys, tree-climbing porcupines, anteaters and the endangered ocelot, and reptiles include iguanas, anacondas and caimans. Nariva is best known, however, for being the main habitat for the locally and globally endangered sub-species of the West Indian manatee, the Antillean manatee (*Trichechus manatus*) or 'sea cow'. Note though, sightings of this elusive mammal are very rare, and fewer than a couple of dozen individuals are believed to remain at Nariva.

The swamp is only accessible by kayak or dinghy in the wet season or on foot in the dry season; to visit you need to be on a guided tour and a have a permit from the Forestry Division. A tour by kayak is particularly recommended as you will paddle silently across fields of giant water lilies, through channels in the thick forest of mangroves and towering silk cotton trees, with monkeys and parrots chattering overhead. Excursions cost around US$100-120, depending on transport arrangements. Contact Stephen Broadbridge at **Caribbean Discovery Tours** ① *T624 7281, www.caribbeandiscoverytours.com*, or Kayman Sagar at **Limeland Tours** ① *T798 5750, www.limeland-tours.com.*

The landscape of the central Trinidad west coast on the Gulf of Paria is marked by sugarcane, citrus and rice plantations that were once the main economic earners of the region south of Port of Spain. But the modern oil and petrochemical industries at Pointe-a-Pierre and Point Lisas are now more important to the economy of Trinidad, and these days the south coast features as many steel mills, and methanol and ammonia plants, as it does agricultural farms. Hardly tourist attractions, but they have made San Fernando and its sprawling satellite coastal suburbs a prosperous area, if a little unremarkable and with a somewhat ugly industrial character. However, this area is still dominated by the Indian community – Indo-Trinidadian history dates back to when almost 150,000 Indians arrived as indentured immigrants between 1845 and 1917 – and is dotted with temples and is rich in religious and cultural festivals. The greatest attraction in the area is the Caroni Swamp, where the spectacular scarlet ibis arrives at dusk to roost; it's an easy excursion from Port of Spain.

Caroni Bird Sanctuary

The Caroni Swamp Visitor Centre is 1 km off Uriah Butler Highway; the (poorly signposted) turn-off is at Caroni Flyover, about 4 km south of the interchange with Churchill-Roosevelt Highway; buses, maxi and route taxis will drop off at the turn-off. Nanan Bird Tours (T645 1305, www.nananecotours.com), operate boat tours from the Visitor Centre, daily at 1600 and returning after sunset, reservations required, US$10 per person, group rates and transport available.

From Port of Spain and the Churchill-Roosevelt Highway, turn right onto the Uriah Butler Highway and across the Caroni River onto the Caroni Plains. This highway continues due south to San Fernando (about 50 minutes from Port of Spain) and a little way beyond, and passes the Caroni Swamp on the right. The 60-sq-km bird sanctuary is a lagoon ringed with mangroves and marshes and is part of the much larger Caroni Swamp, whose geographical boundaries lie between the mouths of the Caroni and Madame Espagnole rivers. It is a RAMSAR Wetland of International Importance and more than 200 bird species have been recorded here, the most famous resident being the scarlet ibis (*Eudocimus ruber*), Trinidad's national bird. During the day these striking birds feed in the forests of Venezuela and then return to the island to roost at dusk, filling the sky and covering the mangroves with a burst of vibrant scarlet red. A two-hour boat trip to see this lovely sight is a fascinating experience, and tours take place in the late afternoon so that you can see thousands of the scarlet ibis, as well as herons and egrets, returning in groups of up to 20 at a time and settling down for the night. Guides will also point out other wildlife, from birds such as eagles and parrots, to crabs, fish and boas living in the mangroves. Although numbers of scarlet ibis have declined as the swamp has been encroached upon, this is still a magical sight.

Tip...
You might like to take a cool bag with drinks, and mosquito repellent is essential for when you get off the boat at the end of the trip.

South to San Fernando

It takes 50 minutes (90 minutes in rush hour) to drive the 54 km from Port of Spain to San Fernando, first on the Uriah Butler Highway then, after Chaguanas, on the Sir Solomon Hochoy Highway. It's a much more comfortable journey on the modern ferry-like Water Taxi service if you are going directly between the downtown areas of each (see page 84). But by road, **Chaguanas**, 26 km south of Port of Spain, is one of the fastest-growing towns on the island. It is not an architectural must, but known for cheap housing and bargain shopping in the several malls. At the centre is the unimaginatively named junction, Busy Corner. On the east of the highway just before you get to town, look out for a large blue statue of the Hindu god, Lord Shiva and a large white statue of Viveka Nanda, a Hindu philosopher. These mark the site of the **Divali Nagar** (City of Lights), an annual exposition of Indo-Trinidadian culture and the celebration of the Hindu Diwali (usually October/November). The **National Council of Indian Culture of Trinidad and Tobago** ⓘ *www.ncictt.com*, is also based here.

After **Chaguanas**, turn off Sir Solomon Hochoy Highway at the Chase Village Flyover, and follow the Orange Field Road towards the coast. On the right is the **Dattatreya Yoga Centre** ⓘ *Datta Dr, off Orange Field Rd, T673 5328, see Facebook, daily 0900-1200, 1700-1900*, which is considered one of the foremost Hindu institutions in the Caribbean and has been built according to the Dravidian style of architecture with several intricate carvings and symbolic figurines. The temple's entrance is guarded by two life-sized elephant statues, and the central feature is the impressive 26-m-tall *murti* (sacred statue) of the monkey deity, Hanuman.

> **Tip...**
> The people at the yoga centre are happy to show visitors around and explain Trinidadian Hinduism, but the temple is an active place of worship so dress appropriately and remember to remove your shoes.

Further south, at Waterloo, is the **Waterloo Temple in the Sea** ⓘ *causeway open daily 0600-1800, but the temple itself is open at the caretaker's discretion*, a small white and blue Hindu temple that has been built in the shallow waters of the Gulf of Paria and is reached by a short causeway. Indentured sugar labourer, Siewdass Sadhu, originally began construction in the 1940s after colonial officials and local landowners prohibited him from building on land. As he considered the ocean to be 'no-man's land', he spent the next 25 years unloading buckets of dirt and rocks into the gulf in an effort to create an artificial base for the temple. He died in 1970 and the government completed and consecrated the temple in 1995, in commemoration of the 150th anniversary of the first Indian arrivals to the country. It is a colourful, octagonal-shaped structure, and at the entrance stands a statue of Sadhu; it is here that you must remove your shoes.

Pointe-a-Pierre Wildfowl Trust

Petrotrin Complex, between Sir Solomon Hochoy Highway and Southern Main Rd, T658 4200, www.papwildfowltrust.org, Mon-Fri 0900-1700, Sat-Sun 1000-1700, reservations must be made in advance to get you through security, free.

Just to the north of San Fernando is the Pointe-a-Pierre oil refinery (the largest in the Caribbean), today run by **Petrotrin**, the state-owned oil company. It was constructed during the Second World War by Trinidad Leaseholds Limited and constituted one of the largest contributions to the war effort by a private company. Its success during the oil boom of the 1970s and 1980s led to a rapid growth of San Fernando and its suburbs. Quite unusually, the 32-ha Pointe-a-Pierre Wildfowl Trust lies within the

Once attached to the South American mainland, and hemmed in between the Caribbean Sea and the North Atlantic Ocean, Trinidad is 12 km northeast of the coast of Venezuela and is separated from it by the Gulf of Paria. Thanks to a combination of Caribbean and South American characteristics, or a unique mix of island and continental ecology, Trinidad's flora and fauna is considerably more varied than that of most West Indian islands. Although it's a rapidly developing and industrialized island, about 40% of its 4828 sq km is undeveloped in three mountain ranges (the Northern, Central and Southern), which are cloaked in tropical forests, woodlands, waterfalls and rivers, while there are flat savannahs in the interior, and the mangrove swamps and coastal waters are fed by the nutrient-rich outflow of Venezuela's Orinoco River.

Within these environments, Trinidad has more than 100 recorded species of mammal, 60 of which are bats; others include the Trinidad capuchin and red howler monkey, brown forest brocket (deer), collared peccary (quenk), manicou (opossum), agouti and armadillo, while a small group of manatees is protected in the Nariva Swamp. There are 1000 flowering plants including hibiscus, poinsettia, chaconia (wild poinsettia – the national flower), ixora, bougainvillea, orchid, ginger lily and heliconia. About 370 tree species can be seen on the island, including pink and yellow poui, frangipani, cassia, pride of India, immortelle, flamboyant, jacaranda and the native purpleheart, mora and crappo. There are 600 species of butterfly and 120 species of reptile and amphibian (40 of which are snakes and few are poisonous), and more than 400 species of marine fish. Trinidad has more bird species than any other Caribbean island, about 430, although the variety is South American, not West Indian. These include hummingbirds, parrots, macaws, the rare red-breasted blackbird, the nightingale-thrush and the motmot. The peak season for birdwatching is November to May, although birding is good all year round, and the most accessible birdwatching sites are the Caroni Bird Sanctuary (page 59), the Asa Wright Centre (page 52), and the Pointe-a-Pierre Wildfowl Trust (page 60).

secured premises of the refinery. This conservation area was established in 1966 and has two lakes dotted with water hyacinths and more than 40 species of tree, which provide a dense canopy over several paths, boardwalks and quiet picnic spots. There's also an interesting museum on Trinidad's flora and fauna, as well as an exhibit on the indigenous Amerindians. More than 85 bird species have been recorded here, including the scarlet ibis, the blue and gold macaw, herons and other wading birds, and, for over 50 years now, the trust has been involved in breeding endangered waterfowl and wetland birds, which are later released into the wild. You can explore on your own, or take a guided tour; both options require advance notice.

San Fernando

Beyond Pointe-a-Pierre you reach Trinidad's second largest city, which is built around a hill that was known as Naparima to the Amerindians, now San Fernando Hill, overlooking a sheltered bay in the Gulf of Paria. A town named San Fernando de Naparima was established by Spanish Governor Don José María Chacón in 1784, in honour of the heir to the Spanish crown. Over time, the 'de Naparima' was dropped, and today's San Fernando ('Sando' to locals) is a busy, hot city, as yet unspoilt by tourism but spoilt by just about everything else. It is the centre for the energy-based industries located in the southwest of the island, and is surrounded by oil, gas and petrochemical refineries, iron and steel and aluminium smelters.

Finding your way around downtown can be a bewildering experience, thanks to a confusing one-way system, few street signs and little parking. San Fernando has lost much of its history; most of its old buildings have been demolished, and the waterfront area is a mess, in spite of continual talk of restoration. However, Harris Promenade – a 500-m pedestrianized street in the centre – is fairly pleasant and has had a facelift in recent times. It's lined with some major buildings including the **Central Police Station**, **City Hall**, the **Our Lady of Perpetual Help Church** and the old **Carnegie Free Library**, and along its centre is a bandstand, a statue of Mahatma Gandhi that was brought from India and erected in 1952, and a section of the last train engine that ran from Port of Spain to San Fernando, which was dismantled in the 1950s. **High Street** and **Coffee Street**, which meet at the eastern end of the promenade, are where most of the shops are. The PTSC Bus Terminus (and other transport) is at **King's Wharf** on the waterfront.

Above the city and around which all the city's roads circle, is **San Fernando Hill** ① *entry off Royal Rd, daily 0900-1800, free*, oddly shaped as a result of quarrying and easily picked out from Northern Range viewpoints or from Chaguaramas. It is now landscaped as a recreation area with lookouts, picnic huts and a children's playground, and you can either walk or drive to the top for a spectacular view of the city and up and down the coast; the offshore islands and the mountains of Venezuela can be seen on a clear day.

East of San Fernando

From San Fernando the main Naparima–Mayaro Road runs east through the rolling hills and gentle forests of the low-lying Central Range and past a string of villages stretching cross-country to Rio Claro and then Mayaro on the east coast (see page 57) – a distance of just under 70 km. It runs more or less parallel to the south coast, most of which is oil field country and fairly inaccessible. Off Naparima–Mayaro Road, beyond and east of St Julien and close to the

> **Tip...**
> It is quite difficult to get east of San Fernando, and south of Sangre Grande, by bus, but there are route and maxi taxis along the central rural roads, or you can hire a car. A full-day circuit of the island can be driven from Port of Spain south to San Fernando, east to Mayaro then north to Sangre Grande and Arima.

village of Hindustan (which is about 4 km southeast of the road), is the **Devil's Woodyard**, a series of small (and disappointing) mud 'volcanoes'. These mounds of watery mud or clay, forced out of the earth by methane gas, occasionally spatter with violent force, but usually it's simply a mild surface upwelling of muddy water accompanied by gas bubbles. This one is considered a holy site by some Hindus, and as such has a few benches, gazebo-type thatched picnic huts and a children's playground for visitors. Some accounts claim that the curious name originated with early European settlers who thought the sound of the gas erupting sounded like the devil chopping wood underground to tend his fires.

Another excursion might be to **Moruga**, a sleepy fishing village among the oil fields on the south coast. A delightful old church stands a short walk from the sea. This is where the arrival of Christopher Columbus' caravels, the *Pinta*, *Niña* and *Santa Maria*, is re-enacted by the villagers at the beginning of August, on the holiday now designated

Emancipation Day. Fishing boats are decked out as the caravels, complete with the red Maltese cross, and Columbus, a priest and soldiers are met by Amerindians; after the meeting everyone retires to the church compound where the revelry continues late into the night. To get to Moruga take Moruga Road directly from St Julien (a distance of 27 km; slow driving).

Southwest peninsula
a massive asphalt lake and an interesting drive down the spine of the southwest peninsula

The south of Trinidad is the backbone of Trinidad's economy. From the natural gas liquefaction and export plant at Point Fortin on the southwest peninsula to the onshore and offshore oil wells at Guayaguayare on the southeast coast, the island has by far the largest resources of crude oil and natural gas in the Caribbean, and it is busily making the most of it. While at first glance the region doesn't look enticing – oil tankers sit offshore and jumbles of pipes, towers and tanks blot the landscape in places – there are a couple of things to see in the southwest such as the curious Pitch Lake, and the Cedros Peninsula, which is dotted with isolated beaches and friendly fishing villages.

Pitch Lake
T651 1232, daily 0900-1700, US$4.50, children (under 12) US$1.80, maxi taxi from King's Wharf in San Fernando to La Brea; say you want to get off at Pitch Lake. By car, from San Fernando take the South Trunk Rd to La Brea and follow signs; a distance of 27 km.

Beyond San Fernando, the South Trunk Road heads down the southwest peninsula to the village of La Brea. A famous phenomenon to visit just after La Brea is the Pitch Lake, some 38 ha of smooth black tar that at times resembles an enormous car park; at 107 m deep it is the third-largest natural asphalt lake in the world, after similar ones in Venezuela and Los Angeles. It is sometimes solid enough to walk on, with care, and watching out for air holes bubbling up from the pressure under the ooze (the guides know which way to go). In the wet season, however, most of the area is covered with shallow pools, when rainwater collects in the cracks and crevices of the lake. These pools contain high levels of sulphur and bathing in them is reputedly good for skin complaints and aching joints; again guides will show you where you can get in, as some are deceptively deep. Cashew trees grow on the pitch and the surrounding land is very fertile with plentiful breadfruit and mango trees. It's also a good place for birdwatching – hummingbirds, herons, sandpipers and kingfishers can all be seen.

Legend has it that long ago the gods interred an entire tribe of Chaima Amerindians for daring to eat sacred hummingbirds believed to contain the souls of their ancestors. In the place where the village sank into the ground there erupted a sluggish flow of black pitch, which gradually became an ever-refilling large pool. The more logical explanation suggests that two geographical faults at one time intersected causing crude oil to seep from fractures in the sandstone beneath the surface. The oil and mud mixture then evaporated over the centuries leaving behind the thick, residual natural asphalt that can be seen today. The **Trinidad Lake Asphalt Company** was established by the British in 1888, and since then the asphalt has been used for supplying manufacturing industries and for road and airport surfacing.

You must explore with an official guide (for safety reasons, and for the lake's history), who you will find at the **La Brea Pitch Lake Tour Guides Association Visitor Centre** inside the car park; a tip is appreciated. Ignore locals who pose as guides outside the entrance – official guides wear orange T-shirts and have ID.

Tip...
The distance between San Fernando and Icaco is 84 km; allow about a 1½- to two-hour drive – longer with stops.

La Brea to Icacos

From La Brea, the South Trunk Road becomes the Southern Main Road, and 3 km south of La Brea is **Vessigny Beach**, which fills up with people from San Fernando at weekends and is a bit of a party beach. It isn't as pretty as some and the sea can be a little murky (polluted from local industry), but there are changing facilities/toilets (TT$2), lifeguards and snack bars open at weekends and holiday times. From here the Southern Main Road continues to **Point Fortin**, a busy town thanks to its liquefied natural gas plant.

The road then winds its way through woodland down the remaining southwest peninsula; the 'toe' of Trinidad here is known as the Cedros Peninsula, a quiet rural and fishing area that is the most southern point in the Caribbean, believed to have been attached geologically to the South American continent millions of years ago. It now lies adjacent to the Venezuelan coastline 11-12 km across the passage of water known as Boca del Serpiente (Serpent's Mouth). This proximity, however, has also led to many drug cartels from South America trying to bring their cargoes via Cedros into the Gulf of Paria; the Venezuelan government routinely sends gunships to patrol these waters.

There are turnings off to quiet beaches and villages. These include **Erin Bay** (on the south coast on Siparia Erin Road about 10 km off Southern Main Road) where there are lots of fishing boats pulled up on the long flat beach, and **Granville** (on the Gulf of Paria about 4.5 km off the road), which has a moderately sloping beach, a car park, toilets and a few holiday homes. At the pretty fishing village of **Bonasse** the beach has calm waters and white and light brown powdery sand backed by almond trees. Stretching around Cedros Bay to Cedros Point, this is the widest beach on the island at low tide, and fronting Main Road is an esplanade with concrete benches and opposite are little bars and shops. Beyond Fullarton, **Columbus Bay** is a 4-km sweep fringed with coconut palms between Los Gallos Point and Corral Point, so-called because Christopher Columbus sailed into the bay on 2 August 1498. The smooth sand here is tan-coloured, the sea clear and the beach is quiet; there is a car park but no other facilities. Three large rocks, the **Three Sisters**, jut out from the sea offshore and erosion has created a rock arch in a smaller bay beyond the river.

The final part of the Southern Main Road is very scenic and goes through hectares of coconut palms and then a region of marsh and swamp (good for birdwatching) to the sleepy fishing village of **Icaco**. The beach is wide and sandy (though there are no facilities) and fishermen here go to the shrimping grounds between Trinidad and Venezuela. Again, on 2 August 1498, Columbus landed here and called it Punta del Arenal or Sandy Point. On a clear day the mangroves of the Orinoco Delta in Venezuela are visible across the water.

Tourist information

Trinidad and Tobago Tourism Development Company (TDC)
Immediately outside the Arrivals exit at Piarco International Airport, T669 5196/6044, www.tdc.co.tt. Daily 0800-2300.
Super friendly and welcoming tourist information office. Be sure to stop here to pick up maps and brochures, and if you haven't already organized accommodation, the staff will phone around and find you a room. They also offer free Wi-Fi and 1 terminal for 15 mins of free internet and printing. There is also a TDC tourist information office at the Cruise Ship Terminal, Port of Spain, open when cruise ships are in dock. The TDC head office is at Level 1, Maritime Centre, 29 Tenth Av, Barataria, T675 7034, Mon-Fri 0800-1600, which while helpful, is off Eastern Main Rd about 6 km east of Port of Spain near San Juan, so not easily accessible for visitors.

Where to stay

Unless otherwise stated, all hotel rooms have a/c, TV and Wi-Fi. Hotel tax of 10% and service charge of 10% is added to bills.

Port of Spain *map page 32.*
Over Carnival, room rates sky rocket, only multiple-night bookings will be taken, and you may well be asked to pay a deposit in advance.

$$$$ Hyatt Regency Trinidad
1 Wrightson Rd, T623 2222, www.trinidad.hyatt.com.
Overlooking the Gulf of Paria, this upscale, high-rise hotel is of a high standard, good for business or leisure, with 428 rooms and suites, contemporary furnishings and all mod cons. There's a good but pricey **Waterfront** restaurant, sushi bar, café, 2 bars (1 is next to the infinity rooftop pool), spa and gym.

$$$$ Radisson Hotel Trinidad
Wrightson Rd, T625 3366, www.radisson.com.
In the downtown business area with good facilities, the 243 spacious rooms are well equipped, some have Juliet balconies, and the suites have living rooms and kitchenettes. Small pool, gym, lobby bar, 2 restaurants, one of which is **360 Degrees**, the Caribbean's only revolving, rooftop restaurant that is open to non-guests for Sun brunch (1130-1430).

$$$$-$$$ Hilton Trinidad
Lady Young Rd, northeast Queen's Park Savannah, T624 3211, www3.hilton.com.
Surrounded by lush greenery, the Hilton has an upside-down layout to incorporate views of the city and Gulf of Paria – the public areas and lovely pool are at the top of the property and the 418 warmly decorated rooms and suites are on lower levels down the hillside. The main restaurant serves Caribbean and international cuisine, the stylish **Luce** serves wine and sushi (see page 78), there's a coffee shop, lobby bar, tennis courts and gym.

$$$ Courtyard Port of Spain (Marriott)
Invaders Bay, Audrey Jeffers Highway, T627 5555, www.marriott.com.
Overlooking the Jean Pierre Stadium and adjacent to **MovieTowne** (see page 80) for shops, restaurants and entertainment, this business hotel is sandwiched between office buildings and the busy highway, but has good and modern Marriott standards. The 119 rooms and suites have all mod cons, some have kitchenettes and pull-out sofa beds, and there's a pool, gym, and **The Centro** restaurant for hot and cold breakfasts and light suppers.

$$$ Kapok
16-18 Cotton Hill, St Clair, northwest Queen's Park Savannah, T622 5765, www.kapokhotel.com.
Casual hotel with a colourful façade and 94 comfortable rooms with big windows, mini-fridges and coffee makers, some

studios have kitchenettes. The excellent **Tiki Village** restaurant serves Chinese and Polynesian cuisine including dim sum, also light meals are available at the **Kava** bar downstairs, which has a brick pizza oven, and there's a small pool and shopping arcade.

$$$-$$ The Carlton Savannah
2-4 Coblentz Av, Cascade, T621 5000, www.thecarltonsavannah.com.
Smart white block close to Queen's Park Savannah, and one of the better of the large business hotels with good service and amenities. 157 rooms, the top 3 floors have balconies, and suites have additional living/dining areas and kitchenettes. 2 restaurants (**Casa** and **Relish**), a jazz/blues bar, rooftop cocktail lounge, and pleasant pool with poolside bar.

$$$-$$ The Chancellor
5 St Ann's Av, off St Ann's Rd, St Ann's, T623 0883, www.thechancellorhotel.com.
In a modern, colonial-inspired building with pillars and gables, this relaxed hotel is conveniently located behind the Royal Botanic Gardens. The 30 rooms are spacious and tiled throughout, although the wooden furniture is a little cheap. There's good service, a nice leafy swimming pool area and the reasonable **Waterfall Bistro and Bar.**

$$$-$$ Coblentz Inn Boutique Hotel
44 Coblentz Av, Cascade, T621 0541, www.coblentzinn.com.
Well-run small hotel with a guesthouse feel, the 16 rooms are not overly big and not all have windows but they are themed and individually named with interesting furnishings and colours – some may find it quirky, others not modern enough. Friendly staff and a good restaurant with a creative international and Caribbean menu and outside tables in a peaceful garden area.

$$$-$$ Kiskadee Korner
9 Rapsey St, St Clair, T221 1546, www.kiskadeekorner.com.
Tucked away in its own private lane off Rapsey St, this bright, cheerfully decorated

and very popular guesthouse has 7 rooms – from a small standard one to a 2-bedroom apartment – each named after an island bird and clustered around a delightful little garden and courtyard, plus there's a swimming pool and deck and the **Kiskatea Kafé** serves delicious breakfasts. Quiet and relaxing and within walking distance of restaurants. Minimum 2-night stay.

$$ Culture Crossroads Inn
Corner Bengal St and Delhi St, St James, T622 8788, www.culturecrossroadstt.com.
In the lively suburb of St James within walking distance of restaurants and bars and the **Long Circular Mall** (see page 80), this is a cheerful and modern family-run guesthouse in a brightly painted orange building. The 13 neat rooms are individually named after Trinidadian Carnival musicians and dancers past and present – owner Colin is a legendary soca performer and a mine of local information and will point you to some excellent local street food spots.

$$ Forty Winks Inn
24 Warner St, Newtown, T622 0484, www.fortywinkstt.com.
Charming little guesthouse in a narrow house on a back street within walking distance of Queen's Park Savannah and a number of restaurants, small with only 5 rooms but comfortable and colourful, a cute little patio area on the roof, breakfast room, and you can make your own tea/coffee and use the kitchen fridge.

$$ The Gingerbread House
8 Carlos St, Woodbrook, T627 8170, www.trinidadgingerbreadhouse.com.
The prettiest guesthouse in town in a lovely 1920s traditional Trinidadian home painted a jaunty blue and white with high ceilings and a timber fretwork wraparound terrace and 3 light and airy guest rooms. Breakfast included, plunge pool, sun deck and garden, friendly hosts and a few mins' walk from Woodbrook restaurants.

$$ Heritage Inn
7 Coblentz Av, Cascade, T621 5663,
www.heritageinntrinidad.com.
Immaculate, with plenty of character and
peaceful corners to relax, like the upstairs
lounge and deck, and some fantastic
artwork decorating the walls, this pleasant
guesthouse is a few mins' walk from the
Queen's Park Savannah. 10 rooms, some are
triples, quiet flowering gardens and pool,
good hot breakfasts and coffee all day. Ask
Sandra about her 3 economy rooms (she
usually only advertises these at Carnival),
from US$80, which are still very comfortable
but have a private bathroom in the corridor.

$$ Hotel Normandie
10 Nook Av, off St Ann's Rd, St Ann's,
T387 1242, www.normandiett.com.
In a complex with craft and fashion shops,
a mid-range business place with 69 rooms
with coffee/tea maker, swimming pool,
the **Ciao! Restaurant** offers international
dishes, while **Café Trinidad** serves breakfast,
lunch and snacks. Service and cleanliness
criticized however, but sensibly priced.

$$ Inn at 87
87 Woodford St, Newtown, T622 4343,
www.innat87.com.
The 9 rooms here are small and fairly simple
but spotless with tiled floors, colourful
fabrics and prints on the walls and are well
priced from US$105. Breakfast room with a
generous buffet, a couple of outside tables
on a wooden deck, and an easy stroll to
restaurants and the central sights.

$$ L'Orchidée Boutique Hotel
3 Coblenz Gardens, off St Ann's Rd, St Ann's,
T621 0618, www.trinidadhosthomes.com.
A few mins' walk from Queen's Park
Savannah, this well-run guesthouse has
12 neat and well-equipped rooms, some
can accommodate extra beds, an excellent
breakfast is included and other meals can be
ordered from local restaurants and eaten on
the patio. Not especially modern but homely
in a mid-20th-century French colonial house.

$$-$ Samise Villa
47 St Ann's Rd, St Ann's, T682 9589,
www.samisevilla.com.
A little further out of town than the other
accommodation in St Ann's, but route taxis
run along the road outside. Denise, the
helpful and gracious owner, offers 4 homely
en suite B&B rooms, simple but quiet, some
have bunk beds and sleep 3 to 5, there's
a back patio to sit on under mango trees.
Singles from US$30, doubles from US$65.

$$-$ Thanna's Place
25 Erthig Rd, Belmont, T225 6582,
www.thannas.com.
This affordable family-run B&B is a 5-min
walk east of the Queen's Park Savannah and
has 7 rooms; en suite doubles/twins from
US$85, with shared bathrooms US$75. The
whole house is spotlessly clean, the walls
painted in different colours brightening
the mood, and a little outside courtyard
with flowering plants. A good continental
breakfast with eggs/pancakes is included,
tea/coffee all day, and guests can use the
microwave and fridge in the kitchen.

$ Melbourne Inn Trinidad
7 French St, Woodbrook, T623 4006,
melbourn@caribsurf.com.
As the owner even says, "nothing fancy,
just clean", which just about sums up this
popular budget hotel in a blue house with
16 rooms of varying size, en suite, fans, some
have microwaves and fridges, and there's a
small outdoor seating area in a tiny garden
overlooking the street. Doubles from US$40,
triples from US$75.

Western Main Road to Chaguaramas
map page 28.

$$$ Crews Inn Hotel & Yachting Centre
Point Gourde, Chaguaramas, T634 4384,
www.crewsinn.com.
Snugly nestled in Chaguaramas Bay with
pretty views of the yachts in their own
marina, this casual mid-range place has
46 rooms in pink blocks with balconies or

patios, ask for one of the neatly refurbished ones, well run and with good facilities including a nice large pool, gym, kids' play area, **Caffe Del Mare** and **Lighthouse Restaurant** (see page 75). **Econo Car Rentals** (see page 85) has an office here.

$$-$ D'Lime Inn
75 Benjamin St, Diego Martin, T221 0876, www.dlimeinn.com.
In the Diego Martin Valley, this small inn has 5 self-catering rooms, basic decor but adequate, a small swimming pool in pretty garden, and supermarkets and restaurants are just around the corner. Owners Cathy and Clyde are very hospitable and can cook delicious local food on request, and Clyde is a Calypso musician who will show you his recording studio and tell you all about Trinidad's music heritage.

North coast *map page 28.*

$$$-$$ Second Spring Bed & Breakfast Inn
Lamp Post 191, Paria Main Rd, Blanchisseuse, T669 3909, www.secondspringtnt.com.
This rustic spot was built some years ago and is showing its age but will appeal to those who want a peaceful day or 2 (no Wi-Fi or cell reception) enjoying the tremendous views over the crashing waves from its isolated clifftop position, as well as birdwatching and nature walks. The cottage (2 adults and 2 children) and the 3 studios have kitchenettes and wooden decks; breakfast (extra) of fruit, home-made jam and bread is available; otherwise bring all food as shops and restaurants are some distance. It's a little tricky to find as it actually lies on a secondary road running parallel to the main coastal Paria Main Rd. Doubles from US$70.

$$ Monique's Guest House
114-116 Saddle Rd, Maraval, T628 3334, www.moniquestrinidad.com.
A reasonable budget stop on the way to the north coast beaches and with easy access from Port of Spain, this roadside B&B/small

hotel is in 2 adjacent buildings set on an attractive hillside surrounded by greenery. The 20 rooms sleeping 1-4 have very dated furnishings but the larger ones have verandas and kitchenettes. **The Pink Anthurium Restaurant & Bar** serves good local food and staff are helpful and hospitable.

$$-$ Laguna Mar Beach Resort
Paria Main Rd, just before and west of Spring Bridge over the Marianne River, Blanchisseuse, T669 2963, www.lagunamar.com.
Owned by German-American Fred Zollna, quiet and peaceful, surrounded by forest and birds, no TV, close to the beach and lagoon, and a good base for the hikes to Three Pools or to Paria Bay. There are 2 buildings here each with 6 rooms and a separate 4-bedroom self-catering cottage, **Cocos Hut** restaurant and bar. Singles from US$45, doubles from US$65 and extra person US$15.

East of Port of Spain to Arima
map page 28.
Useful for the airport.

$$$ Asa Wright Nature Centre
Blanchisseuse Rd, 14 km north of the Eastern Main Rd at Arima (see also page 52), T667 4655, www.asawright.org.
2 main-house rooms in colonial style, with high ceilings, wooden furniture and floors, and 24 standard rooms and bungalow in the gardens, all designed to be private and secluded with verandas for birdwatching; 80% of guests in high season are birdwatching groups. Rates include all meals including afternoon tea, rum punch, tax and service. Wi-Fi in the main house.

$$$ Regent Star Hotel
118-119 BWIA Blvd, Piarco International Airport, Piarco, T669 7827, www.regentstarhotel.com.
Newly opened in 2016 and now the closest hotel to the airport, located on the roundabout on the approach road – a 1 km walk and shuttle buses run every 30 mins. 158 tastefully designed rooms, reasonable restaurant/bar, and they are in the process

of adding a gym and 2 swimming pools (check the website for progress), but for what it is now, rates from US$150 may seem a little overpriced.

$$$-$$ Crosswinds Villa B&B
La Pastora, Upper Santa Cruz, T785 0698, www.crosswindsvilla.com.
Comfortably elegant and with a banana plantation as a backdrop, this upscale B&B in a gorgeous red-tiled Spanish-style house is a 35-min drive northeast of Port of Spain (follow Saddle Rd from either the city or San Juan). 5 spacious rooms, each with high ceilings and lovely sitting/dining areas, and pool in a relaxing landscaped garden that attracts birds and butterflies. With notice, dinner can be provided for US$15.

$$$-$$ Holiday Inn Express
1 Exposition Dr, Trincity, Piarco, T669 6209, www.hiexpress.com.
Just south of **Trincity Mall** (see page 75) this is useful with excellent standards but unremarkable in a purpose-built block which is oddly quite isolated in a field next to the Churchill Roosevelt Highway. The 61 rooms have tea and coffee facilities, some have rollaway beds, and there's a swimming pool. It's a 10-min drive from the airport with free transfers, buffet breakfast included and there's a free shuttle to the mall for restaurants.

$$$-$$ Piarco Village Suites
22 Ramcharan Dr, Piarco, T758 2190, www.piarcovillagesuites.webs.com.
A 3-min drive from the airport, transfers included in the rates, this well-regarded B&B is in a smart bright yellow house in an upscale residential neighbourhood with a spacious lawn area. 6 rooms (some can fit in extra beds), kitchen for everyone's use with fruit, coffee and tea, and the generous breakfast will set up you up for the day.

$$ Airport Inn
Factory Rd, Piarco, T669 8207, www.airportinntrinidad.com.

Good homely B&B run by hospitable Sita Singh, rates include airport transfers, 5 small but comfortable rooms, 1 is a triple and 1 a quad, generous breakfasts and, like Piarco Village Suites, above (which is around the corner), a short drive/taxi ride to Trincity Mall on Churchill Roosevelt Highway (see page 75) for restaurants.

$$ Xanadu Tropical Resort
Lopinot Rd, Arauca, T646 8628, www.xanadutt.com.
A peaceful country retreat surrounded by tropical forest but still a 10- to 15-min drive from the airport (transfers available). 11 neat, tiled rooms of varying size, breakfast is US$12 extra and other meals are available on request. There's a lovely pool with a bar. You can book a day room here for use before/ after a flight for US$60.

$$-$ Pax Guest House
At The Abbey of Mount St Benedict (see page 50), north of the Eastern Main Rd in St Augustine, T662 4084, www.paxguesthouse.com.
Built 1916, this, the oldest guesthouse on the island, features extra high ceilings, wooden floors, characterful verandas with hummingbird feeders, and there are ceiling fans and windows that open wide (no a/c is needed). 18 rooms; the ground floor ones are en suite, the upstairs one have basins and shared bathrooms but better views, delicious home-cooked meals (see also page 76 for details of lunch and tea), and lovely views of central Trinidad as well as of the occasional monk. Doubles from US$65.

$ Chateau Guillaume
3 Rawle Circular, Arima, T667 6670, www.cguillaumme.caribsurf.net.
Run by Matthew and Joan William, this comfortable and spotless B&B has 2 doubles (US$65) and 2 triples (US$80), a pretty fruit-filled garden, excellent breakfast, and you can use the kitchen or eat at restaurants in Arima. Very helpful; Matthew will act as tour guide if needed and provides airport

transfers. It's about a 30-min drive from here to the Asa Wright Nature Centre.

Northeast coast *map page 28.*
After the end of turtle-watching season and before Christmas, roughly 1 Sep to 15 Dec, room rates drop significantly at Grande Riviere and around.

$$$$ Anise Resort & Spa
Paria Main Rd, Sans Souci, T670 4436, www.aniseresortandspa.com.
This family-run all-inclusive little resort in the village of Sans Souci has 11 rooms, neat as a pin, in a house with sea views that feels as if you are staying in owner Kirsta's home. Activities include forest hikes for birdwatching, turtle-watching excursions, there's a lovely infinity pool, good spa facilities, and it's walking distance from the idyllic beach in Sans Souci Bay where sun loungers are set up. Rates from US$305 include all meals and the food is varied and delicious.

$$$ Acajou Hotel
209 Paria Main Rd, Grande Riviere, T670 3771, www.acajoutrinidad.com.
Set between the Grande Riviere River and the beach, there are 6 delightful wood and bamboo cabanas here designed and built by a French architect, each surrounded by lush greenery with a deck and hammock. Very relaxing and peaceful and the delicious food (meals need to be ordered in advance) is made with organic products from the garden or from the local farmers. Activities include turtle- and birdwatching, fishing and snorkelling.

$$$ Le Grand Almandier
2 Hosang St, Grande Riviere, T670 1013, www.legrandealmandier.com.
Run by Wendy and Cyril James, this delightful inn-style place among almond trees is directly on the turtle-watching beach and the great advantage of staying here (and at **Mount Plaisir Estate Hotel** next door) is that, if you rise at first light, there's a very good

chance of seeing the turtles in the morning too. 10 comfortable rooms, some with sea- (and turtle-) facing balconies, most can accommodate up to 3 or groups/families of up to 6. Breakfast is included, and the good restaurant (open to all 0700-2200) specializes in Creole-style dishes (including delicious whole fish) and can provide picnics for hikes and excursions. Cyril will take you fishing, on boat trips to secluded beaches, hiking and birdwatching, and there are free kayaks to use on the river.

$$$-$$ Hosanna Toco Resort
Paria Main Rd, in the village of Trois Roche, just east of Toco, T674 9873, www.hosannatoco.com.
In a hillside position in pretty gardens with panoramic ocean views across to Tobago, this low-key and well-priced place has 6 units – from a tiny wooden double to a large 2-bed sea-view apartment sleeping up to 5 – simply furnished but adequate and all self-catering. It's a 20-min drive to Grande Riviere for turtle watching, and there are steps down to a small, sandy beach that has rock pools.

$$$-$$ Mount Plaisir Estate Hotel
Hosang St, Grande Riviere, T670 2217, www.mtplaisir.com.
Next door to, and on the same beach as **Le Grand Almandier**, above, this has 13 beachfront rooms in a pleasant, double-storey timbered building which can sleep up to 4-6 (each additional person is US$20). Rustic locally made furniture, restaurant/bar with a brick oven to bake bread and pizzas, another bar on the beach, and again, activities include nature trails, birdwatching and canoeing on the Grande Riviere river. Doubles start from US$100, additional person US$20.

$$ Playa del Este
Toco Main Rd, Salybia, T691 2632, www.playadelesteresort.com.
Old-fashioned with very dated decor, but the 40 rooms in blocks are set in beautifully

landscaped grounds (pay a little more for ocean view), and each has coffee maker, microwave and fridge. There's a swimming pool, small gym and restaurant/bar. Like **Salybia Nature Resort** next door, there's a great view over Saline Bay from its elevated position, but the beach here is only a skinny stretch of black sand.

$$ Salybia Nature Resort
Toco Main Rd, Salybia, T691 3210 or 668 7767, see Facebook.
1 of the 2 mediocre places next door to each other in Salybia (both are more suited to the local conference market) with 21 plain but bright, ocean-view rooms in orange double-storey blocks with balconies/patios and a villa sleeping up to 7. Neat gardens with a decent large pool that has a waterfall and swim-up bar, restaurant/bar. Turtle watching can be arranged through **Nature Seekers** (see page 53).

$$-$ J&J Big Yard Guest House
Toco Main Rd, Cumana, T670 2117, www.jandjbigyard.com.
A somewhat inexplicably named newly built guesthouse in the village of Cumana, this has 6 rooms and apartments sleeping up to 4 (6 if there are children), some with 2 bedrooms and full kitchens. It's in a block above a supermarket and bar next to the road, but the back of the property comes as quite a surprise – there's a lovely swimming pool with lounging area looking straight into the trees.

$ Mc Haven Resort
Corner Bristol St and Thomas St, Grande Riviere, T670 1014, see Facebook.
A neat and affordable guesthouse up the hill in the village and run by hospitable Ingrid (whose daughter works at the **Grande Riviere Nature Tour Guides Association** (GRNTGA) office, which is just a short walk away). 6 basic but spotless tiled rooms arranged along a communal balcony, use of kitchen, tasty local meals available and bar where the excellent village band, **Roots and Branches**, often performs.

East coast *map page 28.*

$$-$ RASH Resort
Gould St, Mayaro, T630 7274, see Facebook.
There's nothing very appealing about staying on the east coast for international visitors, and Mayaro has a clutch of aged concrete self-catering beach resorts aimed at weekending Trinidadians from Port of Spain. The RASH is the best of a bad bunch and the only one with direct beach access, with 1- and 2-bed apartments, simply furnished and old, only the 2 upstairs front ones have balconies and sea views. Swimming pool, no restaurant but there's grocery shopping and fast-food joints nearby. A problem here is parking; cars are parked in a compound nose to tail. Similar setups nearby are **Queen's Beach Resort**, **Radix Beach Resort** and **Sunset Beach Resort**.

South of Port of Spain *map page 28.*

$$$ Tradewinds Hotel
38 London St, San Fernando, T652 9463, www.tradewindshotel.com.
Up on a hill in a fairly quiet residential area, this is the best option in San Fernando in terms of comfort and facilities, but it's a corporate haunt with not much character. The 41 rooms and suites are modern and bright, some have kitchenettes, and there's a bar, restaurant (a buffet breakfast is included), gym, pleasant pool with seating and loungers, and a small shop selling snacks, wine and rum. An airport shuttle service is available.

$$ Cara Suites Hotel
Southern Main Rd, Claxton Bay (just north of Pointe-a-Pierre), T659 2272, www.carasuites.com.
This large conference-style place has 100 rooms, comfortable and recently renovated with fridge, microwave and tea and coffee facilities, although Wi-Fi is only in the public areas. The **Metropolitan** restaurant has a decent menu, bar and pool with good views over the Gulf of Paria,

particularly at sunset. Standards are good and staff attentive. However, it's in the industrialized area around Pointe-a-Pierre.

$$ Royal Hotel
46-54 Royal Rd, T652 3924, San Fernando, www.royalhotelltt.com.
Tired and needs maintenance and designed for local business travellers but one of the few central options in San Fernando in a hilltop garden with pool and nice outdoor seating area for breakfast. 62 rooms, some have balconies and are bright, others don't and are dark, and water in showers is lukewarm at best. Intermittent Wi-Fi and basic restaurant and bar.

Restaurants

In out-of-the-way areas there is often no phone signal and therefore credit cards may not be accepted. Take plenty of cash when you go out for a meal, just in case. A 10% service charge is usually added to restaurant bills.

Port of Spain *map page 32.*
All the shopping malls and cinema complexes have food courts with communal seating and a varied and good selection of counters selling cheap food from Chinese to **KFC**. More elegant and costly dining can be found in the business hotels and individual restaurants scattered around the city. Evening street food stalls can be found at Ariapita Av in Woodbrook (see box, page 74), Western Main Rd in St James and the southeast corner of Queen's Park Savannah, and there's no shortage of chain fast-food restaurants from **Wendy's** to **McDonalds**.

$$$ Aioli
Ellerslie Plaza, Rapsey St, Maraval, T222 3291, www.aiolitrinidad.com. Mon and Sat 1830-2300, Tue-Fri 1130-2300.
Just off Saddle Rd about 400 m from the northwest corner of Queen's Savannah. Mediterranean inspired-menu for lunch including some gourmet club sandwiches

and pastas, and international bistro-style menu for dinner with the likes of mussels and duck. Modern decor yet cosy and intimate. The chef is on hand to talk to customers and service is good.

$$$ Angelo's
38 Ariapita Av, Woodbrook, T628 5551, see Facebook. Mon-Sat 1130-2230.
A small restaurant in an older house on busy Ariapita Av, and only reserved parking available 2 doors down and indoor seating, but the typical French/Italian cuisine is exceptional and beautifully presented. Superb meat and fish like pork and salmon, home-made pastas and decadent desserts. Refined service too.

$$$ Apsara
13 Queens Park East, T623 7659, www. apsarattt.com. Mon-Sun 1100-1500, Mon-Sat 1800-2300.
Very expensive but tasty food in a pleasantly elegant dining room, with an authentic North Indian and tandoori rather than Indo-Trini menu, and everything is made from scratch. Save room for a kesar pista kulfi, a traditional frozen dessert flavoured with pistachios, cardamom and saffron.

$$$ Joseph's
3a Rookery Nook, Maraval, T622 5557, www.josephstnt.com. Mon-Fri 1100-1430, Mon-Sat 1800-2200.
An upscale family-run Lebanese restaurant offering excellent mezza with baba ganoush, hummus and tabbouleh, and house specialities such as lamb, escargot and red snapper as well as Lebanese wine. Excellent service and beautiful ambience in the stylish interior or outside patio. Pricey but good for a special occasion.

$$$ Texas de Brazil
MovieTowne, Audrey Jeffers Highway, Invaders Bay, T623 0022, www.texasdebrazil. com. Thu-Sun 1100-1500, daily 1700-2230.
A US chain of *churrascarias*, this is a carnivore's delight but is also known for the vastness and freshness of the salad bar. The

meats can be a bit salty for some tastes, but the service is very attentive and the caipirinhas are excellent.

$$$-$$ Buzo Osteria Italiana
6 Warner St, Newtown, T223 2896, see Facebook. Mon-Sat 1130-2300.
Italian-owned by a chef from Urbino, real Italian pasta, pizza and desserts. Open kitchen with cheerful chefs, and contemporary design with bare brick walls and moody lighting, popular with young professionals, especially for the Fri evening lime.

$$$-$$ Jaffa at the Oval
2nd floor, Queen's Park Oval, 98 Tragarete Rd, T622 6825, see Facebook. Mon-Thu 1145-2230, Fri-Sat 1000-1600.
This restaurant is in the pavilion of the cricket club but is open to the public. They do a good weekday business lunch buffet with a great choice of desserts (US$30), Sun brunch buffet (US$40) and Wed afternoon tea (US$24). Good quality, tasty and reasonably priced and a good place to bring children who get big discounts.

$$$-$ Chaud Café & Wine Bar
Damian St, 1 Woodbrook Place, T628 9845, www.chaudcafe.com. Mon-Sat 1100-2300.
Light lunches or café patisserie and snacks followed by wine bar and small dishes at night, an eclectic international menu based on Lebanese mezze as much as Spanish tapas, although you can also get a substantial ribeye steak and fries. It isn't great for vegetarians but their meat dishes are tasty. Good brunch on Sat 1100-1700. Pleasant deck for outdoor drinking or quiet dining room.

$$ Hakka
4 Taylor St, Woodbrook, T622 0004, www.hakkarestaurant.com. Mon-Thu 1100-2300, Fri-Sat 1100-2400, Sun 1200-2200.
Fusion Chinese and Indian cuisine with a Trini twist, lots of flavour and spices, good-sized portions, most dishes around US$9-12. Dim lighting, red and black colour scheme, indoor and outdoor seating and the advantage of parking space in busy Woodbrook.

$$ Jenny's on the Boulevard
6 Cipriani Blvd, Newtown, T625 1807, see Facebook. Mon-Sat 1000-2300.
Wide variety of mainly Chinese dishes, but also standard American staples like wings and ribs, and a few pasta dishes thrown in for good measure in an elaborate setting in a lovely blue house with fretwork and a wooden terrace. The service can sometimes be awful, in which case you're better with takeaway. Lively pub-style bar downstairs where the Fri lime starts after work around 1700.

$$ More Vino, More Sushi
23 O'Connor St, Woodbrook, T622 8466, www.morevino.com. Mon-Wed 1100-2330, Thu-Sat 1100-0100.
As the name suggests, a wine bar and sushi spot with long menus of both, plus good cocktails and a nice ambience in a modern and stylish environment. After-work lime most nights and a late bar, and security guards walk you to their own parking close by. There's a second branch in San Fernando.

$$ Tamnak Thai
13 Queens Park East, T625 0647, www.tamnakthaitt.com. Mon-Fri 1100-1500, Mon-Sat 1800-2300.
Thai restaurant with a good choice of authentic dishes – the Wed lunchtime set menu is good value at US$14.50 – although the service doesn't always match up to the excellent food and beautiful setting with pretty outdoor area overlooking the Savannah. **Apsara** is upstairs.

$$ Town Restaurant & Bar
51 Cipriani Blvd, Newtown, T627 8696, www.towntrinidad.com. Mon-Thu 1100-2200, Fri-Sat 1100-2300, bar later.
Modern and elegant with a wide menu of Chinese and international dishes, specialities include the Hoisin duck and Hong Kong shrimp or roast pork, generous shared platters or half portions make it good value. Basement and outdoor parking and it's below **51 Degrees** nightclub (see page 78).

Liming like a Trini on De Avenue

Port of Spain's most popular restaurant and nightlife district is Ariapita Avenue in Woodbrook – also known as 'De Avenue' – which is densely lined with restaurants representing just about every international cuisine there is, from Italian and Thai, to Mexican and Jamaican. It's also the place for bar-hopping at the numerous bars and clubs ranging from sophisticated cocktail lounges to raucous sports bars. In the evening, it's well known too for street food, when roadside vendors set up stalls selling typically Trini specialities such as *doubles* (fried bread filled with curried chick peas, often served with *chado beni* – similar to coriander – sauce and pepper), and *rotis* (thin, flexible flatbread with curried meat and vegetables), as well as more internationally recognized items such as fast-fried, chicken-in-a-box, hotdogs and waffles. Generally, the longer the queue, the better the food is. Ariapita Avenue is pretty easy to find (the neon after dark should give you a clue) but if you're driving, parking can be a problem. Rather go by taxi, make firm plans as to where and what time you want to be picked up, and remember your hotel name, address and phone number (as well as your taxi drivers). Note that, as with most places in Trinidad, most establishments are closed on Sunday. The whole of De Avenue is a free Wi-Fi hotspot – so it's easy enough to take selfies and post them while you're liming.

$$-$ IrieBites Jerk Centre & Grill
71A Ariapita Av, Woodbrook, T622 7364. Mon-Thu and Sat 1000-2100, Fri 1000-2200, Sun 1000-1400. Also at 153 Western Main Rd, St James, T622 6725. Mon-Sat 1000-1800, www.iriebitesjerk.com.
Specializes in Jamaican jerk and barbecue meats, combo meals of meat and side bites of your choice, the side dishes can be ordered in larger portions for vegetarians, relaxed atmosphere and always buzzing.

$ Creole Kitchen
22 Boissiere Village, Maraval, opposite Ellerslie Plaza, T622 9905. Mon-Fri 0730-1700, Sat-Sun 0730-1800.
Just off Saddle Rd and a 5-min walk from the northwest corner of Queen's Savannah. Popular with local workers for lunch, home-cooked Trini and Creole food, cafeteria-style and takeaway, generous portions; be prepared to queue. The calalloo soup is delicious and there's also mac and cheese, stewed chicken and fish and the like.

$ D'Bocas
68 Independence Sq, Brian Lara Promenade, T627 3474, see Facebook. Mon-Fri 0930-2330.
Catering for office workers and shoppers, this canteen is good for fish dishes and chicken, with other meats on different days, such as pork or goat, and good Creole vegetables and salads (breadfruit, green bananas, callaloo, sweet potato, pigeon peas), lunchtimes from 1030, cafeteria-style or take-away. Local fruit juices or *mauby* to wash down the 'belly-full' meals. Fri from 1830 there's live entertainment and DJ.

$ Dianne's Tea Shop
119 Long Circular Rd, Maraval, T223 3832. Mon-Fri 0700-1700, Sat 0800-1700, Sun 0900-1400.
In a quiet area of Maraval, just beyond the **Trinidad Country Club**, this lovely little tea shop in a bright white house with a warm atmosphere offers breakfasts, including eggs benedict, classic English and yogurt with granola, lunches of filled paninis and pastas, and high tea (US$13.50) with finger sandwiches, scones and cakes.

$ Hott Shoppe
20 Mucurapo Rd, St James, T622 4073.
Mon-Sat 1000-2130.
A little out of the way (about 400 m south of the **KFC** on Western Main Rd) but worth seeking out for some of the best rotis in Port of Spain, which are of a slightly heavier texture than some and are full of flavour. During the day you may have a long wait, and watch out for the hot sauce.

$ Patraj Roti Shop
161 Tragarete Rd, St Clair, T622 6219.
Mon-Sat 1000-1630, Sun 1000-1400.
Another good roti option (try the conch or shrimp) and a good place to pick up a snack if you're watching cricket at the Oval. Very tasty and medium spicy by Trini standards (though you can add the hot pepper sauce). There's another branch in San Juan.

Western Main Road to Chaguaramas
map page 28.

$$$-$ Lighthouse Restaurant & Caffe Del Mare
Crews Inn Hotel & Yachting Centre (see page 67), T634 4384. Sun-Thu 0800-2000, restaurant until 2200, Fri-Sat 0800-2100, restaurant until 2200.
The food on the (short) menu at the upstairs Lighthouse is average, bland – frozen fries, bottled barbecue sauce and the like – and overpriced. But the Caffe Del Mare downstairs on the boardwalk offers a delicious assortment of treats from healthy salads and mini pizzas, to cranberry scones and chocolate cake. There's free Wi-Fi and international newspapers like *The New York Times* and *The Telegraph*. Popular with yachties, the location is great with a fantastic view of the marina and sunset.

$$ Sails Restaurant & Pub
Power Boats Marina, Western Main Rd, T634 1712 www.sailsrestpub.com. Mon-Fri 1100-2200, Sat-Sun 0800-2200, bar open later.
Great setting and unpretentious atmosphere with outdoor picnic table right next to the

water's edge at this private marina, but the service is poor – you can wait a long time for a meal or even a beer. Good food, though, especially the grilled fish, seafood, kebabs and burgers. DJs entertain on some nights.

$$-$ Zanzibar by the Sea
Peake's Yacht Services, Western Main Rd, T634 3346, www.zanzibartt.com.
Sun-Thu 1130-2330, Fri-Sat 1130-0100.
Towards the end of the yacht-lined Western Main Rd, this friendly sports bar/restaurant has giant TV screens and a cheery pub atmosphere, large portions of food like buffalo wings and spicy shrimp wraps, and an over-the-water deck with sea views. The sister outlet, **Zanzibar**, is at MovieTowne, Audrey Jeffers Highway, Invaders Bay.

East of Port of Spain to Arima
map page 28.
Along either Eastern Main Rd or Churchill Roosevelt Highway, all the dormitory towns from the capital to Arima have plenty of choice for fast food – mostly of the chicken-in-a-box variety (which Trinis love) and you won't travel more than a couple of kilometres without seeing a **KFC**. The other type of cuisine there is no shortage of is Chinese – just about every main road has a restaurant/takeaway. Recommended to look out for is **Rituals Coffee House**, a popular franchise well known for its good coffees, fruit teas and smoothies, as well as tasty and fresh cookies, bagels and panini sandwiches. They also run **Pizza Boys** and **Church's Chicken**, which are usually attached/close by. There are several branches in Port of Spain, most shopping malls and towns in central Trinidad have them, including Arima, Arouca, Curepe and San Juan, and there's one at Piarco International Airport.

$$ Bootleggers
Trincity Mall, corner Churchill Roosevelt Highway and Trincity Main Rd, Trincity, a 5-min drive west of Piarco International Airport, T640 8448, see Facebook. Mon-Thu 1100-2300, Fri-Sat 1100-0100, Sun 1500-2300.

Sports bar and grill, with an unexciting menu of ribs, steaks, Tex Mex, etc, but useful if you happen to be in the mall and want to sit down in a real restaurant and not the food court. Happy Hour is 1700-1900, when it's popular with liming shoppers (and shop workers).

$$ Rasam
Grand Bazaar, corner of Uriah Butler Highway and Churchill Roosevelt Highway, Valsayn, T645 0994, see Facebook. Mon-Sat 1100-2130.
Dark red old-fashioned decor, but long menus of Indian, Chinese (Hakka) and Thai food, very tasty, large portions, and staff are willing to assist and make recommendations. Fri Thai dinner buffet and Sat Indian and continental dinner buffet (US$29.50). No alcohol. There's also a branch of **Rituals Coffee House** in the shopping mall.

$$-$ Valpark Chinese Restaurant
Valpark Shopping Plaza, Morequito Av (off Churchill Roosevelt Highway), Valsayn, T662 4540, www.valparkchineserestaurant.com. Daily 1100-2300.
One of the better Chinese restaurants in the area with decent modern decor and a well-cooked and nicely presented Cantonese menu including the likes of chicken corn soup, pepper shrimps and barbecued ribs. It's nextdoor to **Mario's Pizza** (daily 0930-2130; takeaway or sit down), which has a children's play-park. Valpark also has a **Rituals Coffee House**.

$ Pax Guest House
The Abbey of Mount St Benedict (see page 50), north of the Eastern Main Road in St Augustine, T662 4084, www.paxguesthouse.com.
Just down the hill from the abbey's church, this delightful guesthouse (see page 69) does good afternoon tea daily 1500-1800, US$6, with 3 types of tea, or coffee or juice, home-made bread and jams, sweet and savoury pastries, and cakes; while lunch, 1200-1400, US$11, is soup, salad

and sandwiches. Both must be booked in advance. Meals are taken in the elegant dining room with teak wooden floor and antiques, or on the delightful and peaceful terrace with hummingbird feeders.

South of Port of Spain *map page 28.*
The suburbs and towns on the southern arteries – Uriah Butler Highway, Sir Solomon Hochoy Highway and Southern Main Rd – have plenty of modern franchise restaurants (**KFC**, **Burger King**, **Pizza Hut** and the like, and Chaguanas and San Fernando also have branches of popular American chain **TGI Fridays**). There's not a great choice of anything else but, thanks to the large Indo-Trinidadian community in this region, you won't have to go far to find a roti shop, and there's a decent choice of Indian (and Chinese) restaurants.

$$$ Krave
Tarouba Plaza, Tarouba Rd, San Fernando, T658 5728, www.krave.tt. Tue-Fri 1100-1500, 1800-2215, Sat 1700-2215, Sun brunch 1030-1500.
Some consider Krave as the best restaurant in southern Trinidad and it certainly has a contemporary, fresh menu of European and Mediterranean cuisine, plus excellent sushi – although it's expensive. Stylish interiors, good cocktails and winelist, and easy to find near the Marabella Roundabout on San Fernando Bypass.

$$$-$$ Art d'Manger
18-24 Quenca St, San Fernando, T657 8033, see Facebook. Mon-Sat 1130-2230.
Formerly **L'Attitude** and now under new management, this remains one of the best restaurants in San Fernando, offering pleasant outdoor seating and continental dishes ranging from paninis and soups, salads and pasta for lunch, and more sophisticated meat and fish dishes for dinner. Good choice for vegetarians and delicious desserts (try the cheesecake or white chocolate mousse).

$$$-$ Woodford Café
Price Plaza, Chaguanas, T627 2233, see Facebook. Mon-Wed and Sun 1130-2330, Thu-Sat 1130-0200.

A modern venue with a lively bar scene on Fri and Sat nights with a bit of everything on the long menu, from salads, sandwiches and burgers, to pasta, seafood and grills. Appetizers with a drink are popular for an evening lime, and there's a brunch on Sun when kids eat for free. Also at MovieTowne, Invaders Bay, Port of Spain.

$$ More Vino, More Sushi
33 Scott St, San Fernando, T223 8466, www.morevino.com. Mon-Wed 1100-2330, Thu-Sat 1100-0100.

Popular wine bar and Japanese restaurant also offers spirits and cocktails and is known for its excellent sushi and sashimi, all well-seasoned and with good consistency. Has an outside deck downstairs, which can get crowded, but quieter seating upstairs. 2nd branch in Woodbrook, Port of Spain.

$$ Passage to Asia
7 St Ives St, Chaguanas, T672 2701, www. passagetoasiatt.com. Daily 1000-2200.

Unprepossessing exterior on a dingy street, but completely different inside and the wonderful smells greet you as you enter. Well known for its authentic and richly flavoured Indian dishes made from scratch by Indian chefs, and there's also Creole, Thai and Chinese; food is presented 'fusion' buffet-style on Fri and Sat from 1800.

$$ Soongs Great Wall
97 Circular Rd, San Fernando, T657 5050, www.soongsgreatwall.com. Mon-Thu 1100-2200, Fri-Sat 1100-2230.

At the base of San Fernando Hill not far from the Royal Hotel, in a giant pagoda-styled building lit up at night and an interior of patterned screens and huge oriental pots. Chinese food, good long-serving reputation

and a long menu – best known for their fried shrimp wontons and lobster dishes.

$$-$ Buffet King
Centre Point Mall, Ramsaran St (off Southern Main Rd), Chaguanas, T671 8795. Daily 1100-1530, 1830-2200.

Located upstairs in a shopping mall, this long-serving canteen-style place offers daily lunch (US$15) and dinner (US$21) buffets with over 50 dishes heaped in big silver catering trays, with salad bar and desserts including ice cream, cheesecake and sugary cakes. There are dozens of shops/malls around this junction with the highway (the main Chaguanas exit) including a large branch of **Massey Supermarket**.

$$-$ Canboulay Restaurant & Lounge
13 Sutton St, San Fernando, T653 2138, see Facebook. Mon-Thu 1100-2300, Fri-Sat 1100-0200.

Just off Independence Av, a good downtown place to try traditional Trini food, like crab and dumplings, cow heel, callaloo soup and pig tail. They also serve anything from burgers and pasta to pepper steak and pork loin. The name comes from the Canboulay riots in 1881, a protest against attempts by the British police to crack down on Carnival celebrations.

$$-$ Pêche Pâtisserie
74 Caroni Savannah Rd, Chaguanas, T222 8508, see Facebook. Tue-Fri 1900-1630, Sat-Sun 0830-1700.

The French-trained chef here produces authentic French breads, croissants, brioche and fabulous pastries and petit fours. This café is the place to come for breakfast or lunch, offering good coffee and hot chocolate, fresh juices, sandwiches, salads and main courses, often with Trini ingredients, such as saltfish, with a French twist. Quite a bit north of Chaguanas with easy access off the highway.

Bars and clubs

Trinidad has plenty of evening entertainment and the atmosphere will be natural and the hospitality generous; it will not always be luxurious but the local rum is likely to flow freely. The after-work lime is a popular activity and places run late (any opening hours listed are likely to be vague). Fri has a bigger crowd than Sat but no night is completely quiet, with the exception of Sun – very much a day of rest (and family time) when most places are closed and even taxis drivers may well take the day off.

In downtown Port of Spain, venues tend to be fun but more rough and ready, and the several lively bars on and close to **Brian Lara Promenade**, are generally very dirty and dingy. Another popular strip is along **Western Main Rd** in St James; often called 'the city that never sleeps' because of its thumping music, sidewalk vendors and straightforward, down-to-earth drinking dens. By far the smartest places are along **Ariapita Avenue** in Woodbrook ('De Avenue', see box, page 74), the preferred destination of the well-heeled liming Trini and some venues are very sophisticated. Out of the city, every town from Arima to Chaguanas in the urban regions of the island has plenty of bars, while the rural areas have basic roadside watering holes known as rum shops, quintessential gathering points for the local communities throughout the Caribbean.

Port of Spain *map page 32.*

51 Degrees
Above Town Restaurant & Bar, 51 Cipriani Blvd, Newtown, T627 0051, www.51degrees. biz. Mon and Wed-Sat 2100-0500.
Dance floors, a VIP lounge, sophisticated lighting and sound, this offers 'themed' nights (usually sponsored by a drinks company) and club and radio DJs; see the Facebook page for what's on. Cover charge at the weekends from about US$18. Street vendors for burgers, hotdogs and doubles set up late outside.

Aria Lounge
Corner Fitt St and Ariapita Av, Woodbrook, T225 2742, see Facebook. Thu-Sat 2200-0430.
A modern club with a strict dress code and expensive drinks, dark and loud and busy at the weekends. Regular events, cover charge from US$15 depending on the time of night and what's on; ladies free on Fri.

Drink Lounge & Bistro
63 Rosalino St, Woodbrook, T223 7243, see Facebook. Tue-Thu 1100-2400, Fri 1100-0200, Sat 1800-0200.
A vibey lounge, popular for the Fri evening lime, regular events like their 'Pavement Cooler Party', which spills out on to the street, and also good for food with an open kitchen; brunch, burgers, sandwiches, tapas and good thin-crust pizzas with toppings such as chorizo and roasted vegetables.

Luce
Hilton Trinidad, Lady Young Rd, northeast Queen's Park Savannah, T688 5823, see Facebook. Tue-Thu 1700-2300, Fri-Sat 1700-2400, Sun 1700-2200.
A bar at the Hilton with outdoor terrace offering fantastic views of the Queen's Park Savannah and the city lights and a comprehensive choice of wines and champagnes along with a sushi bar and 'lite bites' menu. Expensive, but you can't fault the location.

Shakers Cocktail Bar
43 Ariapita Av, Woodbrook, T624 6612, www. shakerstrinidad.com. Mon-Sat 1100-0200.
Also known as **Shakers on the Avenue**, the (mostly rum-based) cocktails here are inventive with cheeky names like 'Cruisin' Thru Life' and 'Dude, Where's My Car', and there's also a good choice of international wine, flavoured coffees and food from snacks such as spicy chicken wings and fried mozzarella sticks to pub grub like lasagne and pot pies. In one of Ariapita Av's lovely old houses, there are tables in the leafy garden.

Stumblin On The Avenue

42 Ariapita Av, Woodbrook, T223 5017,
see Facebook. Tue-Sat 1500-0400.
Bar with a good outdoor area on the
fretwork terrace of another fine old Port
of Spain house, with a variety of drinks
including cocktails and whiskeys (as well
as the usual rums), and DJs later play soca
and other music.

Trotters

Corner Maraval Rd and Sweet Briar Rd, St
Clair, T627 8768, www.trotters.net. Sun-Thu
1130-2400, Fri and Sat 1130-0200.
A great liming spot and local version of an
American sports bar with anything from
basketball to football showing on the big
screens (it's packed on important match
days), with tacos, pizzas, burgers and steaks,
and a British Sun pub lunch menu. Reference
to trotters is globe, not pigs'.

Tzar Nightlife

33 Carlos St, Woodbrook, T684 8927, www.
tzarnightlife.com. Wed-Sat 2200-0500.
This swanky nightclub is geared towards a
more mature, professional crowd, and has
chic decor and a great drinks menu. There's
also a rooftop bar that not only allows
dancers to cool off, but has a great view
down on to bustling Ariapita Av.

San Fernando *map page 28.*

Carnival City Ultra Sports Lounge

Gulf City Mall, South Trunk Rd, La Romain,
T223 1194, See Facebook. Wed-Thu 1600-
2400, Fri 1600-0400, Sat 1300-0400.
This is probably the most modern nightclub
in southern Trinidad with sophisticated
lighting and plenty of giant TV screens
(packed when there's an important football
final on). Regular events, not just club parties
but jazz and local crooners too. Tickets/cover
charges from US$15.

HI RPM

Gulf City Mall, South Trunk Rd, La Romain,
T223 8282, See Facebook. Tue-Thu 1300-2400,
Fri-Sat 1300-0300, Sun, 1600-0100.

Cavernous dance club and bar, attracting a
lively, youngish crowd, good mix of music
from rock and pop to techno, after-lime
party on Fri and popular with students on
Sat from early in the afternoon until the early
hours of Sun morning. Cover charge from
US$15; ladies free on Fri.

The Rig Restaurant & Lounge

South Trunk Rd, La Romain, on the opposite
side of the road from Gulf City Mall, T687
6992, www.therigtnt.com. Daily 1100-2400.
Pub/restaurant with large screens for
watching sports and varied music – live
bands on Wed, karaoke on Thu. The menu
consists predominantly of Chinese and
grilled dishes, and again it's popular for after-
work limes with drinks specials from 1600.
As the name suggests, the interior is built of
scaffolding to make it look vaguely like oil
rigs. Sharing the same building/entrances
is **LIV Nightclub**, T653 9129, see Facebook,
Fri-Sat 2200-1600, open at the weekends,
which often has visiting DJs from Jamaica
and Dominica.

Entertainment

Cinemas

Going to the movies is very popular in Trinidad,
especially if combined with a quick meal. Film
releases are about the same time, or not far
behind, the US. Show times are generally from
1100-2100 and listings are on the websites.
Tickets cost around US$7.50-9, US$10-13 for
a 3D movie, children (under 12) half price.
Caribbean Cinemas, *Trincity Mall (see*
Shopping, below), corner Churchill Roosevelt
Highway and Trincity Main Rd, Trincity, near
the turn-off to Piarco International Airport,
T640 7473, www.caribbeancinemas.com.
A 10-screen multiplex with 2 food courts in
the mall. There's another 12-screen multiplex
on Tarouba Link Rd, Southpark, San Fernando
(just off the San Fernando Bypass), T653 1122,
next to a Pizza Hut.
Digital IMAX Theatre, *1 Woodbrook Pl,*
entrance on Damian St, Woodbrook, T299
4629, www.imax.tt. A huge 3D screen

showing the latest releases and occasional documentaries; you pay a higher price to sit in a leather seat here. There are restaurants in 1 Woodbrook Place.

MovieTowne, *Audrey Jeffers Highway, Invaders Bay, west of Port of Spain, T627 2002.* With 10 screens, the **Platinum Cinema & Lounge** has a bar and waiting service for the plush reclining seats (which also have blankets). Also in the complex are shops, nearly 20 restaurants, bars and fast-food joints, many of which have tables in the open-air courtyard. There's another MovieTowne at Price Plaza, Endeavour Rd, Chaguanas, T627 8277, with 9-screens. Price Plaza is right next to, and easily accessed from, Uriah Butler Highway, and also has a **Pizza Hut**, **Rituals Coffee House** and **TGI Fridays**; www.movietowne.com.

Theatres

Although Carnival and its associated events is a huge attraction, there's not a big performing arts scene in formal auditorium-type theatres, but there are a few venues that host the occasional recitals, concerts and drama. Listing of events can be found at www.buzz.tt.

Central Bank Auditorium, *Eric Williams Plaza, Edward St, Downtown, Port of Spain, T623 0845, www.central-bank.org.tt.*
Little Carib Theatre, *corner White St and Roberts St, Woodbrook, Port of Spain, T622 4644, see Facebook.*
Naparima Bowl, *19-21 Paradise Pasture, San Fernando, T652 2526, www.naparima bowl.com.*
Queen's Hall, *1-3 St Ann's Rd, Port of Spain, T624 1284, www.queenshalltt.com.*

Shopping

The main Port of Spain shopping areas with arcades (shopping plazas) are **Frederick St**, **Queen St**, **Henry St** (all especially good for fabrics, and where shoppers go for Carnival costumes) and **Charlotte St** (fruit and vegetables). In particular, look for **Excellent**

City Centre – the modern façade of the main entrance of this arcade/department store is on Independence Square (Brian Lara Promenade), but at the Frederick St entrance and inside, you can see the lantern skylights, columns and balustrades of George Brown's 100-year-old architecture (of Gingerbread houses fame; see box, page 38). In southern Trinidad, arcades line **Chaguanas Main Rd** and on **High St** and **Coffee St** in San Fernando. However, Trinidadians do most of their shopping in large modern malls, with their a/c and secure parking, of which there are several – the better ones are:

The Falls at West Mall, *Western Main Rd, Westmoorings, T632 1239, www.thefalls atwestmalltt.com. Mon-Sat 1000-1900, Sun 1200-1800.* This attractive mall, the best in Port of Spain, features a vast skylight over the entire roof, lots of fountains and greenery, more than 100 shops (some international brands), a good choice of individual cafés and a food court.
Gulf City Mall, *Gulf View Link Rd, off South Trunk Rd, La Romaine, San Fernando, T657 9251, www.gulfcitymalltt.com. Mon-Thu 1000-2000, Fri-Sat 1000-2100, Sun 1400-1900.* The largest mall in southern Trinidad with 250 shops, a food court and crop of chain restaurants, including **TGI Fridays**.
Long Circular Mall, *Long Circular Rd, St James, Port of Spain, www.lcmtt.com. Daily 1000-1900.* Over 100 shops including a **Tru Valu** supermarket, a food court on the ground level and the decent **Sing Ho** Chinese restaurant on Level 5 (1000-2400).
Trincity Mall, *corner Churchill Roosevelt Highway and Trincity Main Rd, Trincity, T640 2329, www.trincitymalltt.com. Shops daily 1000-1900, restaurants and cinema later.* A 5-min drive west of Piarco International Airport, this advertises itself as the largest shopping mall in the English-speaking Caribbean, and it could well be with over 300 shops, including the biggest supermarket in Trinidad – **TruValu Grand Market** – plus 2 food courts, and **Caribbean Cinemas** (see

above). The majority of the shops however, are of the made-in-China variety.

Arts and crafts

Souvenirs include mini steel pans, Carnival dolls, ornaments made from coconuts and calabashes, jewellery, packs of dried seasonings and cocktail mixes, soaps and lotions. However, there's not a great tourist market for such items so they are not always easy to find. But there are some shops worth seeking out and street vendors hawk trinkets at the beaches when there's a cruise ship in and at Carnival time.

101 Art Gallery, *84 Woodford St, Newtown, T628 4081, www.101artgallery.com. Tue-Fri 1200-1800, Sat 1000-1400.* Owned by Mark Pereira, this long-established fine art gallery showcases Trinidadian artists in styles from watercolours to abstract. Can ship internationally.

B&Tees' Native Spirit, *Long Circular Mall, St James, Port of Spain, T622 7969, www.native spirittees.com. Mon-Sat 1000-1900, Sun 1200-1800.* Original and locally made screen-printed and embroidered T-shirts and other clothing and accessories such as caps and beach bags. Colourful Caribbean designs and Trinidad and Tobago logos. Also outlets in Gulf City and Trincity malls.

Bambu Gift Shop, *Level 2, The Falls at West Mall, Westmoorings, T632 7567. Mon-Sat 1000-1900, Sun 1200-1800.* A good variety of handcrafted items made across the Caribbean – sculptures, ceramics, original paintings, hammocks, wind chimes, steel pans, batik and jewellery.

Rainy Days, *Ellerslie Plaza, Bossiere Village, Maraval T622 5597, see Facebook. Daily 1000-1700.* Colourful shop selling local arts and crafts including pottery, batik and jewellery, plus books and local music CDs.

Selection House, *corner Frederick St and Prince St, Port of Spain, T623 7088. Mon-Fri 0830-1700, Sat 0900-1500.* On the edge of Woodford Square, this a/c shop offers one of the city's most comprehensive selections of souvenirs including T-shirts, carnival-inspired dolls, wood and copper products, hand-painted pottery and miniature steel pans.

Sun Tings, *12 Frederick St, Port of Spain, T625-5901. Mon-Fri 0830-1700, Sat 0900-1500.* Similar to **Selection House**, with another good selection of mini steel pans, straw hats, T-shirts and locally made chutneys and relishes.

Food

The largest supermarket chains are **JTA Supermarkets**, **TruValu** and **Hi-Lo Foods Stores**, but **Massy Stores** (www. massystorestt.com; also in Barbados and rapidly spreading though some of the other Caribbean islands) are by far the best and have in-store bakeries, the larger ones have pharmacies, and there are several 'express' outlets. Fresh produce markets offer a wide variety of fish, meat and fruit and veg, but locally grown fruit and veg is often heavily sprayed (wash well or peel). The **Central Market** in Port of Spain is to the southeast of South Quay in an area called Sea Lots – so-called as at one time the government parcelled lots of land near the sea as a commercial area. However, there is also an impoverished squatter community living here, crime is an issue and it's best avoided. There are also sizeable markets in **San Juan**, **San Fernando**, **Chaguanas**, **Princes Town**, **Arima** and **Sangre Grande**. Best to visit any market early, from 0600-1100.

Music

Crosby's Music Centre, *54 Western Main Rd, St James, Port of Spain, T622 7622, see Facebook. Mon-Fri 0900-1800, Sat 0900-1330.* A great choice of Trini music CDs, plus DJ equipment, electronics, gadgets and appliances.

Just CDs, *Long Circular Mall, St James, Port of Spain, T622 7516, and MovieTowne, Audrey Jeffers Highway, Invaders Bay, T625 3472. Open mall hours.* A wide range of local and international music in a number of genres, including calypso, reggae, classical, opera, R&B, pop and jazz.

Panland, *corner Eastern Main Rd and Dorata St, Laventille, opposite House of Angostura (see page 49), T627 0185, www.panlandtt.com. Mon-Fri 0700-1600.* Serious musicians should head to this factory shop, which produces the island's best steel pans in all sizes; 'accessories' include carrying cases, sticks, stands and how-to-play manuals.

Rhyner's De Music Store, *Piarco International Airport, in the duty free shopping area (you can shop when you arrive as well as on departure), T633 6283, www.rhyners.com.* Rhyner's Record Shop was one of the oldest record shops operating in Trinidad and Tobago, on Prince St, Port of Spain, and was founded in 1938 by Mr Hilton Rhyner, who ran the store until his death in 1981. The company now runs the shop at the airport and sells music online. This is one of the most comprehensive collections of Trinidad and Tobago's music there is, including soca, chutney, calypso, steel pan and gospel.

What to do

Cricket

Queen's Park Oval, *Tragarete Rd, west of Queen's Park Savannah, T622 3787, www. qpcc.com.* Cricket is hugely popular, and the iconic Oval has hosted more Test matches than any other ground in the Caribbean. It also currently has the largest capacity, with seating for about 18,000, and is the oldest – it first hosted a Test match in 1930 when England toured the Caribbean, though cricket matches have been played here since 1891 and the pavilion dates to 1896. Today it is owned by **Queen's Park Cricket Club** (**QPCC**) who have opened the simply fascinating (for cricket fans) **Cricket Heritage Museum**, which documents the Oval's and West Indies ('Windies') cricket team history, with lots of archives, photographs and memorabilia; open by appointment only and guided tours take about 45 mins. For information on fixtures, see www.windiescricket.com. Take a

cushion, sunhat/umbrella, whistle (!) and drinks if sitting in the cheap seats.

Diving

Because of the silt washed around the island by the outflow of Venezuela's Orinoco River, Trinidad does not have the clear blue waters typically associated with the Caribbean, and underwater visibility is not as good as that of Tobago. However, the plankton and nutrients in the current attract huge manta rays and other large pelagics so, if you can see, there is lots to see. Most diving is off the Chaguaramas Peninsula and the Bocas islands, where it is more protected and the water is clearer, with some interesting underwater formations.

Dive TnT, *Coral Cove Marina, Western Main Rd, Chaguaramas, T634 2872, www.divetnt.com.*
Rick's Dive World, *Tropical Marine Plaza, 106 Western Main Rd, Chaguaramas, T634 3483, www.ricksdiveworld.com.*

Fishing

The seasons for sport fishing in Trinidad are sailfish: Nov-Apr; kingfish, African pompano and Spanish mackerel: Jun-Sep; dolphin fish and wahoo: Oct-May; tarpon, tuna, shark and other species can be fished all year round. Most offshore fishing takes place along the north coast and in the Gulf of Paria, while tarpon fishing is good off the Bocas islands. Charters can be arranged, for deep-sea fish or bonefish and tarpon in the mangroves and flats. Prices for deep-sea fishing are around US$500-600 per day from the marinas in Chaguaramas for a fully equipped charter boat. **Fishing TnT** (www.fishingtnt. com) has a full list of operators in both Trinidad and Tobago, but you can of course negotiate lower fees with private fishermen. Trinidad plays host to several international tournaments, including the annual **Wahoo Tournament** in Mar, the **Kingfish Tournament** in Jun and the **Tarpon Bash** in Aug. Contact the **Trinidad and Tobago Game Fishing Association** (T632 6608, www.ttgfa.com), for more information.

Football

A favourite sport of the nation, football (soccer) is played locally and many players from Trinidad and Tobago play for top clubs in Europe and the USA. The main stadiums for the Trinidad and Tobago national football team, the **Soca Warriors** (www.socawarriors.net), and the **T&T Pro League** (www.ttpro league.com) are Hasely Crawford (Port of Spain), Marvin Lee (Macoya), Larry Gomes (Arima), Ato Boldon (Couva) and Manny Ramjohn (Marabella). For fixtures, check the website of the **Trinidad & Tobago Football Federation (TTFF)**: www.ttfootball.org.

Golf

There are several golf courses on Trinidad; information can be found from the **Trinidad & Tobago Golf Association** (T629 7127, www.ttgolfasscocaiation.org).
Chaguaramas Golf Club, *Tucker Valley Rd, Chaguaramas (see also page 44), T347 2762, see Facebook. Daily 0700-1800*. This is the best of the small courses, with its par-67, 9-hole and 18-tee boxes, which was built by US servicemen stationed there during the Second World War; it has some glorious trees and bamboo and is close to Edith Falls and Macqueripe Bay. The **Parlez Restaurant** at the club house is a good place for a drink and snack. US$15 for 18 holes, US$7.50 for 9.
Millennium Lakes Golf & Country Club, *Sunrise Loop Rd, Trincity (close to the mall), T640 8337, www.millenniumlakes.com. Mon-Fri 0700-2100, Sat 0600-2100, Sun 0600-1800*. Prepare for a challenging game at this 18-hole Championship PGA-designed par-71 course close to Piarco International Airport. Green fees for 18 holes US$35-70, depending on the day of the week, and there are also golf carts for hire and a driving range. Note: the lakes are home to caimans.
St Andrews Golf Club, *St Andrews Wynd, Moka, just north of Maraval, T629 0066, www.golftrinidad.com. Daily 0600-1800*. One of the loveliest courses on Trinidad, established in 1891, and nestled between the hills in a very picturesque location. The

club house offers good snacks and liquid refreshment and there's a swimming pool. Green fees for 18 holes US$54-90, depending on the day of the week.

Horse racing

Horse racing in Trinidad dates from 1828 when informal races were held at Queen's Park Savannah, known as the Big Yard, and other locations, including beaches. 1897 saw the establishment of the Trinidad Turf Club (replaced in 1976 by the Trinidad and Tobago Racing Authority) and the construction of the race stand on the Savannah, acknowledging the popularity of the sport and the competitiveness of the owners, trainers, jockeys and horses. Rebuilt in 1947 the stand was also used for cricket, football and golf audiences until racing moved to Arima in the early 1990s. Today the grandstand is used for various spectator events, most notably the Carnival.
Santa Rosa Park, *Arima, just off Churchill Roosevelt Highway, T646 2450, www.arima raceclub.com*. Races are held here most Sats and public holidays.

Sailing

Chaguaramas is the main area for sailing and racing, with lots of marinas catering for local and foreign yachts. **Trinidad and Tobago Sailing Association (TTSA)** (T634 4210, www. ttsailing.org), sponsors **Carnival Fun Race** and a weekly racing programme in winter and spring when the winds are at their strongest. It also runs a sailing academy with sailing courses and sailing camps for newcomers. Every Jul/Aug, there is a power boat race from the **Trinidad and Tobago Yacht Club (TTYC)**, Trinidad to **Store Bay**, Tobago.

Surfing

The best swells can be found off the north and northeast coasts in Nov-Mar, although hurricane season can also provide some spectacular waves, and there are also river mouth and reef breaks, good for all level of surfers. The best beaches include

Blanchisseuse, Toco, Balandra, Sans Souci Las Cuevas and Salybia. Check out the website for the **Surfing Association of Trinidad and Tobago (SATT)** (T761 1191, www.surftt.org), for information about where to buy a surfboard and about national and international competitions.

Jason Apparicio Surf Academy, *contact via the website, www.jasonapparicio.wordpress. com.* A former national champion of Trinidad, and US and European pro-surfer (and surfing model), Jason offers lessons for beginners and intermediates all over Trinidad and Tobago; from US$50 half day, US$100 full day, with transport to the beach.

Trinidad and Tobago Surf Experience, *38 Carlton Av, St James, Port of Spain, T355 5691, www.trinidadandtobagosurfexp.com.* Can organize lessons/excursions with boards to the various locations around the island; 3-hr lessons from US$50, board rental only US$25. The meeting point is the office in St James, from where you are driven to the beach.

Tour operators

Avifauna Tours, *T633 5614, www.roger necklesphotography.com.* Tailor-made, birdwatching tours with wildlife photographer and naturalist Roger Neckles – extremely knowledgeable about birds, it's not uncommon to see 90+ species in a day and his enthusiasm is infectious.

Banwari Experience, *T747 8379, www. banwaricaribbean.com.* Customizes tours to suit your interests including hiking and birdwatching, Port of Spain tours with a bit of steel pan and Carnival history, or a tour of the temples and Hindu sites such as the **Dattatreya Yoga Centre** (see page 60) with some Indo-Trinidadian background.

Caribbean Discovery Tours, *T620 1989, www.caribbeandiscoverytours.com.* Run by acclaimed guide, Stephen Broadbridge, who is an expert on the flora and fauna of the island and who offers walking tours, waterfall hikes, cave exploration, kayaking

expeditions, good trips to Nariva Swamp, 'Down de Islands' boat trips, and other tours off the beaten track. Expect to pay from US$80 per person (minimum 2) for a day trip from Port of Spain.

Trinidad & Tobago Sightseeing Tours, *T628 1051, www.trintours.com.* A good professional operator that is well-used to cruise ship groups with guides that speak German, Italian, Spanish and French. Full-day sightseeing tours around Trinidad start from US$80 and go as far west as Manzanilla, plus day tours also go to Grande Riviere; US$80, and there are half-day trips to Maracas and Blanchisseusse; US$45-60, **Asa Wright Nature Centre**; US$70, and Caroni Bird Sanctuary including a boat trip into the mangroves; US$50. They can organize a long-day trip to Tobago taking in the major sights and with time on the beach; from US$190 including return airfares, and transport and a guide can be arranged to go with you on a night out (liming) in Port of Spain.

Transport

Boat
See Getting around, page 133, for details of the ferry service between Trinidad and Tobago.

A Water Taxi service runs between Port of Spain and San Fernando to relieve pressure on the congested roads and this is much the easiest way to travel between the 2 cities. The catamarans are fast and comfortable, and there are 6 45-min crossings a day Mon-Fri (mostly in the mornings for commuters from San Fernando and in the afternoons for the return journey from Port of Spain), but there are no sailings at the weekend; US$2.30 one way. The Water Taxi terminal in Port of Spain is on Wrightson Rd, T624 5137, and in San Fernando, on King's Wharf, Lady Hailes Av, T652 9980. Schedules can be found on the **National Infrastructure Development Company Limited (NIDCO)** website, www.nidco.co.tt.

Bus, maxi and route taxis

PTSC buses The main terminal for **PTSC** buses (T623 2341, www.ptsc.co.tt) is City Gate at the western end of South Quay in Port of Spain. It is a hub for public transport and from here you'll be able to get as far as **Arima**, **Chaguanas**, **Chaguaramas**, **Sangre Grande**, **San Fernando** and **Valencia**. Anywhere beyond these places, you'll have to change vehicles. On the main routes they run roughly Mon-Fri 0500-2100, Sat 0500-2000, and Sun 0600-2000. Buses on more rural routes are extremely infrequent and rarely run at weekends. You can buy tickets at the terminals or look out for the PTSC signs on small shops/kiosks. They cost TT$3 for short journey and up to TT$8 for a trip to the end of a route.

Maxi taxis run on set routes similar to the PTSC buses but have no timetables. They also gather at City Gate (and at numerous other taxi stands around Port of Spain) and are identified by the coloured bands on the sides of the vehicles: **yellow** (Route 1) from Port of Spain to the west of Trinidad including **Chaguaramas**, **Petit Valley** and **Diego Martin**; **red** (Route 2) to the east as far as **Sangre Grande**; and **green** to the south down to **San Fernando**. Other routes from San Fernando are: **black** to **Princes Town**; and **brown** to the southwest, including **Point Fortin**, **Cedros** and **Siparia**. As with buses, fares start from TT$3, but for non-stopping services like Port of Spain to **San Fernando**, fares are TT$20 (US$3) – it is in fact cheaper and quicker to go by Water Taxi.

Route taxis in Trinidad (small shared cars) are not generally found on the main routes from Port of Spain, though they do serve the suburbs and rural areas. Expect to pay TT$3-7 depending on distance, and there is usually the option of paying about TT$2 extra for a short deviation ('off route').

Car hire

Some car hire companies have offices in the Arrivals hall of Piarco International Airport, and those that don't will be able to arrange a pick-up/drop-off there. Expect to pay in the region of US$40-50 per day for a Suzuki jeep or normal/sedan car, US$65 for a more substantial 4-door 4WD, and US$90 for a minibus. See page 135 for further details about hiring a car and driving.

Alamo Rent a Car, airport, T826 6893, www.alamo.com. **Avis**, airport, T669 0905, www.avistrinidad.com. **Budget**, airport, T669 1635, www.budget.com. **Econo Car Rentals**, airport, T669 1119; 191-195 Western Main Rd, Cocorite, T622 8072; Crews Inn Hotel & Yachting Centre (see page 67), Chaguaramas, T634 2154; www.econocarrentalstt.com. **Europcar**, at the Hilton Trinidad, Lady Young Rd, Port of Spain, T621 2159; and the Courtyard Port of Spain (Marriott), Invaders Bay, Audrey Jeffers Highway, T627 5376, www.europcar.co.tt. **Hertz**, Golden Grove Rd, Piarco, T669 6239, www.hertz.com. **Kalloo's Auto Rentals**, airport, T669 5673; the best local operator and well-priced compared to the international franchises, with a desk directly after Arrivals; also at 31 French St, Port of Spain, T622 9073, www.kalloos.com. **Sixt**, airport, T376 0937, www.sixt.com. **Thrifty**, airport, T669 0602, www.thrifty.com.

Taxi

As with Tobago all taxi fares are set by the government and taxi association and fares to all destinations around the island are on a noticeboard at Piarco International Airport. Also here is a dispatcher for the **Piarco Airport Taxi Cooperative Society** (T669 1689). Taxis also meet the Water Taxis in Port of Spain. Otherwise any hotel can phone a taxi for you – if you find a driver you like, get their card and phone number. **Note** Fares between 2200 and 0600 attract a surcharge of 50%.

Tobago

Tobago is 41 km long and only 12 km wide, about the same size as Barbados, but with only a fifth of the population (about 60,000) and a tiny fraction of the number of tourists. It is not as busy and vibrant as Trinidad, but neither is it industrialized or urbanized; instead, the island is charming and beautiful, with a quiet, easy-going way of life in the villages and tiny towns. It is ideal for people in search of relaxation, and Trinidadians regard it as their holiday island. The Crown Point tourist area is concentrated in the southwestern end, about 13 km from the capital, Scarborough. Here, apartment complexes, bars and fast-food joints welcome visitors straight off the plane from Trinidad, given that almost everything is within walking distance of the airport. But, even though it is as close to a typical Caribbean holiday resort as you'll find on Tobago, it is still relatively low-key. Elsewhere, scattered all around the island, are small hotels and guesthouses offering peace and quiet in scenic surroundings. The dense, leafy rainforests on the Main Ridge (highest point 573 m), the mountainous volcanic spine of Tobago that extends for about two-thirds of the length of the island from the northeast tip, are quite wild and provide a spectacular backdrop for the many horseshoe bays around the coast. Beaches are golden, the Caribbean Sea on the leeward side is clear and warm and is backed by wooded coves with fishing boats dotted along the sand, and there is good walking, diving, fishing and excellent birdwatching.

Essential Tobago

Finding your feet

ANR Robinson International Airport is on the southwestern tip of the island at Crown Point (Airport Connector Road, T639 8547, www.tntairports.com/anr), 13 km southwest of the island's capital Scarborough (for Airport information, see page 132.

Immediately outside the Arrivals exit is the desk for the taxi dispatcher for the **Tobago Taxi Cab Co-op Society**; T639 0950. As with Trinidad, all taxi fares are set by the government and taxi association and fares to all destinations around the island are on a noticeboard. Example fares are the airport to hotels in Crown Point US$7.50; Scarborough US$12; Speyside US$45; Plymouth US$15; Castara US$42. Note: fares between 2200 and 0600 attract a surcharge of 50%. All drivers accept Trinidad and Tobago dollars and US dollars cash. Alternatively, you can ask your hotel when reserving a room to send a car to collect you, but these will be taxis too so costs are the same.

Public Transport Service Corporation (**PTSC**; T639 2293, www.ptsc.co.tt) buses between Crown Point and Scarborough turn around on the street just behind the airport. The service costs TT$2 (buy tickets from **Jimmy's Mini Mart** next to the bus stop), and they run at least every hour Monday-Friday 0500-2100, Saturday 0500-2000, and Sunday 0600-2000. On this route they run up Milford Road, so it's possible to reach most of the hotels in Crown Point. The better option with luggage, route taxis also gather on the street behind the airport and run along both Milford Road and Store

Best beaches
Pigeon Point, page 91
Englishman's Bay, page 106
Man O War Bay, page 106
Parlatuvier Bay, page 106
Castara Bay, page 107

Best places to stay
Magdalena Grand Beach, page 109
Shepherd's Inn, page 110
Bacolet Beach Club, page111
Blue Waters Inn, page 112
Castara Retreats, page 114

Bay Local Road and cost TT$3-5 for a short drop around Crown Point and TT$7 to Scarborough. There is usually the option of paying about TT$2 extra for a short deviation ('off route'). Most car hire offices (see page 129) are around Crown Point close to the airport or they will meet you there.

If arriving by ferry from Port of Spain on Trinidad, the **Trinidad and Tobago Inter-Island Ferry Service** (TTIT; T639-2417/4906, www.ttitferry.com) ferry terminal is in the centre of Scarborough on the waterfront. Taxis are available and it's a short walk across the main road (Carrington Street) to buses and route and maxi taxis.

Getting around

Many of the Crown Point hotels are within walking distance or just a short taxi ride of the airport. Scarborough is only a 15-25 minutes' drive from Crown Point and is small enough to walk around, but for trips further afield the options are PTSC buses, regular, route or maxi taxis. From Crown Point these run along Milford Road (route taxis also go along Store Bay Local Road) to Scarborough, where you will have to change vehicles to get to other parts of the island. However, from Milford Road in Crown Point, you may find route taxis going directly to Buccoo via Shirvan Road, where you can change on to another going to Black Rock and Plymouth (thus missing out Scarborough). The final option for exploring Tobago, is to go on an island tour, either in a hire car, with a tour operator (see page 128), or with a taxi driver (if you find one you like). The whole island can be circumnavigated in one day, and a leisurely one at that, with lots of time to stop.

At the southwest end of the island, the flat belt of land between ANR Robinson International Airport and the island's capital, Scarborough, to the east, and the scrappy small town of Plymouth to the northeast, is home to more than 80% of Tobago's population (roughly 60,000 in total). It's also home to the main Crown Point tourist area, the first destination visitors will encounter if they arrive by air (ferry arrivals will immediately spill out on to the congested waterfront at Scarborough). Almost all visitors will spend time in Crown Point before heading up to the less populated and infinitely more scenic mountainous and forested areas to the north and east.

Crown Point *See map, page 92.*

Crown Point is a region of coral scrubland, seldom rising above sea level, and the most built-up and commercialized part of the island. It stretches eastwards from the airport and through the suburbs of Bon Accord and Canaan, all of which run along the parallel Milton Road and Old Store Bay Local Road; both served well with route taxis for getting around. Here there are hotels, resorts and apartment blocks, some within walking distance of the airport (even with luggage), plenty of nightlife and useful facilities like car hire offices and laundromats. This was once the haunt of package holidaymakers from the UK given that airlines such as **Monarch** used to bring planeloads in two or three times a week. But these charter flights stopped a few years ago (mainly because of the UK recession), although **Virgin** and **British Airways** still fly directly to Tobago. But without the high-spending masses of the charter holiday market, Crown Point has suffered a little economically; it has gone a bit to seed and is mostly tatty-looking these days. Its dominant market is now weekending Trinidadians, who hop over on the 20-minute flight, for liming and fishing. Generally, these visitors prefer self-catering in cheap apartments (hence the rash of new building around the airport). Nevertheless, there's always a lively, fun holiday atmosphere at Crown Point, with plenty of restaurants and bars, especially around the junction with Milford Road and Pigeon Point Road, and there are a couple of beaches with decent swimming and snorkelling if you don't mind the crowds.

The ruins of the small **Milford Fort** (the only historical site here) is just a five-minute walk north of the airport, on the ocean end of Old Store Bay Road. It is alleged that a settlement of Dutchmen under the protection of the Duke of Courland was briefly located at the site in 1642, when they wanted Tobago as a first base for their excursions into Guyana, where they were creating colonies on the Demerara and Essequibo Rivers. From about 1770 the British maintained a two-cannon battery here until the island fell to the French in 1781. On their return to the island, the fort was erected by the British in 1811 and was occupied until 1854. Today it is no more than a pleasant garden, but the cannons still point out to sea.

Close by, **Store Bay Beach**, the heartbeat of Crown Point, is really quite tiny, cupped on both sides by small coral cliffs. But it's always busy with locals and visiting Trinis. It's a good place to watch the sunset and brown pelicans are often seen diving offshore. **Store Bay Beach Facility** ① *daily 1000-1730, lockers, changing rooms and toilets TT$2, beach chairs/sun loungers/umbrellas TT$30 (US$4.50) each per day*, has a large car park and stalls for vendors selling T-shirts, beach wraps and souvenirs. There's also a food court for snacks such as fish broth, crab and dumpling, mahi mahi-and-bake, curry goat, rotis and bus-up-shut, ice cream and drinks. Some of the food is delicious and served by always-cheerful ladies; this is a good place to try local specialities. A kiosk operates as the ticket office for the glass-bottomed boat operators for trips to **Buccoo Reef** and **Nylon Pool** for snorkelling (see box, page 94). There is some hassling to sign up to these excursions, as well as from trinket sellers and beach chair touts, and single women have complained of harassment on the beach, but the zeal can generally be neutralized by a friendly "no thanks".

Just north of Store Bay is the small **Coconut Bay**, where a private man-made beach belongs to the **Coco Reef Resort & Spa** (the most upmarket accommodation at Crown

1 Tobago

→ **Tobago maps**
1 Tobago, page 90
2 Crown Point, page 92
3 Scarborough, page 98

Where to stay
Ade's Domicile 22
Adventure Eco-Villas 10
Angel Retreat 13
Arnos Vale Vacation
  Apartments 12
Bacolet Beach Club 8
Blue Haven 25
Blue Mango 13
Blue Waters Inn 1
Castara Cottage 13
Castara Retreats 2

Changrela Cocrico Inn 17
Cholson Chalets 14
Cholson Chalets 6
Cuffie River Nature Retreat 5
Fish Tobago Guesthouse 15
Gloucester Place 18
Grafton Beach Resort 11
Half Moon Blue 16
Magdalena Grand Beach
  & Golf Resort
Man-O-War Bay Cottages 14
Miller's Guest House 7

Moonlight Mountain 23
Naturalist Beach Resort 13
Ocean View Apartment 14
Palms Villa Resort 3
Rainbow Nature Resort 20
Speyside Inn 9
Top O' Tobago 19
Top Ranking Hill View
  Guest House 24

Point, see page 108). It was made from thousands of tons of Guyanese white river sand, and is protected by a breakwater. While this sea wall might be ugly, it has created a mini-reef that is good for snorkelling. The only access is via the hotel and a small charge to go on the beach is applicable.

Pigeon Point Heritage Park

T639 0601, www.pigeonpoint.tt, daily US$3, children (6-12) US$1.50, under 6s free, weekly US$15/7.50, open daily 0900-1700, no entry after 1700 but you can stay later at the bars, beach chairs/sun loungers/umbrellas US$4.50 each per day.

This 50-ha nature reserve has one of the island's most beautiful beaches; dazzling white sand backed by swaying coconut palms and crystal-clear aquamarine water. However, it's also one of the busiest and most developed, and simply heaves at the weekend and on public holidays. But, there are great views of the Caribbean Sea, there are lifeguards on duty and, protected by Buccoo Reef, the calm waters make it ideal for swimming. There is no snorkelling from the shore, but you can take a glass-bottomed boat out from the jetty to Buccoo Reef and the Nylon Pool (see box, page 94). To get to the gated entrance, follow Pigeon Point Road around the coast from its junction with Milford Road – 2 km or a 20-minute walk. Alternatively, route taxis run between this junction and the gate, or another option is to hire a bike from **Easy Goers Bicycle Rental** near the airport (see page 128). From the gate it's a short walk through a sandy area dotted with giant palms, past the **Heritage Pavilion** (used for weddings and conferences), to the main beach (no vehicles are permitted along

Tip...

Look and listen out for the raucous cocrico (also known as the chachalaca), a pheasant-type bird indigenous to Tobago. There are a surprisingly large number of them at urbanized Crown Point; it is believed that many were forced out of the forests during hurricanes and they have bred well. Their loud, grating, repetitive squawk at dawn may well wake you up in the morning.

Restaurants 🍴
Bird Watcher's Restaurant & Bar **1**
Boat House **2**
Cascreole Bar & Beach Club **2**
Cheno's **4**
D'Almond Tree **2**
Fish Pot **3**
Gail's **7**
Jemma's Sea View Kitchen **1**
King's Bay Café **8**

La Tartaruga **9**
Seahorse Inn **5**
Sharon & Phebe's **10**
Shore Things Café & Craft **14**
Suckhole **11**
Waves Restaurant & Bar **5**

Bars & clubs 🍸
Captain Sand Bar **12**
Glasgow's Bar **13**

this stretch, though bikes are). There are huts for shade, tables and benches, lockers, showers, toilets and changing rooms, and a little clutch of shops selling crafts and beach apparel. Food kiosks here sell all things take-out – fried chicken, pizza, rotis, bake and shark, macaroni pie, and ice cream – and there are a couple of beach bars with pool tables and loud music. The northern end is quieter and is a little windier than the main beach, which makes it the best spot for watersports like wind- and kitesurfing (**Radical Sports** is based here, see page 128). Beyond here is a lovely expanse of white sand running around **Bon Accord Lagoon** towards Buccoo. The lagoon is fringed by mangrove wetlands and is an important habitat for many species of bird. It is, however, only accessible by boat, and a small spit of white-coral sand known as 'No Man's Land' has become a popular venue for boozy beach barbecues.

Buccoo

From Crown Point, Milford Road heads towards Scarborough and, once past the suburb of Lowlands, becomes the double-lane Claude Noel Highway; turn left on to Shirvan Road to get to Buccoo. This small, rather tatty but very friendly village is predominantly a

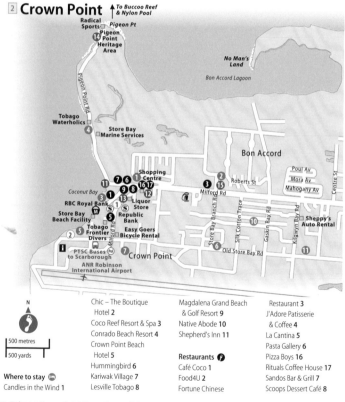

2 Crown Point ↑ To Buccoo Reef & Nylon Pool

Where to stay	Chic – The Boutique Hotel **2**
Candles in the Wind **1**	Coco Reef Resort & Spa **3**
	Conrado Beach Resort **4**
	Crown Point Beach Hotel **5**
	Hummingbird **6**
	Kariwak Village **7**
	Lesville Tobago **8**
	Magdalena Grand Beach & Golf Resort **9**
	Native Abode **10**
	Shepherd's Inn **11**

Restaurants
Café Coco **1**
Food4U **2**
Fortune Chinese Restaurant **3**
J'Adore Patisserie & Coffee **4**
La Cantina **5**
Pasta Gallery **6**
Pizza Boys **16**
Rituals Coffee House **17**
Sandos Bar & Grill **7**
Scoops Dessert Café **8**

N
500 metres
500 yards

base for fishing, but there are a couple of good cheap places to stay (the closest Tobago has to backpacker hostels; see page 110) and it's famous as the location for the weekly Sunday School party (see box, page 122) and annual crab and goat races (see box). Buccoo lies on a peninsula between two bays and their good beaches: Buccoo Bay to the south and Mount Irvine Bay to the north. At **Buccoo Bay**, the long narrow white-sand beach is (like Pigeon Point) protected by Buccoo Reef and the sea is usually calm and good for swimming, but becomes very narrow at high tide. A small beach bar and toilets can be found adjacent to the fishing co-operative where you can watch the fishermen land and prepare their catch. From the jetty, boat captains offer trips out to Buccoo Reef and Nylon Pool for snorkelling (see box, page 94).

The long beach at **Mount Irvine Bay** is split into two by a small headland; the first section is good for swimming and sunbathing and is also referred to as the 'hotel beach' as it's opposite the **Mount Irvine Bay Hotel & Golf Club** (presently very poor and run-down; not recommended for either accommodation or golf). The second section of the beach, a little further north, is where you'll find the **Mount Irvine Bay Beach Facility** ⓘ *car park, changing rooms, showers and toilets; TT$2*, and is where most of the island's sailing tours start from (see page 128). It has good snorkelling – especially for beginners and children as there are plenty of fish to see within wading distance – and it's also Tobago's premier surf spot from December to March; busy with both local surfers and those coming over from Trinidad. Swimmers should be wary of big waves and strong currents during these months and stick to the area demarcated by the lifeguards. There are beach bars and, at busier times, stalls selling rotis, bake and shark and pies, while beach chairs and snorkelling gear can be rented around the lifeguard area.

Black Rock

About 5 km along the coast from Buccoo you come to the village of Black Rock, where the beach at **Stonehaven Bay** is also known as Grafton Beach, given that it's home to the **Grafton Beach Resort** (see page 110). The waves can be very powerful here and you are advised to stay close to the shore to avoid dangerous currents. The right

To Buccoo, Black Rock & Plymouth

Golden Grove

➡ **Tobago maps**
1 Tobago, page 90
2 Crown Point, page 92
3 Scarborough, page 98

⑩

Feeder St

Canaan ⑧

First Citizen Ⓢ Robert St Golden Grove Rd Penny Savers Supermarket Milford Rd Shirvan Rd

Shirvan Plaza ③ ④ Claude Noel Hwy

To ⑨ & Scarborough

Tyson Hall

❷

Skewers **8**
Trinbago Curry House **9**
Watermill **10**

Renmar's Restaurant & Bar **14**
Shade Night Club **15**

Bars & clubs ⑪
Bago's Beach Bar **11**
Colours Restaurant & Bar **12**
Overhang Bar & Lounge **13**

Entertainment ⊙
Jade Monkey Casino **1**
Royalton Casino **2**
Silver Dollar Casino **3**

Tip...
Fishing boats use the more northerly part of Mount Irvine Beach to offload their catch; it's a great place to buy fresh fish including mahi mahi, red snapper and barracuda. The best time to go is around 1500-1700.

ON THE WATER

Buccoo Reef and Nylon Pool

Buccoo Reef, Tobago's largest coral reef, was designated a marine park in 1973. This popular diving and snorkelling site contains a reef system of five flats separated by deep channels. Glass-bottomed boats for visiting this undersea garden leave from Store Bay and Pigeon Point and some go from Buccoo Bay too. The charge is about US$15 for two to 2½ hours, with snorkelling gear provided; wear a hat and plenty of sunscreen. The trips also include the Nylon Pool, an emerald-green, 1-m-deep crystal-clear pool with a sandy bottom in the middle of the sea, created by an offshore sandbar and the still Bon Accord Lagoon. Ideal for swimming, it was named by Britain's Princess Margaret back in 1962, when she visited Tobago on her honeymoon and observed that it was as clear as her nylon stockings. Longer trips also visit No Man's Land, a sandy spit jutting into the lagoon, and include a barbecue and beach party; around US$60-70, worth it if you eat and drink plenty. However, the dragging of anchors and greed and carelessness of divers as well as temperature changes resulting in bleaching of the coral, have tarnished the glory of the once-marvellous Buccoo Reef. But there is still a good variety of fish, including reef sharks and the colourful parrot fish and angel fish, while shoals of squid can also be seen.

From Store Bay, boats leave between 0900 and 1430, and are officially arranged at a kiosk at the Store Bay Beach Facility (at the craft market), although touts for the boat owners may approach you anywhere in the Crown Point area. At the Pigeon Point Heritage Park, they depart from the jetty at 1100 and 1400, and the boat owners are paid directly.

side of the beach (north) can be the calmest and offers reasonable snorkelling. North of Stonehaven Bay, on a headland in the village, are the ruins of **Fort Bennett**. This lookout point offers a panoramic view of the coastline, an advantage when the fort was first built by the Courlanders in 1680 and later when batteries of cannon were positioned there by the British in the 18th century to deter American privateers.

Beyond here a number of side streets in Black Rock lead down to **Great Courland Bay**'s beaches. The central section is very scrappy but there are some calm sections in what is otherwise a fairly exposed stretch of coast. The nicer sloping beach at the northern end (also known as Turtle Beach) is the location of one of Tobago's few all-inclusive resorts, **Turtle Beach Tobago by Rex Resorts** (www.rexresorts.com) and is also the nesting site for leatherbacks (March-August). Turtle-watching excursions can be organized by the hotel for their guests; otherwise contact **Save Our Sea Turtles (SOS) Tobago** (T328 7351, www. sos-tobago.org) to arrange an SOS-trained turtle-watching guide.

Also near Black Rock is the **Grafton Caledonia Wildlife Sanctuary** ① *feeding time 0800 and 1600 (don't bother coming in the middle of the day as you won't see the birds); free but donations appreciated (and needed)*. On a former cocoa estate this is a wilderness of overgrown buildings and tracks and now seriously in decline. To get there, follow signs inland opposite the Grafton Beach Resort. There is a small weathered sign indicating the entrance and a short uphill secondary road that leads to the sanctuary. The bird feeders are at the Copra House, once the drying house for coconut and cocoa, and you can watch blue-crowned motmots, cocricos and other birds emerge from the forest to be fed, a

ON THE ROAD

Goat and crab racing

Tobago is perhaps the only place in the world with a dedicated goat and crab racing track. Replacing a less formal track, it was recently built by the Tobago House of Assembly next to the Buccoo Beach Facility in Buccoo, and has a main covered grandstand, a 90-m grassy track, restaurant and bar and 'stables'. Tobago goat racing is a serious competitive sport that was initiated in 1925 by Samuel Callender (not a Tobagonian but a Barbadian) as a poor man's equivalent to horse racing, which was reserved for the local gentry at the time. Horse racing was an Easter Monday event, and the next day, Tuesday, became dedicated to the racing of goats for the entertainment of the lower classes. Horse racing no longer exists on Tobago, but goat racing certainly does and the event is still on 'Easter Tuesday'. Large crowds attend and before each race the goats are paraded, with commentary indicating the race favourites, and then the goats and jockeys proceed to the starting gates. The jockeys, who run barefoot, wear white silk shorts and brightly coloured jerseys.

Strength and speed are required of a good racing goat and this is achieved by the hard work and dedication of the owners, trainers and jockeys. The animals are trained for at least two months prior to the race and they learn to walk at increasing speeds until they're running in front of the trainer. A swimming routine to build muscles is also a critical part of the training, as is diet. It is thought that nanny goats are better runners. However, billy goats are the preferred choice since they live longer. The jockeys must also train as they must run alongside and be able to match the speed of their goats.

The crab races are an additional event. In these races only the best bred and healthiest looking large blue crabs are entered (although crabs don't take to training so easily), and the jockeys and their crabs are placed in the centre of a large circle drawn in the sand; the first one to be coaxed out of the circle is the winner. These crab races generate almost as much energy and excitement (and betting) as the goat races.

Information about the event is posted on Buccoo Village Council's Facebook page (www.facebook.com/buccoovillage.council); the event begins at 1000 with racing from 1100; except to pay about US$7.50 (half price for children) to join in. Afterwards and when the sun goes down, there's an all-night lime in Buccoo, similar to the regular Sunday School.

tradition that has continued since 1963, when the owner started to feed the wild birds after Hurricane Flora destroyed their woodland habitat. The lack of information and the generally unkempt nature of the place means that it is best to come here as part of a bird tour of the island with a specialist guide. The lovely gentleman who feeds the birds is knowledgeable but is not a guide and is quite shy of visitors.

Plymouth

The main town on this coast is Plymouth, about 14 km from Crown Point via Buccoo. There are limited sites but **Fort James** sits on a well-manicured headland overlooking **Great Courland Bay** (the site of the Courlander settlement in the 17th century). Named after Jacobus (James), the Duke of Courland, it was destroyed and rebuilt several times as a battery and fort, but is the oldest fort site on Tobago. The present fort was erected

BACKGROUND

Tobago's history

Possession of Tobago has been fought over by numerous nations since it was first sighted by Columbus in 1498. He called it Bella Forma, although its present name is a corruption of the word 'tobacco', which the original Carib inhabitants grew on the island. Dutch merchants were the first to establish a colony in 1632; Tobago was identified as a valuable strategic harbour and a source of fertile soil and was regarded as a prize possession by all of its colonial occupiers. Over the years, the island changed hands 31 times between the British, Dutch and French.

From 1672, during a period of stability under temporary British rule, sugar and cotton plantations were established and Africans were imported to work as slaves. The economy flourished and by 1777 Tobago was exporting great quantities of rum, cotton, indigo and sugar, and over 90% of Tobago's 15,000 residents were slaves. However, when the French invaded again in 1781, they forced the British governor to surrender, destroyed most of the plantations, and the island's buoyant economy fell into decline. It was once again recaptured by Britain in 1803 and was finally formally ceded to Britain in 1814 under the Treaty of Paris. Another successful phase of sugar production began. However, a severe hurricane in 1847, combined with the collapse of plantation insurance underwriters in England, marked the end of the sugar trade. Without this highly profitable trade, the island was unable to sustain itself. Britain had no further use for it and in 1889, Tobago's colonial government was abolished and the island was made a ward of Trinidad. This was the groundwork for it becoming a twin-island state.

Without sugar, the islanders had to grow other crops, planting acres of limes, coconuts and cocoa and exporting their produce to Trinidad. But in 1963, Hurricane Flora ravaged Tobago, destroying the villages, crops and an estimated 50% of the island's coconut trees. A restructuring programme followed and attempts were made to diversify the economy; most significant was the development of the tourism industry. Trinidad and Tobago gained independence in 1962 and, under the country's current political system, the central government, located in Port of Spain, sets the budget and allocates funds for the whole country. But Tobago has its own elected governing body called the Tobago House of Assembly, which is given the responsibility to manage the day to day operations on the island.

in the early 19th century. Also here is the **Couronian (Latvian) Monument**. Designed by a local artist, it was erected in 1976 during a cultural visit by Courlanders in exile and represents 'Freedom'.

A much-quoted attraction in Plymouth is the enigmatic tombstone of Betty Stevens (25 November 1783), whose cryptic epitaph reads: "She was a mother without knowing it, and a wife, without letting her husband know, except by her kind indulgences to him."

Just north of Plymouth, the **Arnos Vale Bay** area was once a large plantation and sugarcane was grown on the surrounding hills. Today's Arnos Vale Road through the valley to **Les Coteaux** was used to transport the sugar to the beach for shipment. The plantation house as well as the waterwheel that powered the sugar mill (dating from 1880) became part of the property of the **Arnos Vale Hotel**, but sadly this was damaged by fire in 2015 and is now closed. You can still reach the relatively small **Arnos Vale Beach** via a small track though the woods, to the left of the old hotel entrance but, since the hotel closed down, the beach is unpatrolled and is generally deserted so safety may be an issue.

A more worthwhile attraction is the 5-ha **Adventure Farm and Nature Reserve** ⓘ *2 km from Plymouth off Arnos Vale Rd, 639 2839, www.adventure-ecovillas.com, Mon-Fri 0700-1745, US$4.50*, where you can stroll among fruit trees, picking mangoes and other fruit in season while looking for birds, butterflies, iguanas and other wildlife. Ean Mackay, the owner, has put considerable effort into attracting birds of every type, and over 50 species have been identified, including motmots, cocricos, woodpeckers, jacamars, and five of the six hummingbird species on Tobago. It is no surprise that most of the professional birding guides on Tobago include it in their tours, and you can sit and watch, photograph or film the birds in comfort at the feeders on the veranda. There are cottages to rent in this relaxing spot (see page 111), perfect for birdwatchers who want to rise at dawn.

> **Tip...**
> From Plymouth you can follow Plymouth Road southeast for 6.5 km to Scarborough, or follow Arnos Vale Road and join Northside Road at Moriah to then go on to Castara and the northwest coast.

Scarborough

Tobago's service centre with a patchwork of red roofs, narrow streets and the ferry port

About 13 km northeast of Crown Point along the Claude Noel Highway, Scarborough is the centre of all business activity on the island. It became the capital in 1769 when it replaced the then-capital of Georgetown. Under French rule it was named Port Louis. Although government sits in Port of Spain in Trinidad, Scarborough is the seat of the Tobago House of Assembly, which is responsible for local issues. Boats come into the bay bringing cargo and passengers, there is a lively market and bus and taxi terminals, and a fair degree of traffic congestion around its confusing one-way system. The town, which hugs the shore of Rockly Bay and straggles up its eastern flank, is friendly enough, but is hot, dusty and always thronging so perhaps not worth an extended visit. There are very few places to stay or eat and no souvenir shops, as tourist development has been concentrated elsewhere.

Sights

Lower Scarborough Around the harbour and waterfront, Lower Scarborough is the centre of much of the town's activity. Milford Road skirts the shoreline as it approaches from the west and becomes Carrington Street where you'll find a string of businesses – banks, fast-food outlets, bars and street vendors. Around Wilson Road are the **market** (fish, meat, fruit and vegetables and fresh coconut water, especially worth a visit on Friday and Saturday mornings), the Post Office, the Public Library, the bus terminus, petrol stations, Chinese restaurants, chicken-and-chips joints, roti shops and a couple of shopping malls selling made-in-China wares. New development has included a deep-water harbour and Cruise Ship Terminal.

Botanic Gardens ⓘ *entrances off Gardenside St and Claude Noel Highway, T675 7034, daily 0800-1700, free.* On the hill behind Lower Scarborough, the Botanic Gardens are worth a visit. This is a quiet oasis of brightly flowering shrubs, flamboyant and silk cotton trees, an avenue of royal palms and there's a huge samaan tree with gigantic roots. Dating from 1899, they cover 7 ha of hillside, and there's a good view over the town and bay. The main entrance is from a lay-by on Claude Noel Highway, but concrete steps from Gardenside Street lead up to a side gate from the centre of town.

Upper Scarborough To reach Upper Scarborough, steeply climb either Burnett Street or Castries Street to Main Street, where there are more shops and banks (and a car park opposite Republic Bank). Here you'll come across a small open space known as **James Park**, named after one of Tobago's pioneering political heros, Alphonso Philbert Theophilus 'Fargo' James, who served on the Legislative Council before independence in 1962. He was known as 'Fargo', after a brand of trucks, because of his strength and tendency to crush opponents. Overlooking the park is the **Tobago House of Assembly** ⓘ www.tha.gov.tt, a brown brick building that was built in 1821 when it housed the island's legislature and judiciary. But representative government was abolished in 1877 when the island became a Crown Colony. Also interesting is **Gun Bridge** on Bacolet Street, where the barrels of 19th-century Brown Bess muskets are embedded into the

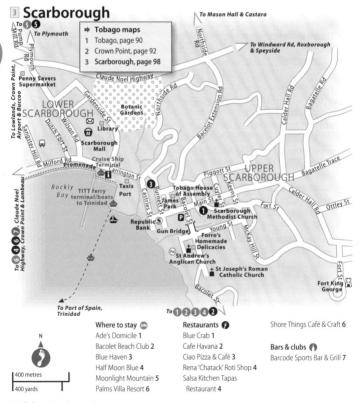

3 Scarborough

⮕ **Tobago maps**
1 Tobago, page 90
2 Crown Point, page 92
3 Scarborough, page 98

Where to stay 🛏
Ade's Domicile 1
Bacolet Beach Club 2
Blue Haven 3
Half Moon Blue 4
Moonlight Mountain 5
Palms Villa Resort 6

Restaurants 🍴
Blue Crab 1
Cafe Havana 2
Ciao Pizza & Café 3
Rena 'Chatack' Roti Shop 4
Salsa Kitchen Tapas
  Restaurant 4

Shore Things Café & Craft 6

Bars & clubs 🍸
Barcode Sports Bar & Grill 7

N

400 metres
400 yards

sides of the bridge as a memorial to the numerous wars that were fought over Tobago; they were relocated from Fort King George when the bridge was widened in the 1950s. Also on Bacolet Street are two churches: **St Andrew's Anglican Church** was built on the foundations of the original church completed in 1819 but blown away by Hurricane Flora in 1963, while **St Joseph's Roman Catholic Church** dates to 1892 and is one of the largest places of worship on the island (it attracts hundreds for mass on Sundays). Another church, the **Scarborough Methodist Church**, can be seen on Fort Street on the way up to the fort. Built by the Wesleyan Methodists in 1826, it was constructed using the bricks that had served as ballast on ships coming to Tobago to collect sugar.

Fort King George ⓘ *T639 3970, the grounds of the fort are open anytime, free, Tobago Museum Mon-Fri 0900-1630, US$3, children (under 12) US$1.50.* From Main Street, you begin the steep climb up Fort Street to Fort King George. You must walk or drive through the old hospital grounds to get to the fort – a new Scarborough General Hospital has recently opened at Signal Hill to the west of Scarborough. Then you emerge onto a glorious headland that offers a panoramic view of Scarborough, southern Tobago, the east coast and the central hills. Building of the fort commenced in 1777 and continued under the French in 1786. Fort Castries was renamed Fort Liberté in 1790 after the garrison revolted, was recaptured by the British in 1793, returned to France in 1801 and, after the island was ceded to Britain in 1802, named Fort King George in 1804. It was decommissioned in 1854. The fort's surroundings are landscaped, and there are a number of historic buildings here, including the Officers' Mess (now a craft shop), the Barrack Guard House (the museum, below), the Magazine (almost hidden under an enormous silk cotton tree) and the Bell Tank (still with water in it and an amazing echo). A military cemetery shaded by palms, samaan trees and vivid flamboyant, and a number of cannons mounted on metal garrison gun carriages can also be seen. In the middle of the parade ground are two very attractive, huge wooden figures by the late artist Luise Kimmé.

At the Barrack Guard House, the **Tobago Museum** has an excellent small display of early Tobago history including Amerindian pottery, military relics, maps and documents from the slave era. Beautifully restored in 2006, the layout and structural design of the renovated buildings has been preserved as it was prior to the hurricane of 1847 – the yellow ballast bricks look almost as good as new. The lighthouse at the top of the fort is relatively new, built in 1958, to guide ships around the reef into Scarborough harbour.

Bacolet Beneath Fort King George on Bacolet Bay is the suburb of Bacolet, reached either by the winding Bacolet Street from the centre of town or from the traffic lights of the Claude Noel Highway and Bacolet Street further east. It is one of the most upmarket suburbs on Tobago and there are a couple of hotels, including the excellent **Bacolet Beach Club** and the rather mediocre **Blue Haven Hotel** (for both, see page 111), which sit next to each other on top of the cliffs at **Bacolet Point**. Below Blue Haven is the small, secluded and very attractive crescent-shaped **Bacolet Beach**, which was used as a location in the *Swiss Family Robinson* film (1960). The beach is only 150 m long, but is relatively wide, and the sand is soft and light. The beach loungers are strictly for use of hotel guests but you can visit the beach bar here for lunch.

Tip...
Go up to the fort for great views of Scarborough sprawling over the hillsides that curve around Rockly Bay; it's a fine place to watch the arrival of the ferries from Trinidad and perhaps a sleek white cruise ship.

ON THE ROAD

The Smiling Assassin

The Dwight Yorke Stadium is located in Bacolet, just to the east of Scarborough, and is used for football and athletics. It is named after Dwight Yorke, the best known and most successful of the nation's footballers, born in Canaan, Tobago in 1971. He played for Aston Villa, Manchester United, Blackburn Rovers, Birmingham City, Sydney FC and Sunderland. When he was with Manchester United (1999-2002), he scored 64 goals in 188 appearances. Yorke captained the Trinidad and Tobago team in the 2006 FIFA World Cup™ in Germany, the smallest country ever to qualify for the finals. However, the team failed to progress beyond the qualifying rounds for the 2010 South Africa and 2014 Brazil FIFA World Cup™. Yorke's older brother, Clint Yorke, is a former cricketer who has represented Trinidad and Tobago as an opening batsman. As a player, Dwight was nicknamed The Smiling Assassin because of his goal-scoring abilities and constant smile.

Northeast from Scarborough

coral reefs, bird islands and sweeping Atlantic beaches

From Scarborough, the Claude Noel Highway thins out to Windward Road just to the east of Dwight Yorke Stadium and the junction with Bacolet Street, and winds its way up to Roxborough, the largest town on Tobago's east (windward) coast. It hugs the Atlantic almost all the way, sweeping up and down through sleepy villages of precarious wooden homes perched on steep hillsides, small roadside kiosks and rum shops. Some of the dark volcanic-sand beaches here are broad and long, but the Atlantic is rough and changeable and this stretch of coastline is not good for swimming. It's scenic, though, with coconut palms bending into the wind and the dark frothy ocean crashing against the shore. Beyond Roxborough, a road climbs up and over the island to the north coast through the brilliantly green forests of the Main Ridge, while Windward Road continues on to Speyside in its lovely location overlooking Tyrrel's Bay and Little Tobago.

Scarborough to Roxborough

Passing Hillsborough Bay and Hope village, Windward Road crosses over the Hillsborough River as it meets the Atlantic. A little further on, at Mount St George, part of the larger suburb of Studley Park, a left fork leads up to **Hillsborough Dam**; built in 1952, this is the source of most of Tobago's drinking water. The reservoir is set in a forested area and is a good location for birding (herons and waterfowl); it is, however, only accessible by permission from the **Water and Sewerage Authority** (T662 2302, www.wasa.gov.tt) and a fee is charged, but if you are on a tour with a birdwatching guide, they can organize a visit. **Mount St George** was Tobago's first, short-lived principal town, then called Georgetown (1762-1769). Just beyond the village is the site of **Fort Granby** on the right at Granby Point. Built around 1765 to protect Georgetown, it is the second oldest fort on the island, and the first British fortification. It was named after John Manners, the Marquis of Granby, a British military hero of the Seven Years' War. The French took over the fort between 1781 and 1787, after which it was abandoned. There isn't anything left of it, except the gravestone of a young soldier, but the site is home to a pleasant picnic site and children's playground with lookouts to both Barbados and Pinfold bays on either side of the windswept promontory. The beach in **Pinfold Bay** next to the fort is also known as **Fort Granby Beach**, and while it's not safe for swimming it's good for a bracing walk.

At Goodwood, you can see local wildlife at the **Genesis Nature Park & Art Gallery** ① *Windward Rd, T660 4668, see Facebook, Mon-Sat 0930-1630, US$9, children (under 12) US$4.50*. This small reserve and art gallery are converted from the garden and living room of local artist, Michael Spencer, whose paintings and sculptures are for sale. Resident wildlife includes two capuchin monkeys, boa constrictors, agoutis, parrots, squirrels, five caiman and an enormous tortoise; children will enjoy it.

Beyond Goodwood but before Pembroke, a turn-off at **Goldsborough Bay** takes you 2 km along a potholed but navigable road to **Rainbow Nature Resort** (see page 112), where you can park. From this rural guesthouse there are worthwhile hikes to two waterfalls. A short 20-minute trail, that in parts goes beneath bamboo 'cathedral' arches, takes you to the **Rainbow Waterfall**; so-called as a rainbow frequently dances in the spray, and where the pool is deep enough to swim when there's been enough rain coming down from the hills. **Twin River Waterfall** is higher up in the Main Ridge rainforest; it takes about two hours of fairly steady hiking to get there from Rainbow Nature Resort. It gets its name from the fact that at its base two rivers join and continue downstream as the Goldsborough River. The trail follows the river upstream and walking is mainly on gravel and small rocks and through some small rapids. The waterfall itself is broken into a series of small cascades and the last one drops into a wide cool pool that is about 3.5 m deep and ideal for swimming.

Beyond Belle Garden, a left-hand turn just before Roxborough takes you to Tobago's most popular waterfall, and there's another route (signposted) from the Roxborough–Parlatuvier Road. The **Argyle Waterfall** ① *T660 4154, daily 0900-1700, US$4.50, children (under 16) US$2.25*, is a 15- to 20-minute walk upstream from the car park at the entrance from the Windward Road. It tumbles for 54 m in a series of three stepped cascades with a big green pool at the bottom where you can swim. The attraction is run by a local co-operative; guides are available, included in the entry fee, but not really necessary as the path is obvious, although they can be most informative. The agile can scramble up the path from the bottom pool to the higher levels and pools and then to the top of the falls. Part of the Main Ridge Forest Reserve, the falls are a good introduction to the rainforest, with a wide variety of trees and flowering plants attracting a wealth of birds and butterflies. There are toilets and a gift stall selling cocoa balls, jewellery and trinkets.

At the junction of the Argyle Waterfall car park, turn left and follow the dirt road up the hills to the **Tobago Cocoa Estate** ① *Cameron Canal Rd, Roxborough, T788 3971, www. tobagococoa.com, 1-hr estate tours by reservation only, US$10.50, children (12-16) US$7, under 8s free*. This lovely old cocoa estate was renovated by Tobagonian Duane Dove, a sommelier, after he acquired the hilly, overgrown land in 2004. The tour shows the way cacao is grown, harvested, fermented, dried and made into cocoa, and visitors are shown the principles of companion planting, using plants such as cassava and plantain which offer temporary shade to the young cocoa trees and can be sold for additional income. Tradition is key here and Dove has built a drying house out of Trinidadian cedar so that the prime cocoa beans never touch metal or concrete, for a better flavour. Cocoa beans from this estate are made into award-winning, single-estate chocolate by artisan chocolatier, François Pralus, in France.

Roxborough itself is the largest village on the windward side of the island, and is strung haphazardly along Windward Road. There are no hotels, guesthouses or decent restaurants but it does have a branch of **First Citizens Bank** with an ATM and car park, small grocery stores, a fish market, and a petrol station with a good shop (**Quick Shop**) for snacks and drinks at the junction with the Roxborough–Parlatuvier Road.

Main Ridge Forest Reserve

The distance between the petrol station on Windward Road in Roxborough and the junction of the Charlotteville–L'Anse Fourmi Road (to Bloody Bay and Charlotteville) and Northside Road (to Parlatuvier and Castara) is just over 12 km and is a beautiful drive though the Main Ridge Forest Reserve. Reaching heights of 573 m, this is the oldest protected forest in the Western Hemisphere, and dates from 1776 when it was declared as a Crown Reserve by an ordinance of the British parliament, shortly after the island fell under British rule. They had realized that the island's water supply could not be guaranteed if the forest was cut down, and the ordinance stated that the reserve was "for the purpose of attracting frequent showers of rain upon which the fertility of lands in these climates doth entirely depend" – perhaps this was the first act of the modern environmental movement and a very early recognition that rainforests are an essential component for watershed. If it hadn't been for this action, the plantation owners may well have plundered the forest for timber, cleared it for cultivation, and destroyed Tobago's vital water source. The forest was severely damaged during the 1963 Hurricane Flora when it was estimated about 75% of the large trees were felled, but since then it has grown magnificently and today the demarcated reserve covers 4047 ha, or about one-third of the entire island (although the total area of forest covers about two-thirds). On the southwest side the land rises gently into the hills, while on the northeast side the steep forests drop sharply to sandy beaches below.

The reserve consists of mostly lower montane rainforest with a largely closed emerald green canopy that attracts rain throughout the year. Of the 220-plus species of bird present on Tobago, about 100 can be spotted in the reserve, including cocricos, collared trogon, motmots, jacamars and hummingbirds. Of these, a recorded 24 species are not seen in Trinidad, including the blue-backed manakin, blue-crested motmot, scrub greenlet and striped owl. Most significant is the white-tailed sabrewing hummingbird that breeds only in northeastern Venezuela and Tobago. It was actually thought to have become extinct on Tobago after Hurricane Flora in 1963, but the population has now largely recovered and locally goes under the nickname of 'Campy'. Mammalian species include armadillos, red squirrels and opossums, and there are numerous species of bat, as well as non-venomous snakes, lizards and frogs. Insects abound too, so ensure you have good footwear on the trails; some bird guides even provide rubber gumboots if it's sloshy underfoot.

About midway along the Roxborough–Parlatuvier Road, right at the top of the reserve, is the newly built **Main Ridge Visitor Centre** ⓘ *daily 0700-1500,* where there are toilets, picnic sites, and local women selling drinks out of cool boxes. Inside there are a few leaflets to pick up and a topography relief map of the island (look out for the places marked by deforestation and the little toy earthmovers demonstrating the point!). Staff here can organize guides for birdwatching; in reality this means they will phone around the guides (some of which are listed under Birdwatching, page 123)

Tip...

From the Main Ridge Visitor Centre look northwest for a marvellous view of Sisters Rocks; a cluster of five rock pillars that rise about 30 m out of the Caribbean Sea. They have long been a navigational aid for fishermen, and are one of the island's top scuba-diving spots.

Flora and fauna of Tobago

Covering 300 sq km, Tobago lies 34 km northeast of Trinidad and is a single mountain mass of volcanic origin (part of the Lesser Antilles Volcanic Arc that forms the eastern boundary of the Caribbean Plate), although at one time, like Trinidad, it was joined to South America. It is dominated by the Main Ridge, which is 29 km long with elevations up to 576 m. There are deep, fertile valleys running north and south of the Main Ridge, and the southwestern tip of the island has a flat coral platform. Forestation covers 43% of the island, there are numerous rivers and streams, and the coastline is indented with bays, beaches, and narrow coastal plains and it has several small satellite islands. The largest of these, Little Tobago, is starfish-shaped, hilly, and consists of 1.2 sq km of impenetrable vegetation. Tobago has a similar number of species of flowering shrubs, trees and ferns as Trinidad, but doesn't attract quite the same numbers of birds; about 220 species compared to 430 in Trinidad (simply because it's further away from South America). However, Tobago does have 24 bird species not found on Trinidad, such as the red-crowned woodpecker, the white-tailed sabrewing hummingbird and the red-billed tropic bird. Also, as the island is smaller, the Main Ridge Forest Reserve and other birdwatching sites are easily accessible and, with excellent guides, birders have a good chance of seing more species in a short time than they would in Trinidad. Even non-birdwatchers will notice the hummingbirds on the feeders, motmots in the bushes and frigate birds over the beach. The island also has 23 butterfly species, 20 species of bat, 16 types of lizards, 14 kinds of frogs and 24 species of snake (all of them harmless).

who live in the coastal villages and may not be more than a 30-minute drive away. Better to pre-arrange one of them to meet you at an allotted time at the Visitor Centre, or at the start of Glipin Trace, or else book on an island birdwatching tour. Of the several trails leading off the Roxborough–Parlatuvier Road, the most popular and easily identified is **Gilpin Trace**, about 2 km from the Visitor Centre back towards Roxborough. The 5-km-long trail starts in the mountains and leads downhill past a small waterfall to Bloody Bay, although many just go along for a short way to enjoy the Main Ridge and turn back. This is the place people are usually brought on birdwatching tours as the guides know in which trees to find particular birds; the route follows an old donkey trail and is not taxing and there is a wide variety of plants and insects to see.

Roxborough to Speyside

Beyond Roxborough, Windward Road goes past the headland of Louis D'or (part of an old sugar estate) and into the village of Delaford. A sweeping corner opens up a spectacular view of coconut-tree-strewn **King's Bay Beach**. You can easily miss the **King's Bay Café** (see page 118) as it looks just like another house perched on the side of the road, but is well worth stopping at for the tasty food on the veranda at the back with its good view of the bay. At the bottom of the hill, a right turn takes you to the beach itself, a lovely horseshoe-shaped 800-m stretch of dark sand shaded by coconut palms and calm, warm water despite it being on the Atlantic; the **King's Bay Beach Facility** has lifeguards, snacks/drinks kiosks and changing rooms/toilets; TT$1.

It's another 6 km from here to the fishing village of **Speyside**, which has a backdrop of forested hills and is set on the broad Tyrrell's Bay with its offshore islets and some of the best coral reefs on the island; far less disturbed than the more famous Buccoo Reef in the southwest. There are places to stay and eat here and it is a good base for excursions: birdwatching, diving (non-divers can take glass-bottomed boats) and snorkelling trips. In 1746, John Piggot purchased a sugar estate in Speyside and the prominent **Speyside Waterwheel** beside the bridge on the road to the Blue Waters Inn dates from the beginning of the 19th century and is a relic of

Tip...
Before descending into the village, stop at the Speyside Lookout at the top of the hill (there's a car park) for a great view of the bay's shifting turquoise sea, spray-covered tiny islets, and Goat Island and Little Tobago (unfortunately, though, the overhead power lines are rather in the way of a good photograph).

the island's sugar plantation days. Scottish-made and erected in the late 18th century, it powered the sugar cane grinding machinery for nearly 100 years until the collapse of the industry at the end of the 19th century. The long, narrow beach lining the village along **Tyrrell's Bay** is somewhat scrappy, given that is very much a working beach for the fishing industry – although there are a couple of good restaurants; **Jemma's** and **Bird Watcher** (see page 118), both with terraces and views across to Little Tobago and Goat Island. The better beach is at **Batteaux Bay** in front of **Blue Waters Inn**, where there is also the jetty for boat tours (see page 112).

At 572 m, **Pigeon Peak** is Tobago's highest mountain. There are two routes to the top through the forest, one steeper, the other longer. Both take about three hours; you will need to hire a guide from Speyside (ask at the hotels).

Little Tobago

Also known as Bird of Paradise Island, 182-ha Little Tobago is the largest and most easterly landmass off the coast of Trinidad and Tobago. Densely forested and surrounded by beautiful reefs, it is a fantastic place for birdwatching, diving and snorkelling. Its highest elevation is 137 m and there are a total of 14.5 km of trails around the island – you could spend anything from one to several hours here. In 1909 Sir William Ingram, a British politician and bird enthusiast, introduced the greater bird of paradise (*Paradisaea apoda*) to the island in an attempt to save the species from overhunting for the plume trade in its native New Guinea. About 45 juvenile birds were introduced to the island. After Ingram's death in 1924 his heirs deeded the island to the Government of Trinidad and Tobago as a wildlife sanctuary. The birds survived on the island until at least 1958 when they were filmed by a National Geographic crew. However, there have been no reliable records of the bird after the 1963 Hurricane Flora and the population is presumed to be extinct. But the island is still excellent for birdlife and more than 50 species have been recorded, including boobies, motmots and, most spectacularly, the red-billed tropic bird found here in the largest nesting colony in the north Atlantic. Often spotted too are the magnificent frigate birds, a large species of seabird that has an enormous wingspan that can exceed 2 m. They occasionally rob other birds of fish, and on Little Tobago can frequently be seen harassing the boobies and terns.

Glass-bottomed boat tours to the reefs for snorkelling and on to the island can be organized from a kiosk in the car park at **Blue Waters Inn** (try Troy at **Top Ranking** or Frank at **Frankie's Glass-bottom Boats**). Departures are at 1030 and 1400 for about 2½ hours; US$20 for just the boat/snorkelling, US$30 if you get off on Little Tobago; children (under 12) half price. It's possible to stay on Little Tobago between boats for birdwatching, picnicking and swimming. Diving can be arranged with **Blue Waters Dive 'N**, at Blue Waters Inn (see page 124).

ON THE ROAD
Goat Island

Between Speyside and Little Tobago is Goat Island. A popular myth claiming that the island's prominent deserted house was once owned by Ian Fleming, the author of the James Bond books, is untrue. The James Bond novels were actually all written at Fleming's house, Goldeneye, in Jamaica. Tiny Goat Island is owned by the government and there is no public access, although Angel Reef, directly in front of it facing Speyside, is a popular stop for snorkelling on the glass-bottomed boat trips, and divers of every level come for its fringing reef wall, which is home to numerous species from trumpet-fish to the Caribbean spiny lobster.

North coast
gorgeous white-sand bays, azure waters and pretty fishing villages on the Caribbean Sea

The route down the leeward coast all the way to Plymouth is refreshingly isolated, the calmer of Tobago's two shorelines with only a few fishing villages dotted along the gentle Caribbean Sea. It has some of the island's most magnificent views and ravishing beaches and is simply a beautiful drive, whether you wind your way around the top from Speyside or begin in Plymouth and head northeast. Construction of the stretch of road between Charlotteville and L'Anse Fourmi was started in the early 1960s but was never completed because of Hurricane Flora in 1963 (when resources were diverted to more urgent projects). For decades it was no more than a goat track, but was finally completed in 2007 and now allows a complete circumnavigation of the island; the only real decision to make is how and when to cut across the central area and include the Main Ridge too.

Flagstaff Hill
After Speyside, the road cuts inland and climbs across to the north coast and Charlotteville. Around halfway, a well signposted right turn takes you along a bumpy but paved road to Flagstaff Hill, overlooking the most northerly tip of Tobago. A magnificent vantage point with panoramic views of St Giles and Melville Islands (which mark the meeting of the Atlantic Ocean and Caribbean Sea) and London Bridge Rock, as well as Charlotteville, it was the site of an American military lookout and radio tower during the Second World War. Sunsets are spectacular here. These islands and rocks, also known as the **Melvilles**, were presented to the government in 1968 by the owner of the Charlotteville Estate, to be preserved as a wildlife sanctuary. They are now one of the most important breeding grounds for seabirds in the southwest Caribbean, and are home to noddy terns, brown boobies, red-footed boobies, red-billed tropic birds and frigate birds, among others.

Charlotteville
After Flagstaff Hill comes the hairpin descent into the fishing village of Charlotteville, with homes sprawling and tumbling down the hillsides to the glistening waters of Man O War Bay with its flotilla of pirogues and diving brown pelicans. Man O War Bay got its name from being a safe anchorage for fighting ships in the 18th century. About 1.6 km of beach stretches along Charlotteville itself; it can be a little smelly and dirty around the area in front of the fishing co-operative, but is great further south near the **Suckhole** restaurant

and beach bar (see page 119), where there is an intermittent lifeguard service, changing facilities, and good swimming and snorkelling. Back from the shore, in the network of (slightly scruffy) streets is a branch of First Citizens Bank with an ATM and a petrol station. There's a good choice of budget guesthouses in Charlotteville, plenty of places to eat fish and fries and the like, a small supermarket, as well as dive shops.

From the northern end of Charlotteville, it is a 20-minute walk uphill on an unsurfaced track (from where you get glorious views of the pristine crescent below you) and over the green ridge of mountains, then down 170 steps to **Pirate's Bay**. (Do not attempt to drive up here as there is no turning space and you'll have to reverse back down.) Named after the shelter that it provided to marauding buccaneers three centuries ago, the beach is magnificent and unspoilt and good for snorkelling. Being on the north coast, however, it can sometimes be affected by strong waves. It has basic toilet/changing facilities, but little else, other than a very friendly vendor selling fruit and coconut water.

A 20-minute walk west around the **Man O War Bay** from Charlotteville (ask for directions) through dense forest takes you to an unassuming hill overlooking the bay. Here is **Campbellton Battery** (also known as **Fort Campbellton**, although it was never a fort), which was built to protect shipping when traders came to collect sugar. Two cannons were installed here in 1777, along with others elsewhere on the coast, during the American War of Independence, to deter American privateers. The guards on duty here would be signalled by mirror from Flagstaff Hill, from where ships approaching from any direction could clearly be seen. Today the battery is a lovely and well-maintained picnic spot with beautiful views of Man O War Bay, Charlotteville and Pirate's Bay.

Charlotteville to Castara

The stretch of road along the north coast between Charlotteville and Castara winds its way through the picturesque fishing villages of L'Anse Fourmi, Bloody Bay and Parlatuvier. It is smooth, traffic is light and the views are very scenic, taking in lovely bays, sandy beaches and rocky headlands, cloaked in thick clumps of bamboo and forest ringing to the sound of birdsong. Note, though, there is no public transport along this route so you'll need to hire a car. **Bloody Bay** is a glorious sheltered bay with golden sands and is nearly always deserted, except for the odd fishermen, although it does have recently installed facilities (changing rooms/toilets/showers; TT$2), a small beach bar, parking and lifeguards. The road across the island from Roxborough through the Main Ridge Forest Reserve joins the north coast road just beyond Bloody Bay; from here it's a distance of just over 12 km to Roxborough. **Parlatuvier** sits on a magnificent, deeply indented bay with a 500-m-long perfect beach, although it shelves deeply (and there are no lifeguards). Its fishing pier and small boats lining the shore make a perfect spot for photographs that typify the gentle life in rural Tobago. Between Parlatuvier and Castara is **Englishman's Bay**, a perfect horseshoe-shaped bay with forest tumbling down the hillsides to the powdery sand and a river running out to the sea. This is one of the prettiest beaches on Tobago and is also perhaps the most photographed for tourist literature of the island. The swimming is excellent and you are likely to have the place to yourself, particularly mid-week. There is a simple

> **Tip...**
> On the northern tip of the island between Charlotteville and L'Anse Fourmi, birdwatchers should keep binoculars handy: this is where the forests of the Main Ridge sink into the sea and there are plenty of jacamars, blue-crowned motmots, collared trogons, orange-winged parrots and cocricos.

shack here, **Eulas** (open most days in the winter months 0900-1500) where Eula and her husband offer cold beers and soft drinks out of a cooler box, simple but tasty meals like fish and fries, channa and rotis, or vegetable rice with plantains. They also sell a few souvenirs made out of coconut shells and beach sarongs/wraps. Even if you don't actually visit the beach or take a swim, the view of the bay as you approach up Northside Road from Castara is nothing short of spectacular and there's a layby to pull in at.

Castara

Castara was named and occupied by the Amerindians; Castara, meaning 'falling waters', refers to the numerous waterfalls along the hillsides. In the 17th century English Puritan colonists called it Charles Bay, and the Dutch, Kalpi Bay. But when the British retook the island and auctioned off sugar estates from 1768, they kept the name Castara. Before the Northside Road

> **Tip...**
> PTSC buses run from Scarborough to Castara about every three hours; note though, they go via Mason Hall and Moriah on Northside Road, and buses do not run between Plymouth and Castara.

was built from Mount Dillon to Castara in 1970, people walked between Castara and Mount St George on the windward coast, or sailed by rum boat to Plymouth.

In recent years tourists have taken this small village to their hearts in a big way, and the outstanding beauty of the area has led to an increase in accommodation, but there are no big hotels yet, and casual and rustic apartments and guesthouses are perched on the hillside above the village. Castara remains a simply charming, friendly and quiet fishing village and that is the attraction. The blue-green bay is dotted with fishing boats and hemmed in by cliffs and forest, and contains two sandy beaches separated by rocks; the main or larger one is **Big Bay**, while the smaller one, **Little Bay**, is also known as Heavenly Bay. Both offer excellent swimming and snorkelling at the thriving offshore reef full of colourful fish, interesting rock formations, rays and turtles. Lifeguards are on duty daily at Big Bay at the **Castara Beach Facility** and, at the southern end, a local lady rents out sun loungers.

A small river comes out at Big Bay and a 10-minute walk inland, it runs over the **Castara Waterfall**, which cascades into a rock pool surrounded by hanging lianas. You can climb the rocks to the top, and the river here runs through a narrow valley above which towers the Main Ridge rainforest, full of birds and butterflies. To get here, simply follow River Road to the football field, and then head upstream on a clearly defined track, at times crossing back and forth across the crystal-clear water. Behind the Big Bay's fish cooperative and lifeguard station, local women produce excellent bread and bakes at the open-air Village Bakery every Thursday and Saturday morning from a traditional clay oven. Watch them mixing, kneading and leaving the dough to prove on banana leaves, before baking. Castara Bay faces due west. **Castara Retreats** (see page 114) is one Tobago's flagship accommodation options. Even if you're not staying, go up to the restaurant/bar for a drink or meal to enjoy a spectacular view of the sunset. There are also hummingbird feeders on the terrace here.

> **Tip...**
> There are a couple of basic grocery shops in the village and one single ATM (no bank) next to the bus stop; however, don't rely on it for cash and, as not many places take cards, it's best to bring cash with you when exploring the north coast.

Castara to Scarborough

The Northside Road climbs up out of Castara and ascends to a height of 421 m at **Mount Dillion**. There's a lookout here with car park and some picnic benches that offers a fabulous vista along the bays of the northwest coast with the waves crashing on the small rocks out at sea. the road then descends in a series of switchbacks through the interior rural villages where houses cling to hillsides and little children play in the streets. At Moriah, there is the option of turning west on the Arnos Vale Road to Plymouth (just over 10 km) or continue on to Scarborough (9.5 km from this junction). An attraction in this area is the **Highland Waterfall** on the Courland River, off a minor road between the villages of Les Coteaux on the Arnos Vale Road and Mason Hill on Northside Road. Like so many of these natural features, it is totally unmarked, so finding it without a guide can be difficult, particularly as this one is located in an area where you are unlikely to find a living sole to ask directions. But if you do, it is a 10- to 15-minute hot hike up from the road (where you can park) alongside an extremely attractive stream to the falls; the pool below offers a perfect location for a cooling dip. This is the highest single-drop waterfall on Tobago and is great for hikers or mountain bikers looking for a spot to call their own. Much more accessible is the **Craig Hall Waterfall** on the left (if going towards Scarborough) of the road at Mason Hall. A short stroll down the concrete steps to the nicely placed seats gives a good view of the falls.

Listings Tobago *maps pages 90, 92 and 98.*

Tourist information

Tourism Information Office for the Tobago House of Assembly (THA)
Opposite Arrivals at the airport (T639 0509, hwww.visittobago.gov.tt, daily 0600-2200). A kiosk also opens at the Cruise Ship Terminal in Scarborough (T635 0934) when there are ships in.
Both offices are helpful and there's a good choice of maps and leaflets to pick up.

Where to stay

Unless otherwise stated, all hotel rooms have a/c, TV and Wi-Fi. Hotel tax of 10% and service charge of 10% is added to bills. There are numerous villas, apartments and condominiums available for rent around the island; many are listed on www.mytobago.info, or contact **Villas of Tobago** (www.villasoftobago.com), or **Abraham Tobago Realty** (www.abrahamrealty.com).

Crown Point *map page 92.*

There is a clutch of small apartment blocks, most of which are inexpensive but basic, on and around Old Store Bay Rd just north of the ANR Robinson International Airport aimed at holidaying Trinidadians. It's quite possible to walk from the airport and find accommodation, but this is not recommended at weekends and public holidays when they are likely to be fully booked.

$$$$ Coco Reef Resort & Spa
Coconut Bay, Milford Rd, T639 8571, www.cocoreef.com.
Modelled on a Bermudan hotel with peach and white walls and red roofs, the 135 rooms, suites and villas on a man-made beach with calm lagoon for good swimming, are set in 4 ha of manicured gardens and lawns with a pretty view of Pigeon Point. Not especially stylish (think wicker furniture and flowery stencils on the walls), but still comfortable with good facilities including tennis, gym, spa, pool, and 2 restaurants.

$$$$ Magdalena Grand Beach & Golf Resort

Tobago Plantations Estate, Lowlands, 7 km from Crown Point towards Scarborough, T660 8800, www.magdalenagrand.com.
If you want a resort hotel, this is the best on the island, and is part of a 300-ha development around Petit Trou Lagoon, with the resort, villas and condominiums, and a championship golf course (see page 126). 200 rooms, 3 restaurants, 4 bars, a casual café, 3 outdoor pools, a spa and gym. The only downside is it's on a very windy bit of coast, but there's a shuttle bus to Pigeon Point. Rates from B&B to all-inclusive and (expensive) day passes available to enjoy all facilities including restaurants and golf.

$$$ Kariwak Village

Store Bay Local Rd, T639 8442, www.kariwak.com.
A little oasis in the main tourist area with 24 simple but comfortable rooms with patios. Allan and Cynthia Clovis started this hotel in the 1970s, concentrating on guests' physical and spiritual well-being. Beautiful and aromatic gardens with flowers, fruits, herbs and vegetables, hammocks, pool and jacuzzi. Activities include a morning stretch, yoga, tai chi and shiatsu, massages and other treatments (also available to non-guests). The open-air thatched restaurant serves excellent wholesome food (see page 115).

$$$-$$ Chic – The Boutique Hotel

16-17 Mt Pleasant Blvd, Bon Accord, T631 8961, www.chictobago.com.
Next door to **The Shade Night Club** (see page 121), although noise doesn't seem to be an issue, and within walking distance of Crown Point, this new, modern hotel with 35 smart rooms and 5 studios, is nicely decorated with splashes of colour, quality linen, lovely large pool with sunbathing area, lobby and pool bar, **Tempo Restaurant** for breakfast and dinner.

$$$-$$ Crown Point Beach Hotel

Old Store Bay Rd, T639 8781, www.crownpointbeachhotel.com.
Prime position on cliffs in 3 landscaped hectares at Store Bay, this old hotel (Queen Elizabeth II visited here in 1966) is within walking distance (even with luggage) of the airport and all 75 rooms and cabanas have patios/balconies, most with kitchenettes and excellent sea views; a little dated but comfortable and well cared for. Great poolside bar with views on to Store Bay Beach (and steps to it) and Caribbean cuisine at the **Simmer Down Restaurant**.

$$ Conrado Beach Resort

9 Pigeon Point Rd, T639 0145, www.conradotobago.com.
This informal seafront hotel is the closest accommodation to Pigeon Point Heritage Park and has been going strong since the 1960s. Still good with super-friendly staff and 31 neat and unpretentious rooms; it's worth paying the extra for sea views and lovely verandas. The **Calypso Reef** restaurant has a small beach with fishing boats moored outside, so better to go to Pigeon Point.

$$ Hummingbird Hotel

128 Store Bay Local Rd, Bon Accord, T635 0241, www.hummingbirdtobago.com.
Pleasant small hotel with a guesthouse feel run by Anglo-Trini hosts, Paul and Linda Mountjoy, a short walk from the centre of things in Crown Point but far enough away to be quiet at night. 10 comfortable rooms, most open on to the lovely swimming pool area with sliding doors, and 2 have sofabeds and kitchen facilities, plus there's a small restaurant/bar for breakfast and (pre-ordered) evening meals.

$$ Native Abode

13 Fourth St, Gaskin Bay Rd, Bon Accord, T639 0162, www.nativeabode.com.
A 5-min drive from the airport, and in a quiet street, this modern, comfortable B&B is in pretty gardens with fruit trees, plenty of birds, hospitable owners and

superb breakfasts. The 5 rooms have mini-kitchenettes, small balconies, super-powerful showers and it's a 20-min walk to the restaurants in Crown Point.

$$ Shepherd's Inn
Store Bay Local Rd, T285 9159,
www.shepherdsinntobago.com.
This exceptionally friendly 20-room hotel, formerly the Toucan Inn, has recently been purchased by congenial Colin Shepherd, who also owns **Sheppy's Auto Rental** (see page 129), which is just around the corner. Now quite delightful with a lovely palm-filled garden and pool area, 12 studios and 1 2-bedroom unit with kitchenette, and 8 cute and well-priced wooden cabanas. A selling point here is, instead of regular cable TV, rooms have Netflix. Great food – a mix of Creole and international – at the wooden pagoda-style restaurant/bar (open to all 0700-2200), where there's live music on Sat evening. Colin also runs **Sheppy's Den**, a 4-bedroom villa just out of Scarborough (www.sheppysden.com).

$ Candles in the Wind
145 Anthony Charles Crescent, T765 5335,
www.candlesinthewind.8k.com.
Straightforward guesthouse with 8 hostel-style rooms on 2 floors, with a kitchen on each floor, plus an attic dorm with 12 beds and a shared bathroom. Convenient, right in the heart of Crown Point with Store Bay Beach and restaurants/bars a short walk away. Owner Andrew is very laid back and always helpful, and knows everything about public transport on the island as well as other tips.

$ Lesville Tobago
Canaan Feeder Rd, Canaan, T639 0629,
www.lesvilletobago.com.
Run by Lestell and Orville Moore (hence the name), 10 studios and 1- and 2-bedroom apartments in a quiet residential area off the beaten track; simple and practical with large rooms and patios, and 2000 sq m of pretty gardens with banana and mango

trees and plenty of birds. Breakfast available. Public transport to Crown Point is close by on Milford Rd.

Buccoo *map page 90.*

$$-$ Fish Tobago Guesthouse
26A Buccoo Point, T309 0062,
www.fishtobago.com.
In a bright building decorated with murals of island scenes, this guesthouse/hostel is a short walk from Buccoo Beach. 8 en suite rooms and self-catering apartments, plus a dorm room with 6 bunks and a bathroom (from US$25 per person), shared kitchen and common lounge with TV, Wi-Fi is available for a fee, breakfast and fresh fish dinners. The hosts will go out of their way to organize tours, fishing with local fishermen and car hire. Minimum stay 3 nights in high season.

$$-$ Miller's Guest House
14 Miller's St, T660 8371,
www.millersguesthouse.com.
Super friendly and spotlessly clean budget spot in a colourful house with balconies, just a few steps away from Buccoo Beach and with good views of the fishing boats. Accommodation in 8 rooms – a single, doubles, triples, 1 4-bed apartment and a dorm room with 6 bunks and a kitchen – all have good bathrooms, and there's a garden and **Luvinia's Restaurant & Bar** with a seaside terrace. Rates from US$30 per bed.

Black Rock *map page 90.*

$$$-$$ Grafton Beach Resort
Stonehaven Bay, T639 0191,
www.graftontobago.com.
In unremarkable and old-fashioned concrete blocks, but set in tropical gardens with a decent range of facilities including squash courts and a large pool with swim-up bar, and 106 bright rooms with balconies and either ocean or garden views. Buffet breakfast, 2 restaurants, a lobby bar and the **Buccaneer's Beach Bar. Extra Divers Worldwide** is based here (see page 125).

Plymouth *map page 90.*

$$$$-$$$ Top O' Tobago
Off Arnos Vale Rd, 3 km northeast of Plymouth, T687 0121, www.topotobago.com.
Perched on a stunning hilltop, the road up here may be quite challenging, a lovely modern and breezy spot with multi-level patios and good views to both the east and west coasts of the island. 3 cabanas sleeping up to 4, plus the main villa that accommodates up to 6, each with kitchen, dining and living areas with tiled floors and high ceilings and their own secluded garden with hammocks and outside showers. There's a pool and it's about a 10-min (steep) walk to Arnos Vale Beach. Rates include a welcome pack of breakfast items. Minimum 2-night stay.

$$ Adventure Eco-Villas
Adventure Farm & Nature Reserve (see page 97), 2 km from Plymouth off Arnos Vale Rd, T639 2839, www.adventure-ecovillas.com.
2 delightful wooden cottages on stilts looking out over the forest with a shared deck, ideal for birdwatching, or a smaller, darker, cheaper apartment attached to the main building. The cottages have a double and single bed, bathroom with tub, living/ dining area with louvre windows which can be opened up completely, well-equipped kitchen, cheerful, painted blue and yellow, surrounded by lush green vegetation, forest noises and birdsong.

$$-$ Arnos Vale Vacation Apartments
Arnos Vale Rd, Plymouth, T639 1362, www.arnosvaleapartments.com.
Run by helpful Victor Forde, the excellent value and very popular 2 2-bedroom and 1 studio apartments here have huge open-plan kitchen/living areas, and beautiful garden with fruit trees and tropical birds which come to the feeders. Sleeping up to 6 this is a good option for families or groups but, like nearby **Top O' Tobago** (above), it's a bit off the beaten track so having a car is a good idea.

$ Changrela Cocrico Inn
Corner Commissioner St and North St, Plymouth, T639 2961, www.changrela.com.
This 1970s concrete block-style inn with 18 rooms and apartments on 2 floors is basic but about the best in Plymouth itself and is friendly and cheap enough. Rooms have tiled floors and balcony but no views, some with microwave and fridge, and there's a pool with barbecue area, bar, meals are available and you can use the kitchen.

Scarborough *map page 98.*

$$$$ The Palms Villa Resort
Signal Hill Old Rd, Signal Hill, T635 1010, www.thepalmstobago.com.
On a 4-ha hilltop estate above Lambeau on the coast, this luxurious development offers 5 villas, each with 3 comfortable en suite rooms, fairly newly built but with pretty colonial-style architecture and large central gardens. Each villa sleeps up to 6 and has broad verandas, a good-sized pool with children's section, barbecue and outdoor eating area. Having a car is useful here. To get here turn off Claude Noel Highway just before the new Scarborough General Hospital.

$$$$-$$$ Bacolet Beach Club
72 Bacolet St, Bacolet, T639 2357, www.bacoletbeachclub.com.
This popular and well-run hotel is owned by former fashion model Gloria Jones-Knapp, and is built on several layers on the hillside with lots of wooden decking. 2 swimming pools are on higher levels, while steep steps go down to the small secluded beach with its own bar. 22 tastefully decorated rooms of different sizes, all have balconies with lovely sea views, and **Cafe Havana** here is excellent (see page 117). Also operates **Le Mans Car Rental** (www.lemanstobago.com) from here for hotel guests only; accommodation and car packages can be good value.

$$$ Blue Haven Hotel
Bacolet Point, Bacolet, T660 7400, www.bluehavenhotel.com.

Built in the 1940s, its heyday was in the 1950s when movie stars like Robert Mitchum, Debra Kerr, Jack Lemmon and Rita Hayworth stayed here while making *Fire Down Below*, *Heaven Knows Mr Allison*, or *Swiss Family Robinson*. The original building perched on the point has been restored and new wings with flying roofs have been built either side, 1 overlooking pretty Bacolet Beach and the other looking out to Scarborough and the Atlantic. All 55 rooms have balcony/patio and are light and bright, and some have a window between the bathroom and bedroom so you can watch the sunset from your tub. Beach bar for lunch, restaurant and pool up the hill with glorious views. Has a certain retro charm but could do with a bit of TLC.

$$$ Half Moon Blue Hotel
73 Bacolet St, Bacolet, T639 3551, www.halfmoonblue.com.
Across the road and under the same ownership as **Bacolet Beach Club**, this small and delightful boutique hotel is in a lovely restored historic wooden building known as 'The Old Donkey Cart House', which was built in the mid-1850s. The 9 rooms have eclectic decor, balconies or bay windows, and high ceilings. The top room is a spacious apartment that can sleep 4-8. There's a pool, the charming bar's terrace has whirring ceiling fans and you can eat here Wed-Sat evenings or across the road at **Cafe Havana** (see page 117).

$$ Moonlight Mountain
Diamond Ridge, Idlewild Trace, off Plymouth Rd, T639 4346, www.tobagoretreat.com.
Perched up in the hills above Scarborough, with views to both the Caribbean and Atlantic and breezes from both oceans, this plantation-style but modern guesthouse with wooden fretwork is set in lush gardens and forest. Used for yoga retreats or just B&B, the 5 rooms open out onto a balcony, 2 with en suite, the others share 2 bathrooms. Plunge pool, hammocks, very relaxing, run by Ginny (yoga teacher) and Kelly (great cook) who also know all the best places to

lime. Massage and reflexology available, breakfast and evening meal by prior reservation, minimum stay 2 nights.

$ Ade's Domicile
19 Old Lighthouse Rd, Bacolet, T639 4306, www.adesdomicil.de.
In quiet, residential Bacelot, a short walk to Bacelot Beach, and with lovely sea views from its hilly position, this cheerful yellow house has 2 studios downstairs with good kitchens and verandas, and 2 1-bedroom apartments upstairs, with balconies and better views. All very spacious, and friendly owners can provide breakfast and advise on local activities.

Scarborough to Roxborough
map page 90.

$$ Rainbow Nature Resort
Lure Estate, 2 km inland from Goldsborough Bay, the turn-off is between Goodwood and Pembroke on Windward Rd, T660 4755, www.therainbownatureresort.com.
The old cocoa house on a picturesque 20-ha estate growing citrus, cocoa, coffee, mangoes and avocadoes, has been tastefully converted into a 4-room guesthouse, 1 a 2-bed unit for families. All meals available and lovely host Shirley will give you cooking lessons while she prepares meals such as calloo soup, crab and dumplings or curries. Very peaceful, children will especially enjoy the farm, and a 20-min walk to both windswept Goldsborough Bay and the Rainbow Waterfall (see page 101) where you can swim.

Roxborough to Speyside *map page 90.*

$$$$-$$$ Blue Waters Inn
Batteaux Bay, Speyside, T660 4341, www.bluewatersinn.com.
Set in lush tropical grounds backing picturesque Batteaux Bay with a view of Little Tobago, this is an isolated and delightfully unpretentious hotel offering great boat trips, snorkelling and diving from its own pier and dive shop, **Blue Waters Dive 'N** (see page 124

for details of these activities). 38 large rooms, smartly decorated with balconies/patios, tea/coffee makers, plus 3 pricier 1- and 2-bedroom bungalows directly on the sand with separate living rooms and full kitchens. The main casual **Drifter** restaurant/bar has a deck overlooking the beach, and **Aqua** is a separate fine-dining restaurant – both offer excellent meals including a good choice of seafood.

$$ Speyside Inn
189-193 Windward Rd, Speyside, T660 4852, www.speysideinn-tobago.com.
This colourful, Caribbean-style hotel and dive resort is 1.2 km from the village centre opposite the turn-off to **Blue Waters Inn**, and has 18 simple but charming and airy rooms decorated in sea-inspired hues, with balconies and Little Tobago views, plus 2 cottages with kitchenettes. Small beach across the road, pool, **Tobago Dive Experience** next door (see page 125), restaurant/bar with good Creole food, seafood and cocktails.

$$-$ Top Ranking Hill View Guesthouse
Tophill St, Speyside, T660 4904, www.toprankingtobago.com.
This small, friendly guesthouse run by Ann and Max Davidson has 2 rooms with fridge and kettle and 3 apartments with kitchenettes sleeping 2-4, with balcony or patio. In a quiet neighbourhood with great views but no meals and it's a 10-min walk down to the beach and restaurants, and quite a climb back up, so a car is a good idea. The expert birdwatching guide, Newton George lives next door (see Birdwatching guides, page 123).

Charlotteville *map page 90.*
There are lots of basic places to stay in the village, it is possible to just turn up and look around as advance reservations are difficult to arrange. However, if you are self-catering, with the exception of fish, which you can buy directly from the boats, Charlotteville's shops are not well supplied so bring provisions with you. Most places in Charlotteville do not have a/c, TV or Wi-Fi.

$$-$ Cholson Chalets
72-74 Bay St, T639 8553, www.cholsonchalets.com.
Right on the beachfront overlooking Man O War Bay – the fishing boats come in across the road – 6 self-catering apartments in 3 jaunty green and white wooden buildings – one is the old family residence with varnished wooden floors and lattice balcony. All are spotlessly clean with bright white linens, fresh fruit and flowers, but the partition walls are a little thin and there can be noise from the street outside.

$$-$ Man-O-War Bay Cottages
Bay St, Campbellton, T660 4327, www.man-o-warbaycottages.com.
On the beachfront in a forested glade close to the lifeguard station, there are 10 rooms here in a clutch of rustic timber cottages ranging from 1- ro 3-bed units, good for groups with lots of single beds, but very basic and old and the kitchen equipment is a bit past its prime. Nevertheless, it's peaceful and inexpensive and close to the popular **Suckhole** restaurant and beach bar (see page 119).

$$-$ Ocean View Apartment
11 Mission Rd, T660 4891, www.oceanview-tobago.com.
This pretty wooden house on the hillside overlooking Man O War Bay has 3 apartments – Seaweed, Seagull and Seahorse – with kitchen and TV and lovely sunset-watching from the verandas. Simple, clean and tidy and run by Kechen Dillon, who is helpful and informative. Extra person sleeping on futon bed US$10.

Charlotteville to Castara *map page 90.*

$$ Gloucester Place
Parlatuvier, www.gloucesterplace.com.
On a hillside just outside Parlatuvier, with a river running along one side of the property with waterfall and swimming hole, this delightful traditional house has 3 B&B rooms (Nov-Apr) and the 2-bedroom self-catering Essex Cottage (all year) in lovely gardens

full of fruit trees which attract lots of birds. Infinity pool, wonderful views over the sea, hospitable owners who can provide a tasty breakfast and other meals on request.

Castara *map page 90.*

$$$$ Castara Retreats
Northside Rd, T766 1010 (reservations/ enquiries, UK T+44-7908-978 477), www.castararetreats.com.
This stunning timber resort has been carefully designed to blend in with the surrounding lush forest and has a stylish rustic chicness about it – it is frequently lauded by the international press as one of the top places to stay on Tobago and rightly so. 15 self-catering units – cottages, treehouses and apartments – spread over 1 ha of hillside. Each is individually named and decorated with gorgeous interiors, with lots of open decks and lovely views of the bay, Castara's 2 beaches and the sunset (even from the beds). Fantastic restaurant (see page 119), yoga and massages can be organized and it's a short walk to the village. Friendly, laid-back service and all needs are catered for by the manager Porridge; who is practically the self-proclaimed mayor of Castara (and known island-wide), who has his own boat for tours and can walk with you to the Castara Waterfall. Highly recommended.

$$ Angel Retreat
Depot Rd, Heavenly Bay, T685 4101, www.angel-retreat.com.
In a wooden block with high ceilings and wooden slatted walls and balconies, and in a marvellous location overlooking Heavenly Bay (the smaller of Castara's 2 beaches). 8 basic but good-sized apartments with 2 queen-sized beds, so can sleep a family of 4, well equipped for self-catering, fans only but breezy and all share the long wooden communal balconies. Has the only swimming pool in Castara and a kiosk for breakfasts and coffees (0830-1100).

$$-$ Blue Mango
2 Bay Rd, T317 4621, www.blue-mango.com.
Simple but charming and owned by friendly Colin Ramdeholl, lovely location built on a cliff-side between the 2 beaches, 5 traditional wooden cottages sleeping 2-6, with kitchen, fan, balconies and hammocks, and the colourful **Clay Kitchen** restaurant where there's a Fri night lime with entertainment from a steel pan band or karaoke.

$$-$ Castara Cottage
Bay Rd, T757 1044, www.castaracottage.com.
Set on the point between the 2 beaches a bit like a treehouse, this has lovely views and gets plenty of breeze through the huge windows. Similarly priced to **Blue Mango**, upstairs are a studio and an interconnecting 2-bedroom apartment while downstairs there is another 2-bedroom apartment. Simply furnished but good kitchens, hammocks and sofabeds are available for extra accommodation.

$$-$ Naturalist Beach Resort
Castara Bay Rd, T639 5901, www.naturalist-tobago.com.
Right on the Big Bay beach with lovely balconies and verandas, this popular spot has 14 varied but spacious and comfortable self-catering apartments, some for families, a little old fashioned but perfectly adequate and very good value. Rates included a buffet breakfast, self-service coffee and day beds on the sand; car hire can be included. Only down side is, despite the great location, the units are not very private, with people walking by.

Castara to Scarborough *map page 90.*

$$$ Cuffie River Nature Retreat
Off Northside Rd between Castara and Moriah, turn off east on the climb up to Mount Dillion if coming from Scarborough, T660 0505, www.cuffie-river.com.
On the western edge of Main Ridge in the heart of rainforest, this has 10 hotel-style rooms with smart decor, tea- and coffee-

making facilities and balconies overlooking the hummingbird feeders in the garden. Fixed menus for breakfast, lunch and dinner; the organic food is very tasty and well prepared. There's a swimming pool with sun loungers and deck. More than 100 bird species have been recorded around the lodge but unfortunately, because of the thick bamboo, the terrain is limited for walking (except for the approach road). Still, guides can be organized and it's wonderfully peaceful and scenic.

Restaurants

In out-of-the-way areas there is often no phone signal and therefore credit cards may not be accepted. Take plenty of cash when you go out for a meal, just in case. A 10% service charge is usually added to restaurant bills. Opening hours listed are for high season; in low season (Jun-Dec) hours may be reduced and restaurants can close for a day or more per week.

Crown Point *map page 92.*
There is no shortage of places to eat in the Crown Point area (some good, some less so) and the highest concentration of restaurants and bars is clustered around the junction with Milford Rd and Pigeon Point Rd. Also here is a small shopping centre with a supermarket and a branch of **Rituals Coffee House** (coffees, smoothies and baked snacks) and co-owned **Pizza Boys** (both Mon-Sat 1000-1900). You can get tasty local snacks such as rotis and bake and shark at the kiosks at the **Store Bay Beach Facility** (see page 89), trading under such names as Miss Esmie's, Miss Jean's, Miss Trim's and Sylvia's Food Shop; competition between them ensures good value and quality.

$$$ Café Coco
Off Pigeon Point Rd, T639 0996, www. cocoreef.com. Daily 1600-2130, bar later.
Pleasant setting with lots of tiles on the walls, fairy lights, ceiling fans, plants and fishponds and run by the **Coco Reef Resort & Spa**, although there is no access directly from there. A short but varied menu from pork ribs and creamy pasta to grilled lobster and cured steak and a good choice of wines and cocktails. Service is inreliable: sometimes exemplary, sometimes non-existent.

$$$ Food4U
Old Store Bay Rd, Bon Accord, T486 3141. Tue-Sat 1900-2400.
Alfresco dining in simple surroundings but the food is elegantly presented, a picture on every plate. Owner Derrick serves local food such as callaloo and crab and dumplings or fresh fish, shrimp, pork and chicken, with tasty morsels of local specialities to garnish the dish. Service can be slow if the restaurant is busy as Derrick seems to do everything, but it is cheerful and friendly, topped off by Derrick's impromptu ad-lib poems about (and to entertain) his guests.

$$$-$$ Kariwak Village
Store Bay Local Rd, T639 8442, www.kariwak. com (see Where to stay). Daily 0700-2130.
Great for a quiet meal away from it all, the open-air, thatched restaurant at this lovely holistic lodge is renowned for excellent food, much of which is made from organic produce. Breakfasts, salads, sandwiches, delicious desserts with home-made ice cream and speciality drinks like cocoa and spiced tea during the day, and 4-course set dinners in the evening (from 1915, reservations required); buffets on Fri and Sat nights.

$$$-$ Watermill
133 Shirvan Rd, Mount Pleasant, T639 0000. Mon-Sat 1200-2200.
The changing daily menu here is written up on a chalkboard that is taken around each table and could include steak, fish, duck, pork tenderloin or lamb, while the callaloo soup, sandwiches, fish and chips, salads, and great desserts like coconut cheesecake are good for lunch. Pricey, but romantic with good service in a fresh open-air setting with loads of ambiance.

$$ La Cantina
Milford Rd, next to the RBC Royal Bank, T639 8242. Daily except Wed, 1130-1445, 1800-2200.
Quality eat-in/take-out pizzeria serving more than 30 types of authentic Italian pizza cooked in a wood-fired oven, plus salads and filled paninis. Generous sizes, tasty toppings, including a good choice for vegetarians, and nice busy vibe with outside tables.

$$ The Pasta Gallery
Pigeon Point Rd, T727 8200, www.pasta gallery.net. Mon-Sat 1800-2200, also Thu-Fri 1200-1400.
Small place with a trattoria feel and warmed with yellow, green and purple washed walls and handmade furniture. Hearty Italian pasta dishes (Alfredo, bolognaise, seafood and the like) and salads, and also good for a glass of wine and snack of tomato and garlic bruschetta.

$$-$ Sandos Bar & Grill
Pigeon Point Rd, T631 2006, see Facebook. Tue-Sun 1100-2300.
A small, attractive terrace with potted palms, this is one of the least bar-ish places along this strip (despite the name). Prices are reasonable for fish with good sauces, grilled steak strips, vegetable and fish broth, a Thai-style larb and really tasty beef/chicken/fish/veggie tacos.

$ Fortune Chinese Restaurant
Milford Rd, Bon Accord, T639 8818. Mon-Sat 1100-2300.
Oddly, while Trinidad has hundreds of Chinese restaurants, there are very few on Tobago. This unremarkable place offers a typical menu and usefully has a car park outside; good to pull in for a takeaway if you are in self-catering accommodation.

$ J'Adore Patisserie & Coffee
Shirvan Plaza, corner Shirvan Rd and Claude Noel Highway, Canaan, T620 8855, see Facebook. Tue-Thu 0700-2000, Fri-Sun 0700-2100.
In a small mall on the corner of Shirvan Rd, this nice little spot for breakfasts offers a great range of cakes and ice creams and different types of Lavazza coffee. Eat-in or take-away.

$ Scoops Dessert Café
Milford Rd, Pigeon Point junction, T631 2233. Daily 1400-2200.
A cheerful kiosk selling ice cream (Häagen-Dazs is more expensive) shakes, sundaes and a surprisingly good variety of cakes, including red velvet and chocolate gateaux; each (expensive) slice is served in a takeaway box. Also juices, teas and instant coffee.

$ Skewers
Milford Rd, Pigeon Point junction, T631 8964, see Facebook. Daily 1000-2200.
Serves grilled Mediterranean-style meat and seafood with tasty Arabian side dishes like hummus and tabbouleh with prices ranging from US$5-9. The brightly lit establishment has tables inside and out or food can be taken away. Often long queues which is always a good sign.

$ Trinbago Curry House
Off Pigeon Point Rd, T350 7817. Daily 1000-1500.
The upstairs deck here is a great spot for a lunchtime curry roti or bus-up-shut (beef, chicken, shrimp, goat or channa for vegetarians) served with dhal and rice, and sometimes there's crab and dumplings. Be careful with the hot sauce though. Service is friendly and prompt and the beer always cold.

Buccoo *map page 90.*

$$$ La Tartaruga
Buccoo Bay, by the pier from where glass-bottomed boats depart, T639 0940, www.latartarugatobago.com. Mon-Sat 1830-2200. Reservations essential.
Tiny Italian restaurant with red and green walls and wooden floor. The owner, Gabriele, cooks with passion and produces excellent and very authentic pizzas and pastas, good vegetarian options like ratatouille or eggplant with Parmigiano cheese, and mains like lamb chops or lobster. Also runs a great little wine shop – Italian and Argentinian labels – which

also sells rums and liquors, home-made pasta, olive oil and Illy ground coffee.

$$-$ El Pescador
14 Miller St, T631 1266, www.leos-pescador.com. Tue-Sun 0800-2200.
Part of **Miller's Guest House** (see page 110), but under separate ownership, simple place on a rustic deck with rickety tables, seafood prepared by Venezuelan chef Leo Larios who often cooks whatever has just come ashore. Also serves breakfast (try the pancakes) and cocktails, all with a fantastic view over Buccoo Bay, especially when the fishing boats come in during the afternoon and at sunset.

Black Rock *map page 90.*

$$$ The Seahorse Inn
Grafton Beach Rd, Stonehaven Bay, T639 0686, www.seahorseinntobago.com. Daily 1200-1530, 1830-2200, happy hour 1730-1830 for drinks. Reservations essential.
Across the road from Black Rock Beach, this elegantly rustic restaurant offers beautifully presented lunches and dinners; lots of lobster, shrimp, catch of the day and yummy desserts. Good portions, friendly service, extensive wine list, you can sit upstairs overlooking the garden or in the bar downstairs. There are also 4 comfortable guest rooms if you want to stay ($$).

$$$-$$ The Fish Pot
Pleasant Prospect, Grafton Rd, T635 1728, see Facebook. Mon-Sat 1100-2300.
As the name suggests, tasty fresh fish reeled in by local fishermen only hours before, well-cooked and seasoned, with a variety of accompaniments, plus light meals like fish chowder or crab cakes, crunchy salads, and desserts. Good choice of wine, cocktails and fruit punches. Located in a cute little house with leafy terrace between Black Rock and Mt Irvine.

$$$-$ Waves Restaurant & Bar
Old Grafton Beach Rd, Stonehaven Bay, T639 4369, www.wavestobago.com. Daily 1100-2200, bar later.
An upmarket beach bar overlooking Grafton Beach with plenty of rum punch and fancy cocktails and a menu of late breakfasts, burgers, salads, wings, tacos, a kids' menu and more sophisticated dinners of grilled fish, lobster, lamb, steak and pork. Great for sunsets on the pleasant deck, friendly staff, and free Wi-Fi.

Scarborough *map page 98.*

$$$ Cafe Havana
100 Bacolet St (part of Bacolet Beach Club), Bacolet, T639 2357, www.cafehavana.org. Daily 1200-1500, 1800-2200.
Lovely old building with open fretwork verandas, large shutters and whirring ceiling fans, and a short but well-thought-out menu of excellent callaloo soup, seafood, steak, Cajun chicken or pork chops, and a good choice of wines and cocktails such as mojitos with fresh lime. Across the road at **Half Moon** (under the same ownership) there's another dining area/bar on the pretty veranda which offers a similar menu (Wed-Sat 1500-2200).

$$$ Salsa Kitchen Tapas Restaurant
8 Pump Mill Rd, T639 1522. Tue-Sun 1800-2300. Reservations only.
Small and intimate with only a clutch of tables on a cute little terrace illuminated by twinkling fairy lights, this offers tapas Tobago-style – 3 per person to share should do and be sure to order the flatbread drizzled with butter, garlic and sea salt – plus a dish of the day that might be lobster, lamb or duck. Food cooked fresh to order so be prepared to sit over a rum punch or 2; pricey, but well worth the wait (or you can pre-order). Difficult to find up a steep hill (Pump Mill Rd is off Plymouth Road to the north of town).

$$ Blue Crab
Corner of Robinson St and Fort St, T639 2737, www.tobagobluecrab.com. Mon-Fri 1100-1500, dinner Wed-Fri, by reservation only.
Specializes in local seafood and Creole cuisine, lunch and dinner is a generous set menu with a choice of fish (always), and

perhaps chicken or pork chops, lots of fresh veg and salad, rice, fried plantains and dumplings; expect to pay around US$25 with a glass of fresh lime juice. Tables are set on an oversized veranda with nice views over the harbour. Alison and Kenneth often do all the cooking and serving, so don't be in a hurry.

$$-$ Ciao Pizza & Café
20 Burnett St, T635 2323, see Facebook. Pizza: 1145-1445, 1800-2200 (closed Sun lunch and all day Tue); Café: Mon 0900-1100, Tue 1000-1700, Wed-Thu 0900-2300, Fri-Sat 0900-2400, Sun 1700-2300.
Located a stone's throw from the ferry terminal, and Italian owned, this offers authentic home-made pizzas cooked in a wood-fired oven, with wide range of toppings, plus pastas and salads, while the wonderful little Italian-inspired café/bar next door serves the best espressos and cappuccinos in town, filled paninis, cakes, croissants and real gelato ice cream.

$$-$ Shore Things Café & Craft
25 Old Milford Rd, Lambeau, between Scarborough and Crown Point, T635 1072, see Facebook. Mon-Fri 1100-1800.
Craft gift shop and café, great place for lunch with hummingbirds feeding outside. The extensive menu includes sandwiches, salads, crêpes and pizzas, as well as home-made desserts like soursop ice cream, mango sorbet and a divine cheesecake. Bar, coffees and juices such as tamarind and lime. Lunch specials on Fri need reservations.

$ Rena 'Chatack' Roti Shop
Old Milford Rd, T635 7684. Mon-Sat 0800-1500.
Not the easiest place to find, tucked into a small parade of shops on the main drag in Scarborough (on Milford Rd just to the west of the junction with Smithfield Rd), but definitely worth the effort to enjoy Rena's cooking. Meat and vegetarian curry rotis and bus-up-shuts, full of flavour and very filling, always packed with locals having lunch.

Roxborough to Speyside *map page 90.*
The restaurants at **Speyside Inn** and **Blue Waters Inn** are open to casual visitors (see page 113).

$$$-$$ Jemma's Sea View Kitchen
Windward Rd, Speyside, T660 4066. Sun-Thu 0800-2100, Fri 0800-1600, closed Sat.
Originally a platform built on stilts around a sea almond tree above the beach, now expanded into a large restaurant but still with good view to Goat Island and Little Tobago from the breezy deck. Good, filling lunch or dinner, Creole dishes including lobster with breadfruit pie a speciality. But it's a popular spot on island tours and suffers from being a little touristy with slow indifferent service. No alcohol but you can BYO.

$$$-$ Bird Watcher's Restaurant & Bar
Windward Rd, Speyside, T639 5438. Mon-Sat 1100-1500, sometimes open for dinner if there is the demand.
Casual village restaurant with plastic tables and simple, limited menu serving wonderful fish, shrimp and whole lobster (enough for 2) from US$30 depending on weight, with traditional sides – rice, pigeon peas and macaroni pie. Chicken and vegetarian options also available. Takes a while to prepare so be patient and have another Carib. Good place to come after a morning's dive or while touring the island.

$$ King's Bay Café
Windward Rd, Delaford, T771 2716, see Facebook. Mon-Tue 1200-1800, Fri and Sat 1200-2000, Sun 1200-1700.
Looks like a simple roadside house, but walk through and you get to a veranda with wonderful view of King's Bay, a perfect location to eat some really good food; known for its excellent tuna burgers and chocolate brownies but the grilled fish caught in the bay below should not be missed. Everything is fresh and delicious.

Charlotteville *map page 90.*

$$-$ Sharon and Phebe's
On the main street at the Campbellton (south) end, T660 5717. Mon-Sat 0900-2300, Sun 1100-2300.
Light and bright with a nice view of the bay from upstairs, very friendly and good and cheap Creole meals; try the flying fish sandwiches and prawns if available, dumplings and curried crab also good, accompaniments include rice and beans, salad and chips.

$ Gail's
To the north of the seafront close to the Pirate's Bay track. Dinner only from 1900, closed Sun.
Small place with a few tables on the front porch of her house and run by charming Gail, a great cook and a genius with fish. She most always has a soup to start (maybe callaloo or pea) and a choice of fish, chicken, sometimes goat with delicious vegetables and salad and cold beers. Come early, at 1900, or she may close.

$ Suckhole
On the beach next to the Charlotteville Beach Facility (lifeguard station). Sun-Fri 1200-1600.
While oddly named, this informal and inexpensive beach bar is a popular stop on island tours for lunch of simple meals like mahi mahi, salad and fries, or vegetables and rice and onion rings; huge portions and a full plate will cost around US$9. They'll rustle up something vegetarian like ratatouille pasta and roasted peppers. Takes a while to prepare if there's a group, but it's a pleasant spot on the beach to wait and they do a mean rum punch.

Castara *map page 90.*

$$$-$$ Castara Retreats
Northside Rd, T766 1010, www.castara retreats.com. See Where to stay, above. Daily 1100-2200.
With a simply stunning view overlooking the bay and great sunset-watching from the multi-terraced decks with hummingbirds visiting the feeders, the food at this top-notch resort restaurant is superb. The menu includes very tasty fish (tuna, wahoo and mahi mahi), vegetarian dishes such as excellent handmade pasta with inventive sauces, plus some Caribbean specialities like jerk chicken. Leave room for dessert, as they use local cocoa and coconut in their creations. Good choice of wines and cocktails and you can also come here for light bites, cappuccino and fresh fruit drinks during the day.

$$ The Boat House
Heavenly Bay, T483 0964. Tue and Thu 1000-1700, Mon, Wed and Fri 1000-2200, bar open later.
Colourful decor, with fabric strips hanging from the ceiling, this casual beach bar serves local food and pizza, but when English owner Sharon is on site, there are also really good set meals for lunch and dinner; usually grilled fish, squid or chicken with an excellent choice of vegetables for about US$18 (vegetarians US$13). Drumming and limbo dancing Wed night, when reservations are needed as it's so popular; US$4 cover charge.

$ Cascreole Bar & Beach Club
Castara Bay Rd, T639 5291. Daily 0900-late.
Lovely spot with bar downstairs and deck restaurant upstairs, Debbie's cooking is delicious and consistent, no menus just 'specials of the day' – fish/goat/chicken – plenty of rum punch and Thu night is party night with a bonfire on the beach; a perfect spot to watch the sun go down.

$ Cheno's
Main St, T704 7819. Mon-Fri 0800-1300, Sat-Sun 0830-1300.
Good place to come for breakfast, whether you want bacon and eggs or local saltfish and coconut bake, or to stop by for home-made ice cream and very good coffees from a proper machine. Very friendly and popular, and also holds occasional Sat night barbecues; stop in in the morning to ask.

$ D'Almond Tree
Castara Bay Rd, T683 3593. Mon-Sat 1230-2100.

Beachside restaurant also known as Vera's after the cook, a little shabby but you can't fault the location just near the lifeguard station with lovely views. No menus, look at the whiteboard, but usually fish (the fishing cooperative is right next door so it couldn't be fresher), grilled chicken/pork or curry goat, and reasonable rotis at lunchtime. No alcohol, but you can BYO or, during the day, go to the small shop 50 m away, or try the fresh juices.

Bars and clubs

Tobago is not as lively as Trinidad and, away from the Milford Rd/Pigeon Point Rd junction in Crown Point (where there are several bars), nightlife consists of little more than small local bars (rum shops) – quintessential gathering points on Tobago and throughout the Caribbean. They are mostly open 'any day, any time' though it is rare to find one open any later than 2200. There are also beach bars on the most popular beaches. The larger hotels offer entertainment in high season (drumming or steel pan) but it is unlikely to set the world alight.

Bago's Beach Bar
Pigeon Point Rd, Crown Point, T631 8487. Daily 1100-late.
A typical Caribbean beach bar, and always fun and loud, this is as popular with locals for the after work lime as it is for tourists and ex-pats. On the beach with sea grape trees for shade, it's a good stop-off on the way back from Pigeon Point Heritage Park to watch the sunset. Good cocktails, rum punch and choice of imported beers. Happy hour 1900-2000, karaoke on Sat.

Barcode, Sports Bar & Grill
Milford Rd, Scarborough, T635 2633, www.barcodetobago.com. Tue-Thu 1100-0200, Fri-Sat 1100-0300, Sun 1800-0200.
Lively sports bar in town with music events, karaoke on Thu, spacious outdoor deck, great setting. Fri lunch is **Sweet Hand Friday** when they serve local food: a meat dish with macaroni pie, peas and rice (1200-1400; arrive

early because it may sell out). At other times wraps, salads, chicken, juices and protein shakes are served. There are TV screens for sports events and a couple of pool tables.

Captain Sand Bar
Battery St, Buccoo, T631 1644. Mon-Thu 0900-2400, Fri-Sun 0900-0100.
Since the building of the new goat and crab racing track near the Buccoo Beach Facility (see box, page 95), Sunday School (see box, page 122) has moved to Battery St, just off Buccoo Main Rd, and this bar is the centre of things and is where the steel pan band performs. But it's open the rest of the week too and has a good selection of drinks and an authentic rum shop setting.

Colours Restaurant & Bar
Milford Rd, near the junction with Pigeon Point Rd, Crown Point, T631 8184. Daily 0900-2400.
A great meeting place as well as a place to watch the world go by in the centre of Crown Point from the shady terrace, very friendly, with a decent selection of drinks (try the lime daiquiri), also wines, and reasonable simple food including coconut bake and saltfish for breakfast, rotis for lunch and grilled strip-loin steak/flying fish for dinner.

Glasgow's Bar
Northside Rd, Parlatuvier, go out of the village up the hill towards Castara. Daily 1200-2430.
Spectacular setting high above Parlatuvier Bay on 2 floors with a panoramic view, great place to sip a cold beer and watch the waves roll in and there are steps down to the beach. Alan Glasgow is a friendly and informative host and concocts a mean rum punch. Sometimes there's food (chicken or fish with rice, plantain, salad, etc), but don't rely on it as the chef is not always there. A great pit stop on a tour of the island or for a sunset cocktail.

The Overhang Bar & Lounge
Milford Rd, Crown Point, T639 8929. Tue-Sun 1400-0500.
Popular with locals and visiting Trinis, this bar upstairs at **Jimmy's Holiday Resort** has

booth-style seating, TVs for sport, good breezy balcony overlooking the Crown Point strip, some food such as burgers and wings with chips, and loud but varied music from soca and reggae to Jamaican dancehall.

Renmar's Restaurant & Bar
Pigeon Point Heritage Park, Crown Point, T631 8768, www.renmarstobago.com. Daily 1000-2300.
The principal bar along the beachfront places at Pigeon Point, always a holiday atmosphere, plenty of rum and cocktails, indoor seating or sit on a bar stool with your feet in the sand. Offers a lunch (Sun-Fri 1200-1530) of Tobago's favourite dishes like stewed goat, baked chicken, fried fish and macaroni pie with rice, lentils, peas, dumplings and mixed vegetables/salad; try to go early because it does run out on busy beach days.

The Shade Night Club
Bon Accord, Crown Point, T294 2811. Wed-Thu 1700-2200, Fri-Sat 1700-0500.
Nightclub and place to party, beside **Chic – The Boutique Hotel**, and the only place on the island with an open-air dance floor. It has a thatched bar and is pleasantly set among trees in the compound, and DJs play soca, rock and reggae. The crowd tends to be a mix of Tobagonians, Trinis and visitors, but it also has a reputation as a bit of a pick-up joint. Happy Hour 1700-2000; also on offer is sushi and wine as an after-work lime on Fri.

Sundowner's Bar/Simmer Down Restaurant
Crown Point Beach Hotel, Old Store Bay Rd, Crown Point, T639 8781, www.crownpoint beachhotel.com. See Where to stay, above. Daily 0700-2400.
You can sip a cocktail at the open-air, poolside Sundowner's Bar for a great view of the sunset beyond Store Bay. Happy Hour 1700-1900 and on Fri and Sat there's a DJ later in the evening. The food is not fantastic at the restaurant, but there's a decent and filling Sun brunch; US$16.50.

Entertainment
Casinos
The casinos on Tobago are not at all plush and verge on tatty, although all of the key elements are there – table games such as black jack and roulette, slot machines, and bars where you can get a late drink. You need to show your passport to get in and they offer free pickups/drop-offs from hotels in the Crown Point area.
Jade Monkey Casino Bar & Grill, *Milford Rd, Crown Point, T631 0044, see Facebook. Mon-Thu and Sun 1700-0100, Fri-Sat 1800-0300.*
Royalton Casino, *next to Crown Point Beach Hotel, Old Store Bay Rd, Crown Point, T631 8500, see Facebook. Daily 1000-0300.*
Silver Dollar Casino, *Shirvan Plaza, corner Shirvan Rd and Claude Noel Highway, Canaan, T631 2002, www.silverdollaryourcasino.com. Mon-Sat 1200-0400, Sun 1800-0200.*

Cinema
MovieTowne, *Gulf City Mall, Lowlands, T627 8277, www.movietowne.com.* 4-screen movie theatre, open from 1200 and with late shows Fri, Sat, plus there's a food court in the mall.

Shopping
Arts and crafts
Batiki Point, *opposite the Buccoo Beach Facility, Buccoo, T631 0111. Mon-Fri 1100-1800, Sun from 1800 during Sunday School.* A cavern of colourful local and imported crafts. Owned by Tina Friman from Finland. Colourful wall hangings depicting local life, beautiful Indian sari/sarongs and jewellery, mini steel pans, and batik clothing, beach wraps and T-shirts.
Shore Things Café & Craft, *25 Old Milford Rd, Lambeau, between Scarborough and Crown Point, T635 1072, see Facebook. Mon-Fri 1100-1800.* Run by Giselle Beaurn and her team, this brightly coloured café (see page 118) also sells an excellent range of crafts, local artwork, jewellery, clothing and CDs of local music, all in a lovely setting overlooking the ocean.

ON THE ROAD

Sunday School

There is nothing religious about this event – Sunday School is a loud, vibrant street party in Buccoo popular with tourists, visiting Trinis, and locals who come from as far away as Castara and Charlotteville. It starts about 2000 every Sunday evening with live steel pan music, followed at about 2300 by a DJ playing until as late as 0400. The music, ranging from Jamaican dancehall and reggae to soca and calypso, is very loud and infectious. This is the main night-time activity on the island, and a great place to see Tobagonians lime and let their hair down. Don't miss it. However, do take precautions. Go by taxi and arrange a time to be collected or at least get your taxi driver's phone number; guard your pockets from theft; be prepared for sexual approaches even if you are already with your partner; take a small amount of cash and leave all valuables behind – rum and beer are cheap, as are the snack stalls and barbecue outlets.

Store Bay Beach Facility Craft Market, *see page 89, daily 1000-1730*. The 35 or so booths here sell imported clothing, beach wraps and souvenirs, including jewellery, calabash and wooden sculptures, tacky Rasta hats, and trinkets carved out of coconut shells. Many of these vendors also turn up at Buccoo's Sunday School from around 1900 to 2300.

Food

Most villages on Tobago have one or more small shops selling the basic supplies, and perhaps a stall selling fruit and vegetables, but the range is minimal. If you're driving and staying in self-catering accommodation, then it's best to go to one of the (few) supermarkets in Scarborough or the southwest. The exception is fish; almost every village on the coast has a small fish market (cooperative) where you can get it cleaned and filleted too. The Scarborough Market is at its busiest and liveliest on a Fri or Sat morning before 1300, and specializes in fish, fruit, vegetables and local foods such as hot pepper sauces, tamarind balls and packets of blended spices.

Forro's Homemade Delicacies, *The Andrew's Rectory, at St Andrew's Anglican Church, Bacolet St, Scarborough, T639 2485. Mon-Fri 0900-1600*. Local condiments, preserves and sauces are cooked and bottled in a cottage industry started by Eileen Forrester, wife of the Anglican Archdeacon of Trinidad and Tobago. Gift boxes of tropical fruit jellies, tamarind chutney and hot sauces are a wonderful souvenir of the island.

Gourmet Foods at RT Morshead, *off Shirvan Rd, Mt Pleasant, T639 8855. Daily 0800-1800*. More upmarket than **Penny Savers**, below, with imported and higher-priced foodstuffs, including cheeses and deli meats, wines and spirits.

Penny Savers Supermarket, *at 3 locations: Milford Rd, Canaan, T639 8992; Main Rd, Carnbee, T639 8816; and Wilson Rd,*

> **Warning...**
> Puncheon is a high-proof heavy type of rum produced in Trinidad and Tobago; common local brands are Forres Park, Caroni and Stallion, and they are 75% alcohol by volume. After enjoying a few rum punches at the beach bars and rum shops, you might be tempted to take home a bottle of rum as a souvenir. However, bear in mind that all civil aviation authorities ban the transport of alcohol where the percentage of alcohol by volume is greater than 70% (140 proof) in either checked-in or cabin luggage. Ensure you buy a bottle that's less than 70% and not the fiery 75% Puncheon.

*Scarborough, T639 5549. Mon-Sat 0800-2000,
Sun and holidays until 1300.* This is the main
supermarket on the island; the Canaan store is
the largest, has a car park and ATM, and in the
small mall directly opposite there's is a good
pharmacy and wine store. If you're in self-
catering accommodation around Crown Point,
you can get a route taxi here along Milford Rd.
Tobago Chocolate Delights, *next door
to Shore Things Café & Craft (above), Old
Milford Rd, Lambeau, between Scarborough
and Crown Point, Lambeau, T370 1907, see
Facebook. Mon-Fri 1230-1600.* A Trini by birth
but of French parentage, Jean Claude Petit
hand makes chocolate bars and individual
dark, milk and white chocolates using cocoa
produced in Tobago; the Coconut Rum
Cream is an ideal souvenir to take home,
but fillings also include hazelnut, amaretto,
crème de menthe and orange brandy, and
he plays around with local flavours such as
mango and tamarind jelly – delicious.

Shopping malls
Gulf City Mall, *Claude Noel Highway,
Lowlands, T631 1321, www.gulfcitymalltt.com.
Mon-Fri 1000-1800, Sun 1400-1700.* This
modern a/c mall is the sister property to the
one at San Fernando in Trinidad, but it hasn't
been nearly as successful. Although it's
home to MovieTowne and a food court with
the likes of KFC and other cheap takeaways,
there are hardly any shops; many of the units
are empty and there are no useful stores like
a pharmacy or supermarket

Birdwatching guides
Eureka Natural History Tours, *T731 0759,
www.naturetobago.com.* Jason Radix is a
former guide at the Asa Wright Nature Centre
in Trinidad, and has great knowledge not only
of birds, but also reptiles, insects and plants.
A half-day trip will include hiking along the
Gilpin Trail at the Main Ridge, he can organize
trips to the wetlands in the southwest and
the Grafton Caledonia Wildlife Sanctuary,
and a long day to Trinidad to the Asa Wright
Nature Centre and Caroni Swamp.
Newton George Nature Tours, *3 Top Hill St,
Speyside, T660 5463, www.newtongeorge.com.*
A former forestry employee and custodian
of Little Tobago, Newton is the most
experienced and authoritative guide on the
island with an international reputation and
encyclopaedic knowledge; he is also very
friendly and fun to spend a day with. He
and his wife, Dianne, have a 'hummingbird
gallery' on the veranda of their home, where
all of the island's 6 species of hummingbird
come to feed – you can visit (by appointment
only) for US$10 per person and its fantastic for
photography. Newton will go with you on a
glass-bottomed boat trip to Little Tobago for
birdwatching, and his day trip around Tobago
includes wetlands and sewage ponds,
the Grafton Caledonia Wildlife Sanctuary,
Adventure Farm and Nature Reserve and
other birding hotspots. Again Newton can
also arrange an all-day trip to Trinidad.
Peter Cox Nature Tours, *Bon Accord, Crown
Point, T751 5822.* A naturalist, ecologist and
specialist birdwatching guide, Peter Cox is an
enthusiastic and knowledgeable all-rounder
who can tell you as much about the geology

Birdwatching on Tobago

Birdwatching is one of the most popular activities on Tobago. The island is home to about 220 species, and some 90 of these species breed here, including some not commonly seen on Trinidad. The national bird is the rufus-vented chachalaca, or cocrico, a type of noisy pheasant with a look of a turkey about it which makes quite a racket at dawn and dusk. There are six different hummingbirds, often attracted to feeders strategically placed on verandas, where they appear to be unaware of their audience. Blue-crowned motmots flit around spectacularly in the bushes, while the range of seabirds off Little Tobago is impressive, particularly December to July, when the red-billed tropicbirds are breeding. Tobago is on a route for migrating birds, with those from South America arriving between May and September and those from North America from November to March, both escaping winter in their latitudes. At least one birdwatching trip is recommended with a specialist guide who will know where to find species you are interested in, will recognize their calls and be able to identify local and migrant birds. Your guide is also likely to be something of a botanist and can tell you about the plants the birds live on and know where the fruiting trees are that they are feeding on. The best guides take only two to four people so you can move quietly and see more; don't forget your binoculars. There are several rewarding birdwatching locations; the main ones are the Main Ridge Forest Reserve and Little Tobago, but there are less obvious spots like the Bon Accord sewage ponds or the freshwater pools around the Magdalena Grand Beach & Golf Resort. Prices vary depending on arrangements and how many people, but for an idea, expect to pay from around US$25-40 for 1½- to three-hour guided birdwatching trails in the forests of the Main Ridge (if you have your own transport), and US$70-75 for half a day to the Main Ridge and other places (with transport and refreshments). Apart from the ones listed below, you can ask your hotel to recommend a local guide or call in at the Main Ridge Visitor Centre (see page 102).

of the island as the creatures that live on it, whether they are butterflies, lizards, iguanas, snakes, turtles or birds. He offers birdwatching, nature tours, sightseeing and turtle watching in season.

Unique Tours Tobago, *Bloody Bay, T660 7847, www.uniquetourstobago.com*. Friendly Junior Thomas offers guided tours around the island in his 4WD truck for sightseeing and birdwatching, and can also meet you at the Main Ridge Visitor Centre (see page 102) for walks along the trails including the Gilpin Trace (which he knows intimately); gum boots and refreshments included. Junior can also take you to his house in Bloody Bay to watch the hummingbirds at the feeders.

Dive operators

Blue Waters Dive 'N, *at Blue Waters Inn, Batteaux Bay, Speyside, T660 4341, www. bluewatersinn.com/blue-water-diven*. The hotel's dive school is open to all and offers diving out to the reefs around Little Tobago

> **Tip...**
> More information about diving in Tobago can be found from the **Association of Tobago Dive Operators**, www. tobagoscubadiving.com. In the event of emergencies, Tobago's hyperbaric or recompression facility is at the Roxborough Health Centre, T660 5155.

ON THE WATER
Diving off Tobago

The waters around Tobago are known as an unspoilt diving destination and there are several reputable dive shops. Most species of hard and soft corals can be found, and there is a huge brain coral, believed to be one of the world's largest, off Little Tobago, which you can see on a glass-bottomed boat tour. The parrot fish are nibbling away at it, but it is so large that they are not yet doing major damage. The Guyana current flows round the south and east shores of Tobago and supports a large variety of marine life. Dive sites are numerous and varied, with walls, caves, canyons, coral gardens and lots of fish. There is exciting drift diving but it is not recommended for novices. You are swept along the coral reef at up to five knots while, high above, manta rays flap lazily to remain stationary in the current as they sieve out the plankton. Manta rays are not as plentiful as they used to be, because of changes in the temperature of the current; they are best seen between January and March. Eagle rays and southern stingrays can also be seen. The most popular launch sites for dive boats are Arnos Vale Bay north of Plymouth, Pirate's Bay and Man O War Bay at Charlotteville, and Batteaux Bay at Speyside. Buccoo Reef (see box, page 94), Tobago's most famous reef, is usually absent from listed dive sites as its too shallow and better for snorkelling, although some operators use it for training or children's courses. There is, however, a wreck dive lying to the north of Buccoo Reef: the *Maverick*, once a car ferry between Trinidad and Tobago called the *MV Scarlet Ibis*, it was purposely sunk in 1997 and now forms a thriving artificial reef. The boat stands almost perfectly upright on the sandy seabed and while the deck has collapsed, with care you can swim through the hull. For diving expect to pay in the region of: single dive US$55, night dive US$60, two-tank dive US$90, PADI Discover Scuba Diving US$100-110, PADI Open Water Diving course US$495-520.

and Goat Island, and also rents out kayaks, stand-up paddle boards and snorkelling gear. **DiveTnT**, *Main Rd, Charlotteville, T378 4269, www.divetnt.com.*

Environmental Research Institute Charlotteville (ERIC), *Northside Rd, Campbellton, next to Man-O-War Bay Cottages (see page 113), Charlotteville, T788 3550, www.eric-tobago.com.* Has 2 self-catering apartments for divers attached to the dive shop known as the **Shark Shack**.

Extra Divers Worldwide, *Grafton Beach Resort (see page 110), Stonehaven Bay, Black Rock, T639 7424, www.extradiverstobago.eu.*

Tobago Dive Experience, *Windward Rd, near Speyside Inn, 660-5268, www.tobago diveexperience.com.*

Tobago Dive Pirates, *at Turtle Beach Tobago by Rex Resorts, Great Courland Bay, Black Rock, T635 1725, www.tobagodivepirates.com.* The in-house dive school at this all-inclusive resort, but organizes diving for non-guests too.

Tobago Frontier Divers, *near the craft market at Store Bay Beach Facility, Crown Point, T631 8138, www.tobagofrontierdivers.com.* Run by Alvin 'Dougie' Douglas (the current vice-president of the Association of Tobago

Tip...

Snorkelling is excellent almost everywhere, with good visibility. Most of the dive shops and some of the beach hotels rent out snorkelling gear and there are several boat tours on offer.

Dive Operators). Also offers the snorkelling trip to Buccoo Reef (see box, page 94), and great tours in glass-bottomed kayaks to the mangroves around Bon Accord Lagoon, which act as a spawning ground for the Buccoo Reef fish; 2 hrs, US$45.

Fishing

The offshore fishing season is Oct-Jun, with the peak time around Nov when wahoo are plentiful and Feb-May for blue marlin. Other fish caught are white marlin, swordfish, sailfish, tuna, barracuda and mahi mahi. Coastal and reef fishing are on offer all year round, mostly in the Caribbean Sea between Crown Point and Plymouth where you can find tarpon and snapper. Locals on this leeward side of the island fish with a simple line while standing on a rock or jetty and in some villages you can still see seine fishing ('pulling seine') when groups haul in the nets on to the sand; help from visitors is welcome. You could arrange to go out with a local fisherman in his pirogue if you are not bothered by the lack of navigation equipment, life vests, shade, refreshments, etc. It will be a fraction of the price but he will expect to take home most of the catch after you've taken whatever you want to eat. Alternatively, professional fishing charters are available with all the modern equipment at about US$400 for half a day/4 hrs and US$800-900 for a full day of up to 9 hrs for up to 6 people.

Fish Tobago, *at the guesthouse of the same name (see page 110), Buccoo, T309 0062, www.fishtobago.com.*

Grand Slam Charters Tobago, *Grafton Beach Rd, Black Rock, T683 1958, see Facebook.*

Hard Play Fishing Charters, *Buccoo, T639 7108, www.hardplay.net.*

Pops Tours Tobago, *Buccoo, T738 8226, www.popstourstobago.com.*

Golf

There are 2 18-hole golf courses on Tobago; one of them, the **Mount Irvine Bay Hotel & Golf Club** (T639 8871, www.mountirvine

bay.com), is currently very run down and in need of some serious maintenance (both the hotel and the overgrown golf course). **Tobago Plantations Golf Club**, *part of the Magdalena Grand Beach & Golf Resort (see page 109), T387 0288, www.magdalenagrand. com.* The island's best option is a par-72, 18-hole championship course built on a former coconut estate. There is a club house with pro shop and driving range, a golf academy and practice putting green. Green fees are US$72 for 18 holes if you are staying at the hotel and US$90 if you are not, with club rental US$62.50. There are packages available if you plan to play or take frequent lessons. However, if you just want to play for the day, the Golf Pass, 0700-1800, US$85, is easily the best-value option as it includes transportation to/from anywhere within a 20-min drive, breakfast, lunch, clubs, golf cart, an 18-hole round, and house brand drinks at the club house's **Fairways Bar**.

Horse riding

Being With Horses, *14 Galla Trace, Buccoo (near Miller's Guest House), T639 0953, www.being-with-horses.com.* Veronika and Lennon have a calming and caring attitude towards their 6 horses, all of which are rescue horses that had previously been mistreated. For visitors, they run a very enjoyable ride through the mango trees from the stables and on to Buccoo Beach; the highlight is riding/swimming with the horses bareback in the sea (which the horses love). Allow about 3 hrs for the activity, which includes getting to know the horses first, and, quite uniquely, they are permitted to choose their rider. Equally good fun for those that have never been on a horse before to experienced riders. Daily 0900 and 1500, US$95, reservations essential. They also run the **Healing With Horses Foundation** (www.healing-with-horses.org), which provides horse interaction such as grooming, feeding and riding for disabled, blind and deaf children on Tobago (horses help the

ON THE WATER
Yacht services

Being upwind, and to the east, of the main chain of West Indies islands, most private yachts miss Tobago, and some of the waters, particularly on the Atlantic side, can be hazardous. However, some yachts do stop in the bays on the leeward side of Tobago, often on their way to Trinidad's excellent sheltered outhaul facilities (Chaguaramas is stuffed with marinas). **Store Bay**, the largest west-facing bay at the south of Tobago, is generally calm, and the anchorage is just off Pigeon Point Road. The only services for yachts on Tobago is **Store Bay Marine Services** (The Surf Shack, Pigeon Point Road – near the Conrado Beach Resort – Crown Point, T390 5408, see Facebook, Monday-Saturday 0800-1800), which provides repairs and maintenance services, water, a laundry, long range Wi-Fi and provisioning.

children experience a sense of bonding and affection, whilst riding provides physical benefits such as strengthening muscles and improving balance).

Mountain biking
For regular bike hire, see **Easy Goers Bicycle Rental**, page 128.

Tobago is criss-crossed with a network of trails through the mangroves and mountains, up steep hills, along ridges, over streams, past waterfalls and down to beaches to cool off. There are stunning views of bays and beaches, as well as shady, forested paths and the sound of birdsong, and you can stop off to pick fruit for refreshment. The following 2 outfits offer guided tours with mountain bikes and all equipment, plus drinks and snacks, and will plan a tour based upon your experience, skill levels and preference. Routes are normally designed to keep riders off the main roads as much as possible, using back tracks and trails. Expect to pay in the region of US$45 for a 2- to 3-hr ride for beginner/intermediate riders, or US$55 for a 3- to 4-hr ride for experienced/extreme mountain bikers.
Mountain Biking Tobago, T639 9709, www.mountainbikingtobago.com.
Tobago Mountain Bike Tours (aka **Slow Leak Tours**), T332 5872, www.tobago mountainbike.com.

Sailing
Being a small island, it's natural that visitors like to enjoy Tobago's waters from the deck of a boat. The leeward side of the island has lots of great bays, with fantastic snorkelling sites. Most day trips, by catamaran, follow the same basic format: departure from Mt Irvine Bay (or the jetty at Pigeon Point Heritage Park), a sail up the Caribbean coast with possibly a mid-morning snorkelling stop, a longer lunch and snorkelling stop (the lovely Cotton Bay is a popular choice, but its charm can be rather spoilt when there are several boats present), and then a return with possibly another snorkelling stop along the way. This excursion costs in the region of US$80-90, children (under 12) half price, under 6s free, and includes a barbecue lunch, cold Carib beers, rum punch and soft drinks, and transport from hotels in the southwest. There are also other options such as sunset cruises to Nylon Pool or you can charter the boat for a group and decide what you want to do.
Island Girl Sail Charters, T639 6306, www.sailtobago.com.
Picante, T620 4750, www.yachtpleasures.com.
Splash Sports, T682 2919, www.splashsports tobago.com.

Tour operators

A number of tour operators and taxi drivers offer island tours; stopping at the best viewpoints and places of interest, with lunch at perhaps a beachside restaurant; expect to pay around US$80-90. It's a good option if you don't want to hire a car. Other options are birdwatching (see guides, above), visits to the waterfalls and transfers to one of the beaches or Sunday School.

CP Tours, *T496 3286, www.cptourstobago.com.*
Frankie Tours & Rentals, *T631 0369, www.frankietourstobago.com.*
Hans Tours, *T759 2880, www.hanstourstobago.com.*
Harris Jungle Tours, *T639 0513, www.harris-jungle-tours.com.*
Simon McLetchie Tours, *T639 0265, www.tobago-adventure.com.*

Watersports

Frankie Tours & Rentals, *Mt Irvine Beach, T631 0369, www.frankietourstobago.com.* Run by Michael Frank, this company has been going for more than 20 years, and has its own glass-bottomed boat as well as other equipment such as jet skis, boogie boards and kayaks at their kiosk at the Mt Irvine Beach Facility. They also offer island tours and can also arrange fishing and birdwatching trips as well as car hire.
Monkey Business, *Mt Irvine Bay, T703 7213.* Surf lessons and board rental.
Radical Sports, *Pigeon Point Heritage Park, Crown Point, T631 5150, www.radicalsports tobago.com.* A one-stop shop for all watersports at Pigeon Point and the only wind/kitesurfing centre on the island. Buccoo Reef protects the Bon Accord Lagoon and the water can be flat and calm with prevailing cross-shore winds. Conditions for wind/kitesurfing are best Dec-Jun, but there can be strong winds later in the year. Costs for rental are from US$45 for windsurfing and US$85 for kitesurfing per hr and there are daily and weekly rates; additional lessons are from US$70/95 per hr. You can also hire kayaks, US$22 per hr, and hobies, US$50 per hr.
Salty Tours, *Mt Irvine, T360 1325, www.salty tours.com.* Can organize wakeboarding and waterskiing on Bon Accord Lagoon; from US$60 for 1-hr lessons or US$40 per session. As an alternative to the larger catamaran tours, Nigel can also take you in his small boat up the coast for snorkelling and to explore the bays.
Stand Up Paddle Tobago, *at Radical Sports (above), T728 5483, www.standuppaddle tobago.com.* Run by Duane Kenny, who offers a variety of tours and instruction on SUPs and kayaks, from US$60-US$120, along the coast, in the swamps and mangroves, in the lagoon, at night to see the bioluminescence, or further afield to discover deserted beaches and waterfalls. You can rent boards from **Radical Sports** for US$22 per hr.
Tobago Waterholics, *Pigeon Point Rd, close to the entrance of Pigeon Point Heritage Park, T688 7669, www.tobagowaterholics.com.* Waterskiing/wakeboarding, from US$40 for 30 mins; jet skis, US$50 for 30 mins, plus other toys such as kayaks, banana boats and donuts – all for playing off the Pigeon Point Beach and Bon Accord Lagoon. Can also arrange day boat trips across to Grande Riviere (see page 56) on the north coast of Trinidad; from US$120.

Transport

Bike hire

Some hotels rent out mountain bikes to their guests. See also Mountain biking, page 127, for guided tours.

Easy Goers Bicycle Rental, Milford Rd, Crown Point, T681 8025, www.easygoers bikes.com. Daily 0900-1700. Just around the corner from the airport, rents out mountain bikes, road bikes, children's bikes and tandems (easily spotted is the big cage on the side of the road stuffed full of bikes). Rates are US$15-20 per day depending on the season, and there are discounts for weekly hire.

Boat

See Getting around, page 133, for details of the ferry service between Trinidad and Tobago.

Bus, maxi and route taxi

All **PTSC** buses originate from the bus terminal off Sangster Hill Rd near the waterfront in Lower Scarborough (T639 2293, www.ptsc.co.tt). They run along most of the main roads around the island, roughly Mon-Fri 0500-2100, Sat 0500-2000, and Sun 0600-2000. On the busier routes, for example between Scarborough and Crown Point (and the airport), they can run every hour, but on the more distant routes, such as between Scarborough and Roxborough, Charlotteville or Castara, it may be only every 3 hrs. You can buy tickets at the terminal or look out for the PTSC signs on small shops/kiosks. They cost TT$2-3 for short journey and up to TT$8 (US$1.20) for a trip up to the top of the island to, say, Charlotteville. **Maxi taxis** also gather at the terminal off Sangster Hill Rd and run all over Tobago on set routes (and fares) similar to the PTSC buses, but have no timetables. **Route taxis** pick up/drop off passengers at the Sangster Hill Rd terminal and along Milford Rd in Lower Scarborough for the west (Crown Point, airport, Buccoo, Plymouth); TT$3-7 depending on the distance. There are few route taxis that go from Scarborough up the Windward Rd to the northeast of the island; they are small cars after all and usually run shorter distances between the villages along the Windward Rd.

Car hire

Thanks to Tobago being a popular weekend destination for Trinis, there are dozens of car rental firms but not all of them enjoy a good reputation. All will arrange pick up/ drop off at the airport. Expect to pay in the region of US$40-50 per day for a Suzuki jeep or normal/sedan car, US$65 for a more substantial 4-door 4WD, and US$90 for a minibus. See page 135 for further details about hiring a car and driving.

Alamo Car Rental, airport, T826 6893, www.alamo.com. **Carro Rentals**, 19C River Rd Circular, Plymouth, T721 9960, www.carro rentals.com. **Econo Car Rentals, airport**, T660 8728, www.econocarrentalstt.com. **Sheppy's Auto Rental**, off Old Store Bay Rd, Bon Accord, T639 1543, www.tobagocar rental.com. **Sherman's Auto Rentals**, Lambeau, T639 2292, www.shermansrental. com. **Taylor's Jeep & Car Rentals**, Castara, T354 5743, www.taylorstobagoauto rental.com. **Thrifty**, airport, T639 8507, www.thrifty.com. **Tobago Car Hire**, 283 Hummingbird Av, New Grange, T682 2888, www.tobagocarhire.com.

Taxi

As with Trinidad, all taxi fares are set by the government and taxi association and fares to all destinations around the island are on a noticeboard at ANR Robinson International Airport. Also here is a dispatcher for the **Tobago Taxi Cab Co-op Society** (T639 0950). Taxis also meet the ferries in Scarborough. Otherwise any hotel can phone a taxi for you – if you find a driver you like, get their card and phone number. Note: fares between 2200 and 0600 attract a surcharge of 50%.

Practicalities

Getting there 131
Getting around 133
Essentials A-Z 133
Index 142

Getting there

Air

Trinidad and Tobago has two international airports. **Piarco International Airport** ⓘ *Golden Grove Rd, Piarco, T669 4880, www.tntairports.com/piarco*, is 27 km east and inland of the country's capital Port of Spain. **ANR Robinson International Airport** ⓘ *Airport Connector Rd, T639 8547, www.tntairports.com/anr*, is on the southwestern tip of Tobago at Crown Point, 13 km from the island's capital Scarborough. Both are connected by the regular 'Air Bridge' flights with **Caribbean Airlines** ⓘ *www.caribbean-airlines.com*, also see Getting around, page 133. See below for airport information.

Flights from the UK and Europe **British Airways** ⓘ *www.britishairways.com*, fly from London Gatwick to Trinidad. **British Airways** and **Virgin Atlantic** ⓘ *www.virgin-atlantic. com*, have twice-weekly flights from London Gatwick to Tobago – all of the above have touchdowns in Barbados or St Lucia. Flying time from the UK is 11-12 hours. **Condor** ⓘ *www.condor.com*, fly from Frankfurt to Tobago via Barbados once a week. At the time of writing, an option was to fly from the UK to Frankfurt and connect to this flight with **Thomas Cook Airlines** (and others). But, by the time this book is out, **Thomas Cook Airlines** ⓘ *www.thomascookairlines.com*, will be offering direct flights from Manchester to Tobago.

Flights from North America To Trinidad, **American Airlines** ⓘ *www.americanairlines. com*, fly from Miami, **JetBlue** ⓘ *www.jetblue.com*, from New York and Fort Lauderdale, and **United Airlines** ⓘ *www.united.com*, from Houston and New York; all with connecting services from other US cities. None of the US airlines service Tobago, so the option is to connect with the **Caribbean Airlines** 'Air Bridge'. **Caribbean Airlines** also fly to Trinidad from New York, Miami, Orlando, Fort Lauderdale and Toronto in Canada.

Flights from Central and South America To Trinidad, **Copa Airlines** ⓘ *www.copaair.com*, fly from Panama City in Panama; **Surinam Airways** ⓘ *www.flyslm.com*, from Paramaribo in Suriname via Caracas in Venezuela; **Caribbean Airlines** from Caracas in Venezuela, Georgetown in Guyana and Paramaribo in Suriname; and **LIAT** ⓘ *Leeward Islands Air Transport; www.liat.com*, from Georgetown in Guyana. To Tobago, **GOL** ⓘ *Gol Linhas Aéreas Inteligentes; www.voegol.com.br*, fly from São Paulo, Brazil, with one stop in Barbados.

Flights from the Caribbean Caribbean Airlines ⓘ *www.caribbean-airlines.com*, and LIAT ⓘ *www.liat.com*, are the major carriers. Trinidad is a hub for **Caribbean Airlines**, and as well as the 'Air Bridge' to Tobago, offers direct flights to/from Port of Spain and Antigua, Barbados, Grenada, Jamaica, St Lucia and Sint Maarten. LIAT fly to/from Trinidad and Antigua, Barbados, Curaçao, Grenada, St Lucia and St Vincent. Also with LIAT, you can connect to Dominica from Barbados, Puerto Rico from Barbados and

Tip...
As there are few direct flights to either Trinidad or Tobago from the UK and Europe, consider going via an East Coast US city, or to one of the French/Dutch islands in the Caribbean with KLM or Air France – Martinique, Sint Maarten/ Saint Martin or Guadeloupe. You can then fly to Trinidad (and on to Tobago) with Caribbean Airlines/LIAT.

St Vincent, Martinique and Dominica from St Lucia, and Anguilla, Dominica, Dominican Republic, Guadeloupe, Nevis, Puerto Rico, Sint Maarten and St Kitts from Antigua.

Airport information

Trinidad The modern **Piarco International Airport** has plenty of space centred around an attractive atrium, but few comfortable places to sit. Downstairs, the Arrivals/Departures area has ATMs (for local and US currency), several fast-food and coffee outlets, First Citizens' Bureau de Change near the Customs exit (0600-2200), and shops selling snacks, crafts and souvenirs. Air-side and upstairs, are extensive duty free shops (available on the way into Trinidad as well as on departure), more coffee/fast food, a bar, a fairly well-stocked bookshop, and the Millennium Finance Cambio for foreign exchange (0600-2200). If you don't fancy the Subway-, KFC-type places inside the airport, a fine alternative is the 'Local Food Court' on the main road outside for cheaper local food such as rotis and bake and shark, fresh juice and cold Carib beer.

Tobago **ANR Robinson International Airport** is named after Arthur Napoleon Raymond Robinson, the third Prime Minister of the republic. The runway ends right at the shoreline; be sure to get a window seat for lovely views of the aquamarine Caribbean Sea crashing against the rocks on take-off and landing. The airport is very small – it handles very few international flights and the majority of traffic is smaller aircraft, namely the **Caribbean Airlines** 'Air Bridge' from Trinidad. Facilities are therefore limited. The check-in desks are simply on the outdoor concourse next to the road where taxis drop off and where there's also a single snack bar, the tourist office and ATM. Inside there's a small bar, a couple of souvenir shops and a single duty-free shop with limited choice. If you are booked on a large aircraft, such as **Virgin Atlantic**, expect long, slow queues from check-in all the way up the stairs to security and immigration, which can take an hour to clear.

Sea

Cruise ships There are currently no ferry services between the other Caribbean islands or Venezuela in South America, but you can get to Trinidad and Tobago from the north by cruise ship. There are cruise ship terminals in Port of Spain on Trinidad and Scarborough on Tobago.

Yachts Port of Spain and Chaguaramas (Trinidad) and Scarborough (Tobago) are the ports of entry for combined customs and immigration for cruising yachts. In Trinidad, it is recommended you check in at Chaguaramas rather than Port of Spain (see Yachting in Chaguarama Bay, page 44). Each facility is open 24 hours, but normal business hours are Monday-Friday 0800-1600 (an overtime fee is applicable for processing at weekends, public holidays and 1600-0800, so it pays to arrive during normal working hours). A 'clearance out' certificate from your last port is required. After clearing into the country, yachts are free to move between anchorages, but if a vessel wishes to enter Tobago and clear out of Trinidad (or vice versa), the captain must notify the immigration/customs officers at the port of entry. The same goes if you are leaving a boat in Trinidad and Tobago and are departing by air. Further information can be found from the **Yacht Services Association of Trinidad and Tobago** ⓘ *www.ysatt.org*.

Getting around

Air

Caribbean Airlines ⓘ www.caribbean-airlines.com, operates the 'Air Bridge' between Trinidad's Piarco International Airport and Tobago's ANR Robinson International Airport, and there are up to 25 daily flights; US$25 one way, US$50 return, children under 12 half price. Tickets can be bought online or at the airport counter. The 20-minute flights, however, are often heavily booked at weekends and public holidays when it's very popular for Trinidadians to go across to Crown Point on Tobago for some relaxation – at other times tickets can usually be bought the same day and are valid for one year with no penalty for changing dates. Check-in time for the 'Air Bridge' is officially two hours before – this seems excessive for such a short flight but, if you haven't checked in within plenty of time, you could lose your seat to a standby passenger. Bear this in mind when booking an international flight into Trinidad and on to Tobago on the same day.

Boat

Taking the ferry between Trinidad and Tobago is time-consuming and, given that the 'Air Bridge' only takes 20 minutes, it is obviously quicker and easier to fly. Nonetheless, going by sea can be an enjoyable experience with some wonderful views of the islands' coastlines. It is also a way of avoiding the heavy traffic between Port of Spain and Piarco International Airport at peak times of the day. Two fast ferries are operated by the **Trinidad and Tobago Inter-Island Ferry Service (TTIT)** ⓘ Port of Spain Terminal, Wrightson Rd, Port of Spain, T625 4906/3055; Tobago Terminal, Scarborough, T639-2417/4906, www.ttitferry. com. These are the T&T Express and the T&T Spirit, which both take about 2½ hours, can carry 900 passengers and 200 cars. Larger vehicles must go on the cargo/ro-ro vessel, The Warrior Spirit, which also carries foot passengers but takes five hours. Tickets for same-day sailing only can be purchased at the Port of Spain Terminal and the Tobago Terminal; otherwise advance tickets must be bought through travel agents up to the close of business on the day before each sailing. At peak times, such as Christmas, Carnival and Easter, it is best to book well in advance, and weekends too sometimes get booked up quickly. Although holidaying Trinidadians like to take their cars across, it is easier for international visitors to rent vehicles separately on each island. There are more than 40 authorized agents across Trinidad and Tobago and there's a full list on the TTIT website. Prices are about US$8 one way per adult, US$4 for children aged 3-12. Children under three are free, but they must have a ticket. The schedules are on the TTIT website, and there are two crossings per day by both T&T Express and T&T Spirit, with the earliest departures being 0630 and the latest 1700 – except on Wednesdays when the last sailing of the ferries is at 1200 noon. The Warrior Spirit usually crosses once a day. You are supposed to be at the ferry terminals two hours before departure – check-in closes 30 minutes before and you must show your passport, have your luggage tagged and get a boarding pass before you board.

Tip...

On Trinidad, a Water Taxi service runs between Port of Spain and San Fernando to relieve pressure on the congested roads; this is much the easiest way to travel between the two cities (see page 84).

The roads on Trinidad and Tobago connect most points of the islands, which makes the islands relatively easy to get around. There are several multi-lane highways, and secondary and rural access roads, some of which can be narrow and winding on the coasts. Car hire, regular taxis, bus, maxi and route taxis, or an island tour with a tour operator are the options of getting around by road. Neither hitchhiking nor giving lifts to strangers is advised.

Bus

Buses on both islands are run by the state-owned **Public Transport Service Corporation (PTSC)**. The main terminal in Port of Spain, on Trinidad, is the old South Quay railway station, now called City Gate (T623 2341). On Tobago all buses originate from the bus terminal off Sangster Hill Road near the waterfront in Scarborough (T639 2293). Most buses run along the main roads around both the islands from 0500 or

> **Tip...**
> On all PTSC buses you purchase your ticket before boarding the bus. The terminals have ticket booths, while in the more remote areas look out for PTSC signs on small shops/kiosks – it's a good idea to buy a couple or more tickets at a time.

0600 to 2000 or even 2100 on the busier routes, but with far fewer departures on Saturday and Sunday. Check the website (www.ptsc.co.tt) for routes and fares. See also Transport in Trinidad, page 85, and Tobago, page 129.

Maxi and route taxis Maxi taxis work on the same basis as a bus, picking up passengers on a fixed route, except that they are privately owned mini- and microbuses (seating 12-24 passengers, depending on the size of the vehicle). Route taxis do exactly the same except they are privately owned regular cars (seating four and the driver). Despite being individually or company owned, they are registered as public service vehicles and have the necessary insurance and licences. Neither runs to a timetable and while, like buses, they have marked stands, they can also be hailed down from the side of the road and passengers can be dropped anywhere along the route; the driver will often toot to signal if he has a spare seat. For route taxis, there is usually the option of paying extra for a short deviation ('off route').

While maxi taxis run along the main roads, the smaller route taxis may be the only means of transport on some suburban and rural routes, and travelling to remote areas may involve three or more vehicles. This is not really a problem; just ask where the next one stops. The system can be difficult for visitors to figure out, given that local people know every car (and often driver) and where it is going; ask directions for where to assemble for a particular route. Route taxis can also be hard to distinguish from a regular taxi, so ask the driver, otherwise he might assume you want the vehicle to yourself and pay a full taxi fare. See also Transport in Trinidad, page 85, and Tobago, page 129.

> **Tip...**
> Official regular, maxi and route taxis have vehicle registration plates that start with the letter 'H'. Never travel in a 'P' (Private) registered vehicle with someone who claims to be a taxi driver. These bogus taxis are known locally as 'Pirates'; they are unlicensed and not insured for carrying paying passengers and there are obvious safety issues.

Car hire

Driving on Trinidad and Tobago is not especially challenging, there aren't that many roads, and even fewer signposts, although wandering from your intended route is seldom more than a minor inconvenience and you can never get really lost on the islands. Driving is on the left and cars are right-hand drive. All passengers

Tip...
Trinidad's speed limit is 80 kph on highways and 50 kph in built-up areas. But note, on Tobago, the maximum speed limit is 50 kph everywhere; this is not really an issue as distances are short, most of the road around the coast is winding and a slow drive is the best way to enjoy the views.

must wear seatbelts in the front and back seats, and the use of mobile phones is illegal while driving, except in 'hands-free' mode. In the urban areas, petrol stations are located on main thoroughfares, but are scarce in rural areas. There are numerous rental companies on both islands, although some only rent for a minimum of three days. If it's not busy, then you should be able to arrange a car almost immediately, but around Carnival on Trinidad, and at weekends on Tobago when many Trinidadians go across, it is best to make reservations in advance. To hire a car you generally need to be over 23, have a full driving licence (it does not have to be an international licence, your home country one will do as long as it's got a photograph – with an English translation if necessary), and a credit card. Expect to pay in the region of US$40-50 per day for a Suzuki jeep or normal/sedan car, US$65 for a more luxurious vehicle or four-door 4WD, and US$90 for a minibus. Deals can be made for more than seven days' car hire. Basic hire generally only includes statutory third-party insurance; you are advised to take out the optional collision damage waiver premium at US$15-20 per day as even the smallest accident can be very expensive. All drivers must always carry their licence and insurance which may be inspected at police road blocks. Do not leave anything in your car, theft is c ommon. Be careful where you park; in particular Port of Spain police 'wreckers' are diligent and will tow the car away and you will need to pay a fine to retrieve it.

There is a huge choice of car hire companies from the international brands to local companies that may just have a couple of vehicles. Not all are in great condition and may have been used as rentals for up to five years. If you want a smart new car, then go to the likes of Avis or Hertz; but having an older car that may already have a few scratches is not a bad thing on the islands as you will have to worry about it less and mileage is never very much anyway. See page 85 for car hire companies in Trinidad, and page 129 for those in Tobago.

Taxi

Taxis are expensive and rates are set by the government and taxi associations, so there is no negotiation. You can pay about US$10 for a short ride no more than a couple of blocks to US$50 for a half an hour's drive or 15-20 km, and more from one side of the islands to the other. On Trinidad, a trip from Piarco International Airport to Grande Riviere will cost around US$85; on Tobago, a journey from ANR Robinson International Airport to Charlotteville is about US$65. Additionally, fares between 2200 and 0600 attract a surcharge of 50%. All drivers accept TT dollars and US dollars cash, although generally they prefer local currency. Tipping is not obligatory, but is appreciated. On Trinidad, taxis operate from the airport, ferry terminal, main hotels and Independence Square in the centre of Port of Spain. On Tobago, they operate from the airport, ferry terminal and main hotels in Crown Point. Otherwise any hotel can phone a taxi for you. If you find a driver you like, get their card and phone number, and he/she may also offer to be your driver on a tour of the islands.

Tip...
Always book your taxi ahead if you have a flight to catch.

Essentials A-Z

Accident and emergency

Police T999; **fire** and **ambulance** T990.
To report a crime T555, toll-free.
Coast guard T634 4440.

Customs and duty free

Duty-free imports: 200 cigarettes or 50 cigars or 250 g tobacco, 1.5 litres wine or spirits, 50 ml of perfume and 250 ml of eau de toilette. There is no duty on any equipment for your own use (such as a laptops or cameras); see www.customs.gov.tt. Once in Trinidad and Tobago, be careful about buying or accepting any wildlife-derived object such as coral or shell souvenirs. Attempts to smuggle controlled products can result in confiscation, fines and imprisonment under the **Convention on Trade in Endangered Species (CITES)** (www.cites.org).

Disabled travellers

There are few specific facilities for disabled people in Trinidad and Tobago; for example, wheelchairs are not accommodated on public transport, the towns have very uneven pavements and, with the exception of the more modern upmarket hotels, few accommodation options have rooms with disabled facilities. However, it's easy enough to get around on an organized tour or in a rented vehicle and local people will do their very best to help.

Dress

Do not wear military or camouflage clothing; it is illegal. It is also illegal to sunbathe naked or topless and best to keep beachwear for the beach. Light cotton clothing is best for the tropical weather but pack a sweater, cardigan or wrap for cool evenings and some long sleeves and trousers to ward off mosquitoes.

Drugs

Trinidad and Tobago's location close to South America makes it a direct transportation route for cocaine and marijuana. Do not be tempted to dabble in narcotics; all are illegal and the law does not allow for 'personal possession'. Larger amounts of marijuana or any amount of cocaine will get you charged with trafficking and penalties are very severe. If you are offered drugs on the beach, in a rum shop or at a party (like Sunday School on Tobago), be warned, some visitors have been found themselves arrested a few minutes later.

Electricity

110 or 220 volts, 60 cycles AC.

Embassies and consulates

For a list of embassies and consulates in Trinidad and Tobago, visit the website of the Ministry of Foreign Affairs and Communications, www.foreign.gov.tt or see www.embassy.goabroad.com.

Festivals and public holidays

1 Jan New Year's Day.
Feb/Mar Carnival Mon and Tue before Ash Wed (not officially holidays, although government offices, schools, banks and many other businesses are closed on these days). The best carnival parades and music in the Caribbean. See box, page 34.
30 Mar Spiritual Baptist (Shouter) Liberation Day. A public holiday celebrating the right to worship of Spiritual Baptists. The original Baptists in Trinidad were African Americans, former slaves who fought for Britain in the War of American Independence, later settling in Princes Town, Laventille and Caroni district. **Mar/Apr Easter. Good Fri** and **Easter Mon** are public holidays and the long weekend

is one of the most popular for a trip to the beach. **Goat and crab races** are held at Buccoo on Tobago on the Tue after Easter Mon. See box, page 95.

Apr The Tobago Jazz Experience, www. tobagojazzexperience.com. Attracts many international celebrities as well as local and regional performers, with concerts at a variety of venues around the island, plus there's goat racing and lots of opportunities to sample local food.

May Tobago International Game Fishing Tournament, www.tigft.com. Usually takes place over a weekend in mid-May. This 4-day tournament is held in Charlotteville during the prime fishing season.

30 May Indian Arrival Day. A public holiday celebrating the arrival of Indian indentured labourers in 1845, when 225 Indians arrived to work on the sugar plantations to take the place of African slaves after eventual emancipation. It is an affirmation of the contribution of Indo-Trinidadians to the islands, with re-enactments and street parades mostly in southern Trinidad.

19 Jun Labour Day. A public holiday that marks the labour uprising on 19 June 1937, which is generally recognized as the start of the modern trade union movement in Trinidad and Tobago.

July Great Fete Weekend. A huge 5-day end-of-the-month beach party at Pigeon Point Heritage Park on Tobago (which attracts lots of Trinidadians) with DJs and live bands – the Sun is a family day. Often coincides with the **Carib Great Race** – a power-boat race that starts in Carenage (Trinidad) and ends at Store Bay (Tobago).

1 Aug Emancipation Day. First celebrated in 1985, this public holiday marks the freeing of the slaves on this day in 1834.

31 Aug Independence Day. Public holiday marking independence from Britain in 1962. There are military and police parades at the Queen's Park Savannah, followed by 'jump up' through the streets of St James.

Sep Trinidad & Tobago Film Festival (TTFF), www.ttfilmfestival.com. Usually the latter part of the month for 2 weeks, screens feature-length documentary films, short and experimental films from Trinidad and Tobago, the Caribbean diaspora, and Latin American countries in the Caribbean basin. Most venues are in Port of Spain.

24 Sep Republic Day. Public holiday celebrating the day Trinidad and Tobago became a republic on 1 Aug, 1976. It is marked on 24 Sep as this is the date when the first Parliament met under the new Republican constitution.

Oct/Nov Divali, The Hindu festival of lights, is a family affair and involves a lot of good food in Indian homes, with pretty oil lamps or *deyas* burning outside. Divali Nagar ('City of Lights') in southern Trinidad (see page 60) is the major venue for public festivities.

25-26 Dec Christmas Day, **Boxing Day**.

Health

See your GP or travel clinic at least 6 weeks before departure for general advice on travel risks and vaccinations. Make sure you have sufficient medical travel insurance, get a dental check, know your own blood group and, if you suffer a long-term condition such as diabetes or epilepsy, obtain a **Medic Alert** bracelet (www.medicalert.org.uk). A yellow fever inoculation certificate must be produced on arrival if you have arrived within 5 days of leaving an affected area.

Health risks
Insect-borne risks The major risks posed in the region are those spread by insects such as mosquitoes and sandflies. The key parasitic and viral diseases are **dengue fever** and **chikungunya** (also known as chik V). Cases

> **Tip...**
> While swimming, watch out for Portuguese man o' war jellyfish; although a rare occurrence their tentacles can inflict a painful sting. Also, take care not to tread on sea urchins.

of the **zika virus** have also been reported in Trinidad and Tobago from early 2016 (as it has in much of the Caribbean). Although, the risk of contracting any of these is very low, it is always a good idea to protect yourself against mosquitoes; try to wear clothes that cover arms and legs at dusk and dawn (when mosquitoes are most active) and also use effective mosquito repellent. Rooms with a/c or fans also help ward off mosquitoes.

Stomach issues   Visitors may contract some form of **diarrhoea** or intestinal upset. The standard advice is always to wash your hands before eating and to be careful with drinking water and ice. Tap water on Trinidad and Tobago is generally very good, but if any doubt, buy bottled water. Food can also pose a problem; be wary of salads if you don't know whether they have been washed or not. Symptoms should be relatively short-lived. Adults can use an antidiarrhoeal medication to control the symptoms but only for up to 24 hrs. In addition, keep well hydrated by drinking plenty of fluids and eat bland foods. Oral rehydration sachets are a useful way to keep well hydrated. These should always be used when treating children and the elderly.

Sun   Protect yourself adequately against the sun. Apply a high-factor sunscreen (greater than SPF15) and also make sure it screens against UVB. Prevent heat exhaustion and heatstroke by drinking enough fluids throughout the day (your urine will be pale if you are drinking enough). Symptoms of heat exhaustion and heatstroke include dizziness, tiredness and headache. Use rehydration salts mixed with water to replenish fluids and salts and find somewhere cool and shady to recover. If you suspect heatstroke rather than heat exhaustion, you need to cool the body down quickly (cold showers are effective).

If you get sick
On Trinidad, there are hospitals in Port of Spain and San Fernando, as well as several district hospitals and community health centres. All complex medical cases are transferred from Tobago to Trinidad.
Port of Spain General Hospital, 169 Charlotte St, Port of Spain, T623 2951, is a large public hospital.
Scarborough General Hospital, Signal Hill, off Claude Noel Hwy to the west of town, T660 4744, emergency medical services, T639 4444, www.trha.co.tt. This new hospital is the best on Tobago. It has a 24-hr accident and emergency department.
St Clair Medical Centre, 18 Elizabeth St, Port of Spain, T628 1451, is private and more comfortable, but not necessarily better equipped.
West Shore Medical Private Hospital, 239 Western Main Rd, Cocorite, close to the The Falls at West Mall shopping

mall in Westmoorings, T622 9878, www.westshoreprivatehospital.com, is fairly new and very well equipped with a 24-hr accident and emergency department and ambulance service. It is expensive, but the best choice if you have adequate insurance.

Useful websites
www.btha.org British Travel Health Association.
www.cdc.gov US government site that gives excellent advice on travel health and details of disease outbreaks.
www.fco.gov.uk British Foreign and Commonwealth Office travel site has useful information on each country, people, climate and a list of UK embassies/consulates.
www.fitfortravel.nhs.uk A-Z of vaccine/health advice for each country.
www.travelhealth.co.uk Independent travel health site with advice on vaccination, travel insurance and health risks.
www.who.int World Health Organization, updates of disease outbreaks.

Insurance

Before departure, it is vital to take out comprehensive travel insurance. At the very least, the policy should cover medical expenses, including repatriation to your home country in the event of a medical emergency. Hospital bills need to be paid at the time of admittance, so keep all paperwork to make a claim. If you have something stolen whilst in Trinidad and Tobago, report the incident to the nearest police station and ensure you get a police report and case number. You will need these to make any claim from your insurance company.

LGBT travellers

Trinidad and Tobago is one of several Caribbean countries that still criminalizes same-sex sexual activity. However, while in some of these, such as Jamaica and Dominica where there is harsh treatment and criminal sentences, in Trinidad and Tobago the law is not known to have been enforced. The gay/lesbian scene is largely tolerated, although public displays of affection are ill-advised.

Money

US$1 = TT$6.69; UK£1 = TT$8.79; €1 = TT$7.37 (Jul 2016)

Currency
The currency in Trinidad and Tobago is the Trinidadian dollar; TT$ or TTD. Notes are TT$1, 5, 10, 20, 50 and 100. Coins are 5, 10, 25 and 50 (50 cents and TT$1 coins are still in circulation but hardly used anymore). US$ cash are widely accepted by businesses and the official exchange rate is very steady, although most prefer to deal in TT$. Some things, such as hotel rates, air fares and sometimes activities such as diving and tours, are quoted in US$, but you can pay in either. On departure change TT$ back into US$ or other currencies at the foreign exchange bureau at Piarco International Airport (open until 2200); this is advised even if you are going to one of the other Caribbean islands where TT$ will be difficult to exchange.

Changing money
There are ATMs and bureaux de change at both the international airports. On Trinidad there are plenty of banks with ATMs. On Tobago there are fewer; most are in Scarborough and Crown Point and the few around the island in rural areas cannot be relied upon for cash – if you are travelling to the northern end of the island make sure you take enough cash with you. The easiest currencies to exchange are US$, UK£ and euros, but banks also generally change

> **Tip...**
> ATMs generally only dispatch notes in increments of TT$100, which are often too large for people to have change – break bigger notes when you can and save small change for taxis, snacks, drinks, souvenirs and the like.

Eastern Caribbean, Barbados and Canadian dollars, and the Swiss franc.

Credit, debit and currency cards

Credit and debit cards are widely accepted by the large hotels, restaurants, airlines, car hire firms, tour operators and shops. An additional levy of 5% may be charged by some businesses, so check first if paying a sizeable bill. Visa is the most widely accepted card, followed by MasterCard; AMEX and Diners far less so. Pre-paid currency cards allow you to pre-load money from your bank account, fixed at the day's exchange rate. They look like a credit or debit card and are issued by specialist money changing companies, such as **Travelex**, **Caxton FX** and the **Post Office**. You can top up and check your balance by phone, online and sometimes by text.

Opening hours

Banks: Mon-Thu 0800-1400, Fri 0800-1200, 1500-1700.
Shops: Mostly Mon-Fri 0800-1700. If they open on Sat they usually close at 1500. On Trinidad, the large modern shopping malls generally open Mon-Sat 1000-1900, Sun 1200-1800. In the rural areas, small grocery shops and kiosks are often open daily, but more like whenever the vendor feels like it.

Safety

The people of both islands are, as a rule, exceptionally friendly, honest and ready to help you. Most visitors will not experience any issues and will have a safe and enjoyable stay, so there is no need to get paranoid about your safety. There is, however, a high level of gang-related violent crime in Trinidad, particularly in the inner-city neighbourhoods east of Port of Spain's city centre: **Laventille**, **Morvant** and **Barataria**. Other places to be avoided are **Sea Lots** (where the Central Market is), a rough squatter area on the shoreline to the southeast of South Quay and, even rougher,

Beetham Estate, a slum area elongated west to east between the Beetham Highway and the Eastern Main Rd. Central Port of Spain is fairly safe, but is quiet at night, apart from around Independence Square, so exercise caution and avoid the area around the **port** or **City Gate** bus terminal except when making a journey. As sleepy as it appears, do not underestimate the risk of crime in Tobago. There have been opportunist thefts and muggings in the **Crown Point** area, and parts of **Scarborough** are known to have drug problems and associated crime issues.

The general common sense rules apply to prevent petty theft: don't exhibit anything valuable and keep wallets and purses out of sight; use a hotel safe to store valuables, money and passports; lock hotel room doors; don't leave items on hotel or villa balconies when you go out; at night, avoid deserted areas, including the Queen's Park Savannah in Port of Spain and the beaches in Tobago, and always take taxis. If you are driving, avoid travel outside major populated areas at night as erratic driving by others can be a problem, avoid stopping if at all possible and keep doors and windows locked.

Tax

VAT stands at 15% on goods and services, but is usually included in the final price of the product. A hotel tax of 10% is levied on all room rates, as is a service charge of 10% – most B&Bs, guesthouses and hotels lump tax and service together, charging 20% on the rack rate. In restaurants, VAT is usually included but the 10% service charge isn't and will be added to the final bill; there is therefore no need to tip extra unless you want to.

Telephone

Country code: 1-868. The main company providing fixed line and internet services is **Telecommunications Services of Trinidad & Tobago (TSTT)**, www.tstt.co.tt. Its mobile service division is **bmobile**, www.bmobile. co.tt, while **Digicel**, www.digicelgroup.com, and **Flow**, www.discoverflow.co, are Caribbean-wide cellular and internet providers. Local SIM cards and start-up packs are available to purchase at phone shops (including at the airports) and cost TT$25 (US$4), but are also preloaded with a minimum of TT$100 (US$15) credit, so cost from TT$125 upwards (around US$19).

Time

Atlantic Standard Time, 4 hrs behind GMT, 1 hr ahead of EST.

Tourist information

The most useful and helpful tourist information offices are immediately outside the Arrivals exit at Trinidad's Piarco International Airport; operated by **Trinidad and Tobago Tourism Development Company** (**TDC**), T669 5196/6044, www.tdc.co.tt, daily 0800-2300, and opposite Arrivals at Tobago's ANR Robinson International Airport; operated by the **Tobago House of Assembly** (**THA**), T639 0509, hwww.visittobago.gov.tt, daily 0600-2200. Other offices for both of these respectively are in Port of Spain and Scarborough (and kiosks operate in their Cruise Ship Terminals). Both websites also have excellent information.

Useful websites
www.discovertnt.com   Publishers of the annual booklet of the same name that is available to pick up for free from all the tourist offices and many hotels.
www.gotrinidadandtobago.com
Website of the Ministry of Tourism, and *Discover Trinidad and Tobago*.

Visas

All visitors are required to have passports, valid for 3 months after your planned departure from Trinidad and Tobago in the case of travellers from the USA and EU; 6 months past your travel date for visitors from

Tip...
Even though you may not always get asked for it, all travellers need to be able to produce a return or onward ticket from Trinidad and Tobago, proof that you can support yourself during your stay (a credit card will suffice), and an address at which you will be staying (the hotel on your first night should be enough).

other countries. Visas are not required for tourist visits of up to 90 days by nationals of Caricom (except Haiti), most Commonwealth countries, West European countries, South Africa and the USA. Citizens of some Commonwealth countries do need visas. In the case of Australia and New Zealand citizens, visas should be applied for before leaving home (takes 24 hrs), although a 'visa waiver' can be obtained on arrival for a fee currently of TT$400 (US$60). For other nationalities visas must be obtained from a Trinidad and Tobago Mission abroad or, where there is no office, at a British Embassy or Consulate in a non-Commonwealth country. Fees vary according to nationality.

Entry permits for 1 to 3 months are given on arrival; a 1-month permit can be extended at the **Immigration Offices** (Head Office at 67 Frederick St, Port of Spain, T868-625 3571, Mon-Fri 0600-1700; 2 Knox St, San Fernando, T868-653 6691, Mon-Thu 0800-1415; Agricola Building, Plymouth Rd, Scarborough, T868-635 0430; www.immigration.gov.tt).

Casual employment is prohibited but business visitors are allowed to work without a work permit for up to 30 days once in any 12 consecutive months. For periods longer than 30 days, business travellers must obtain a work permit for a specified period of time and for attachment to a particular company or institution. To apply, contact the **Ministry of National Security** (52-60 Abercromby St, Port of Spain, T868-623 2154/44, www.nationalsecurity.gov.tt, Mon-Fri 0800-1600).

Index

*Entries in **bold** refer to maps*

A

Abbey of Mount St Benedict 50
accident and emergency 136
accommodation 18
  price codes 18
Adventure Farm and Nature Reserve 97
air travel 131, 133
Angostura bitters 50
Argyle Waterfall 101
Arima 49, 51
Arnos Vale Bay 96
Asa Wright Nature Centre 52
Avocat Falls 48

B

Bacelot 99
Balandra by the Bay 54
Balata Bay 46
Bamboo Cathedral 44
Batteaux Bay 104
B&Bs 18
Big Bay 107
birdwatching 13
Black Rock 93
Blanchisseuse 47
Bloody Bay 106
Blue Basin Waterfall 41
boat travel 133
Bonasse 64
Brasso Seco 48
Buccoo 92
Buccoo Bay 93
Buccoo Reef 90
Bush Bush Island 58
bus travel 134

C

Campbellton Battery 106
car hire 135
Carib Brewery 49
Carnival 12, 34
Caroni Bird Sanctuary 59
Castara 107
Castara Waterfall 107
Chacachacare 45
Chaguanas 60
Chaguaramas Military History and Aerospace Museum 42
Chaguaramas Peninsula 41
Chagville Beach 42
Champs Fleurs 49
Charlotteville 105
climate 11
Coconut Bay 90
Columbus Bay 64
Craig Hall Waterfall 108
Crown Point 89, **92**
cruise ships 132
Cumana 54
customs and duty free 136
cycling 13

D

Devil's Woodyard 62
Dial 51
Diego Martin Valley 41
disabled travellers 136
Divali Nagar ('City of Lights') 60
dress 136
drink 22
drugs 136
Dunstan Cave 52

E

East coast 57
electricity 136
embassies and consulates 136
Englishman's Bay 106
Erin Bay 64

F

Falls at West Mall 41
ferry travel 133
festivals 12, 136
fishing 13
Flagstaff Hill 105
flora and fauna 61, 103
food 20
Fort Bennett 94
Fort Campbellton 106
Fort George 39
Fort Granby 100
Fort Granby Beach 101
Fort James 95
Fort King George 99

G

Galeota Point 57
Galera Point 54
Gasparee Caves 45
Gaspar Grande 45
Genesis Nature Park & Art Gallery 101
Gilpin Trace 103
gingerbread houses 38
Goat Island 105
goat racing 95
Goldsborough Bay 101
Grafton Caledonia Wildlife Sanctuary 94
Grande Riviere 56
Gran Tacarib 48
Granville 64
Great Courland Bay 94
Guayaguayare 57
guesthouses 18

H

health 137
Highland Waterfall 108
hiking 13
Hillsborough Dam 100
hotels 18
  price codes 18
House of Angostura 49

I

insurance 139
itinerary 9

K

Keshorn Walcott Toco Lighthouse 54
King's Bay Beach 103
Knowsley 38

L

La Fillette 47
Las Cuevas Bay 47
La Vache Point 46
LGBT travellers 139
Little Bay 107
Little Tobago 104
Lopinot Complex 51
Lower Manzanilla 57

M

Macqueripe Bay 43
Macqueripe Beach 43
Main Ridge Forest Reserve 102
Man O War Bay 106
Manzanilla 57
Maracas Bay 46
Maracas Lookout 46
Maracas Valley 50
Maracas Waterfall 50
Maraval 46
Marianne Bay 47
Marianne River 47
Matelot 56
Matelot Falls 57
Matelot River 48
Matura Beach 53
Mayaro 57
Mayaro Bay 57
menu reader 23
Milford Fort 89
money 139

FOOTPRINT

Features

Angostura bitters 50
Birdwatching on Tobago 124
Buccoo Reef and Nylon Pool 94
Carnival 34
Early Aviation at the Savannah 36
Flora and fauna of Tobago 103
Flora and fauna of Trinidad 61
Gingerbread houses 38
Goat and crab racing 95
Goat Island 105
Leatherback turtles 54

Limin' 22
Liming like a Trini on De Avenue 74
Little Apple of Death 138
Menu reader 23
Music 14
Roti 21
Sunday School 122
The Smiling Assassin 100
Yachting in Chaguarama Bay 44
Yacht services 127

Monos Island 45
Moruga 62
Mount Dillion 108
Mount Irvine Bay 93
Mount St George 100
Mount St Pleasant 43

N

Nariva Swamp 58
Northeast coast 52
Nylon Pool 90

P

Paramin 46
Paria Bay 48
Paria Falls 48
Parlatuvier 106
Petite Riviere 48
photography 16
Pigeon Peak 104
Pigeon Point Heritage
  Park 91
Pinfold Bay 101
Pirate's Bay 106
Pitch Lake 63
Plymouth 95
Pointe-a-Pierre
  Wildfowl Trust 60
Point Fortin 64

Port of Spain 27, **32**
  Anglican All Saints
    Church 38
  Emperor Valley
    Zoo 35
  Independence
    Square 31
  Magnificent Seven 36
  Museum of the City
    of Port of Spain 33
  National Academy for
    the Performing Arts
    (NAPA) 38
  National Museum
    and Art Gallery 39
  Queen's Park
    Savannah 35
  Woodford Square 28
public holidays 136

Q

Queen's Hall 36

R

Rainbow Waterfall 101
restaurants 20, 72, 115
  price codes 18
Rio Seco Waterfall 53
road travel 134
Roxborough 101
Royal Botanic Gardens 35

S

safety 140
sailing 14
Saline Bay 53
Salybia 53
Salybia Matura Trace 53
San Fernando 61
San Fernando Hill 62
Sangre Grande 57
Santa Rosa Roman
  Catholic Church 51
Scarborough 97, **98**
  Botanic Gardens 97
  Lower 97
  Upper 98
Scotland Bay 45
scuba-diving 15
sea travel 132
self-catering 18
Speyside 103
Speyside Waterwheel
  104
Spring Bridge 47
St Joseph 49
Stonehaven Bay 93
Store Bay Beach 89

T

tax 140
taxis 135
telephone 140
Three Pools 47

Three Sisters 64
Tobago 86-129, 90
  listings 108
Tobago Cocoa Estate 101
Tobago House of
  Assembly 98
Tobago Museum 99
Toco Beach 54
tourist information 141
transport 131
Trinidad 24-85, 28
  listings 65
Tucker Valley 43
turtles 54
Twin River Waterfall 101
Tyrico Bay 47
Tyrrell's Bay 104

V

Valencia 52
Vessigny Beach 64
visas 141

W

Waterloo Temple in the
  Sea 60
watersports 15
weather 11
Williams Bay 42

Y

yachts 44, 127, 132

Credits

Footprint credits

Editor: Felicity Laughton
Production and layout: Emma Bryers
Maps: Kevin Feeney
Colour section: Patrick Dawson

Publisher: Felicity Laughton
            Patrick Dawson
Marketing: Kirsty Holmes
Sales: Diane McEntee
Advertising and content partnerships:
Debbie Wylde

Photography credits

Front cover: John de la Bastide/
Shutterstock.com
Back cover top: PHB.cz (Richard Semik)/
Shuterstock.com
Back cover bottom: Lizzie Williams
Inside front cover: Shane P White,
Rolf Richardson/SuperStock.com,
Nina B/Shutterstock.com.

Colour section
Page 1: George H.H. Huey/SuperStock.com.
Page 2: Altin Osmanaj/Shutterstock.com.
Page 4: Wolfgang Kaehler/SuperStock.com,
Gail Johnson/Shutterstock.com.
Page 5: Shane P White.
Page 6: Adam Woolfitt/SuperStock.com.
Page 7: bcampbell65/Shutterstock.com,
Michael Newton/SuperStock.com,
Shane P White, LOOK-foto/SuperStock.com.
Page 8: martino motti/SuperStock.com.

Duotones
Page 24: Stephen Beaumont/
Shutterstock.com.
Page 86: stifos/Shutterstock.com .

Printed in Spain by GraphyCems

Publishing information

Footprint Trinidad & Tobago
2nd edition
© Footprint Handbooks Ltd
September 2016

ISBN: 978 1 911082 05 7
CIP DATA: A catalogue record for this book
is available from the British Library

® Footprint Handbooks and the
Footprint mark are a registered
trademark of Footprint Handbooks Ltd

Published by Footprint
6 Riverside Court
Lower Bristol Road
Bath BA2 3DZ, UK
T +44 (0)1225 469141
F +44 (0)1225 469461
footprinttravelguides.com

Distributed in the USA by
National Book Network, Inc.

Every effort has been made to ensure that
the facts in this guidebook are accurate.
However, travellers should still obtain advice
from consulates, airlines, etc about travel
and visa requirements before travelling.
The authors and publishers cannot
accept responsibility for any loss, injury
or inconvenience however caused.